Harry Potter
Collector's
Handbook

WITHDRAWN

D0032778

Published by

Krause Publications, a division of F+W Media, Inc.
700 East State Street • Iola, WI 54990-0001
715-445-2214 • 888-457-2873
www.krausebooks.com

To order books or other products call toll-free 1-800-258-0929
or visit us online at www.krausebooks.com or www.Shop.Collect.com

This book is unofficial and unauthorized. It is not authorized, approved, licensed or endorsed by J. K. Rowling, her publishers, or Warner Bros. Entertainment Inc.

Cover image of Ron Weasley at Hogwarts (T6-HPDD-01), Harry Potter at Hogwarts (T5-HPDD-02), and Hermione Granger at Hogwarts (T6-HPDD-02), courtesy Tonner Doll Company, Inc.; used with permission.
See page 122 for more information.
Photography by Storm Photo, Kingston, New York, www.stormphotoinc.com.
©Tonner Doll Company, Inc. All rights reserved. www.tonnerdoll.com/harrypotter.htm

Library of Congress Control Number: 2010923675

ISBN 13: 978-1-4402-0897-3
ISBN 10: 1-4402-0897-2

Designed by Katrina Newby
Edited by Mary Sieber

Printed in China

Harry Potter Collector's Handbook

William Silvester

Other fine titles from Krause Publications

Legendary Yankee Stadium

Dames, Dolls & Delinquents

1000 Comic Books You Must Read

The Ultimate Guide to G.I. Joe

Warman's Sterling Silver Flatware

200 Years of Dolls

Vintage Fashion Accessories

Fine Vintage Watches

Hot Wheels Variations

Collecting Rocks, Gems & Minerals

Horror Movie Freak

Barbie Doll: A Rare Beauty

Contents

Foreword

I will never forget sitting in an executive meeting at Warner Bros. and hearing about Harry Potter for the first time. On the way home from work that night, I bought *Harry Potter and the Sorcerer's Stone* and finished it in a single sitting. I immediately fell in love with the story of Harry and the magical world at Hogwarts, never realizing the adventures that laid ahead of me working on this property.

As vice president of design for the Warner Bros. Stores, my team was responsible for designing the first Harry Potter product. At that time the initial film had not yet been cast, so we had to develop art for all the main characters and settings from the stories. The pinnacle of our whirlwind development was a trip I took to London with Fred Bode, my senior character illustrator, for a long meeting with J.K. Rowling finessing Fred's drawings of the characters and scenes. I had never worked with a creator who had such a clear vision in her head of her characters and their world. I felt like Rowling could describe intricate details of each character and every corner and crevice of Hogwarts. It was an incredibly inspiring day, and her passion for the world she had created helped me understand her intent to always respect the property more than trying to make piles of money from merchandising.

As you look through this book, you may marvel at all of the collectibles that have been produced from the Harry Potter properties, but what you may not realize is that for every product produced, there are piles of ideas that never saw the light of day in an effort to stay true to the property and what it represented to its fans.

After the closing of the WB Studio Stores, I acquired the license to continue the fine art business for WB with the intent of Harry Potter being an important part of our program. Over the last eight years we have had the opportunity to publish over three dozen wonderful Harry Potter illustrations by Mary GrandPré. These works include both scenics she had illustrated from the HP stories, to the actual book cover artwork she did for the U.S. books. We have also released film inspired images from artist Jim Salvati and the Witches and Wizards of Harry Potter individual character studies from the films. I am very proud to be the publisher of such beautiful, meaningful works.

I am by nature a collector and a huge fan of the Harry Potter series, so I understand people's desire to own something that reminds them of the characters and stories they love so much. My family and I own a number of Harry Potter collectibles, including the exquisite timeturner (produced by Noble Collections) I presented to my daughter when she dressed up as Hermione for Halloween one year. When you are a fan, it is a pleasure to own something that reminds you of your passion. To be able to hang a signed print of your favorite book cover in your home or wear a timeturner around your neck keeps the stories alive in your world. In a world full of challenges and difficult times, J.K. Rowling's stories let us enter a magical world and escape in Harry's story. I feel very fortunate to have experienced that magic, and through the artwork share it with you.

Ruth Clampett,
Former Vice President of Design
for Warner Bros. Stores

Photo courtesy Clampett Studio Collections   ClampettStudio.com and WildsvilleGallery.com

Ruth Clampett (right) with Harry Potter books author, J.K. Rowling.

Acknowledgments

In my search for information and images of the Harry Potter collectibles, I had the great pleasure of corresponding with a number of wonderfully helpful people. They are listed below, in no particular order, with my sincere thanks for all they have done to assist in the researching of this book.

Victoria Mielke, Arabella Figg's Hogwarts Express website, for permission to use all the information on her website, an incredible source for early items.

Doug Blaine, for images from Bachmann Trains.

Kate Harvey, rights executive, Bloomsbury Publishing, for information and incredible images of the book covers.

Liz Davignon, eBay store: bondlizbond, for images from Bonds Corner.

Ruth Clampett, Clampettstudio.com and Wildsvillegallery.com, for images of artwork and for writing the fantastic foreword.

Lucy Rogers, Christopher Little Literary Agency, for information and permission to use excerpts.

Chuck Pint, Chuckpint.com/dicers, for information on dicers.

Susan Nielsen, photo stylist, and Melinda Seegers, manager, consumer services, Department 56, for information and images.

Jeanne Haffeman, director, licensing, Elope Inc., for information and images.

Captain Coder, figurerealm.com, for information and images from his website.

Gary Tulk, Fuburiver Investibles Inc., for information and images on early Harry Potter wands.

John "Dev" Gilmore, vice president, product development and design, Gentle Giant, for images.

Janice de Vera, product research and graphics coordinator, Gund, for images.

Matt Polakoff and Joe Fay, Heritage Auction, HA.com, for information, catalogs, and images.

Louise Tinagero, marketing department, Kurt S. Adler Inc., for images.

Seth Reisman, Rubie's Costumes, for information and images.

Kristen Moran, Scholastic Publications, for information and images.

Tony Roscelli, marketing, and Jared Gustafson, vice president, marketing, Screenlife, LLC, for information and images.

Deb Martino, Sylvan Lane Shoppe, for images.

Tom Courtney, art director, Tonner Doll Company Inc., for information and images.

Debbie Weiss and Stephanie Chefas, Wonderful World of Art Gallery, for information.

And the following individual Potterphiles:

Megan Barrow, for her invaluable assistance and images from her collection.

Austin Hall-Silvester, for borrowing from his collection for images.

Natacia "Danceingfae" Louvier, Padfoot, and PotterNerdJordan, for images from their collections.

Harry Silvester, for borrowing from his collection for images.

Jason Silvester, for his Photoshop expertise.

Winnie Silvester, for encouraging me to take on the project and standing beside me throughout it.

Introduction

Welcome, Muggles, to the magic, mystery, and merchandise of the wonderful wizarding world of Harry Potter.

I must admit that I was not a Harry Potter fan from the beginning. The first three books had already been written and become phenomenal successes before I joined Potterdom. It was the hype surrounding *Harry Potter and the Goblet of Fire* that drew me into the fold in 1999. My curiosity about the Boy Who Lived and a copy of *Harry Potter and the Philosopher's Stone* I had purchased as a gift tempted me to find out just what all the excitement was about. I am not a stranger to books aimed at young people; I have often been to Narnia, Middle Earth, Redwall, Prydain, Xanth, and the wonderful worlds of Disney, and so I approached Ms. Rowling's books with the hope that here would be another thrilling adventure. I was not disappointed. Hooked from the first paragraph, I promptly devoured the first three books and waited impatiently for the fourth.

During the next few years I experienced the anticipation of Christmas as the date of every new release drew closer. With agonizing slowness, Rowling wove her magic into the seven books of the series and then teased us more with three smaller books, a tiny prequel, and with the possibility of a *Harry Potter Encyclopedia* some time in the future.

The merchandising of Harry Potter did not begin in earnest until 2000. That was the year that Warner Bros. took on the task of converting the written word of Rowling to fantastic images on the silver screen. Scores of licensees took advantage of the worldwide love affair with Harry Potter, his friends, and his enemies to manufacture everything from pens to diamond timeturner necklaces. At first collectors grabbed up all things Harry Potter, but in time, as the amount of merchandise became overwhelming to all but those with the deepest of pockets, collectors started to focus more on specific items. For the most part, such is the market today. Many longtime collectors still have the merchandise from the early days, but their newer collectibles are selected with more care.

In this book readers will find hundreds of listings, images, and secondary market values for Harry Potter collectibles. An index is provided to make it easy to find whatever you're looking for, from rare first editions worth thousands of dollars to commonplace toys, ornaments, stamps, coins, t-shirts, jewelry, and costumes. In many cases there is a fine line between primary and secondary market items as something bought in a store one day can be sold in an online auction the next. On any given day, typing "Harry Potter" into the search box on eBay will bring up over 10,000 items for sale. The values listed in this book are based on an average of prices realized in various online auctions, prices charged in online stores, and the retail values of new products over the past year. This book has attempted to be as up-to-date as possible with listings dealing with every book and movie released until mid-2009. As much as is possible, only licensed items are listed for I do not want to encourage piracy and knockoffs by giving them a legitimate value.

While I have attempted to include as many collectibles as possible, I have not listed "everything" Harry Potter. Instead I strove to produce a general guide to what is available on the secondary market, with an eye towards the unpredictability of market fluctuations. Many of the items are cross collectibles, desired by both the Potterphile and the general collector, so competition for specific items can be costly.

This book is written for all who love Harry Potter, whether collectors or not. Harry Potter fandom is a huge international community that is blessed with many wonderful sites on the Internet to keep it informal, close knit, and vibrant.

Despite the fact that J.K. Rowling has stated there will only be seven books, and the last of the eight movies is only a year away, the magic of Harry Potter is far from nearing an end. Every day young readers are discovering the wizarding world as children introduce their friends or siblings to the books. Parents continue to snuggle beside their youngsters to transport them to Privet Drive, perhaps for the first time, as they themselves board the Hogwarts Express for a nostalgic revisit. I have no doubt that somewhere in the world, at this very moment, someone is reading for the very first time, "Mr. and Mrs. Dursley, of number four, Privet Drive, were proud to say that they were perfectly normal, thank you very much."[1]

William Silvester, Nov. 30, 2009

---

[1] Harry Potter and the Philosopher's Stone, copyright © J. K. Rowling 1997, used with permission of Bloomsbury Publishing.

J.K. Rowling:
The Woman Behind the Wizard

Photo courtesy Raincoast Books

The train from Manchester to London came to an abrupt halt. A voice announced that there was some kind of mechanical problem and it could be some time before it was corrected.

Sitting in one of the long strings of cars was a young woman named Joanne Rowling. She was not in a hurry, so the news of the breakdown did not upset her unduly. In fact, she welcomed it for she looked upon the trip as a private time when she could indulge her love of writing. She looked for her pen and pad but discovered she did not have them with her, so instead she stared out the window at a herd of grazing cows and let her imagination entertain her. Harry Potter popped into her head.

"I saw Harry incredibly clearly. The idea basically at that point was wizard school and I saw Harry very, very plainly," she would later say.[1]

Joanne spent the rest of the waiting time thinking about the world this boy would inhabit. She conjured up Hogwarts School of Witchcraft and Wizardry and began populating it with eccentric teachers, ghosts, and gifted children. By the time she disembarked at King's Cross Station, she had the basic story worked out in her mind.

---

[1] Feldman, Roxanne. "The Truth about Harry," *School Library Journal*, September 1999

Chipping Sodbury General Hospital in Yate, Gloucestershire, England was the birthplace of Joanne Rowling on July 31, 1965. Her parents, Peter and Ann Rowling, and later a sister, Diane, moved a number of times in her early years from Yate to Winterbourne to Tutshill. Her greatest love was writing and telling stories, and though quiet and reserved, she graduated from school as Head Girl.

Furthering her education at Exeter University, she studied French and lived in Paris for a year. Later she was employed at Amnesty International and held a variety of secretarial jobs. None of these held any great interest for her, and she continued to write whenever an opportunity arose.

Her 26th year was one of emotional turmoil. Her mother had been diagnosed with multiple sclerosis, her relationship with her boyfriend was not going well, and she was out of work. Harry Potter was the only real joy in her life. She began creating the wizarding world, utilizing every spare minute.

But dreams did not put food on the table nor pay the rent, so Rowling took a job teaching English as a second language in Oporto, Portugal in September 1990. She found a comfortable apartment, discovered that she enjoyed her job, and settled into a routine of teaching and writing. In December her mother died, and the loss was reflected in her writing about the orphaned Harry Potter.

Romance now entered her life in the form of TV journalist Jorge Arantes, whom she married, and just before her 28th birthday she gave birth to her daughter, Jessica. By this time she had completed the first three chapters of *Harry Potter and the Philosopher's Stone* with the rest of the book as a rough draft.

Unfortunately, her marriage did not work out and she separated from her husband and returned to Britain with her daughter. Her sister, Diane, lived in Edinburgh, Scotland, and it was here that Joanne continued her writing while looking for another job. Whenever she could, Rowling wheeled her baby to Nicolson's Café, owned by her brother-in-law, and spent the hours writing while the child slept. Finally, after five years of writing, she was able to finish the book.

The book was rejected on her first attempts to market it, but literary agent Christopher Little saw the potential, and so did Bloomsbury Press, who paid her a $4,000 advance in October 1996. A few months later Rowling was awarded a Scottish Arts Council grant that enabled her to buy a computer and write *Harry Potter and the Chamber of Secrets*. Her biggest break came in April of the same year when Scholastic Books bid $105,000 for the American rights to *Philosopher's Stone* (changing the name to *Sorcerer's Stone*). Now she was able to quit her job and become a full-time writer.

Harry Potter and the Philosopher's Stone was published in Britain in late June 1997 with an initial print run of only 500 books. Joanne was asked to use her initials instead of her name for fear that boys would not want to read a book written by a woman. She adopted her grandmother's name, Kathleen, as a second name, and the book was published as written by J.K. Rowling.

The book was a huge success and garnered several awards. When the time came to publish the second book in the series, *Harry Potter and the Chamber of Secrets*, the print run was increased to 10,000. Meanwhile, book one was printed in the United States with a run of 50,000 copies, and American readers had to resort to buying book two online as *Chamber of Secrets* did not come out in the United States until the summer of 1999.

Now Rowling had two books on the top of the bestseller lists, and they were soon to be joined by a third, *Harry Potter and the Prisoner of Azkaban*. So popular were the books that when Rowling made a three-week book tour of the United States, the venues were mobbed by excited fans.

The year 2000 was to be a particularly exciting one for Potterdom as it was announced that Warner Bros. had signed a contract to make the Harry Potter books into films. The films would trigger the beginning of Harry Potter merchandising. In July of the same year, the fourth book in the series, *Harry Potter and the Goblet of Fire* was published simultaneously in the United Kingdom and the United States with a combined first run of five million books.

Potter fans were now in for a long wait as Joanne worked on the fifth book that would not be released until 2003. In the meantime, two of the schoolbooks used at Hogwarts, *Quidditch Through the Ages* and *Fantastic Beasts and Where to Find Them* were published to benefit the British charity, Comic Relief. The first of the Harry Potter films, *Harry Potter and the Sorcerer's Stone*, was also released, setting record grosses on both sides of the Atlantic. Rowling ended the year on a happy personal note when she married anesthesiologist Neil Murray.

Harry Potter and the Chamber of Secrets was released on film in November 2002, again setting box office records. The long wait for book five was finally over in mid-2003 when *Harry Potter and the Order of the Phoenix*, the longest of the books, was finally published. Joanne and Neil became the proud parents of her second child, David.

Prisoner of Azkaban opened in theaters in May 2004 with a

new director and a different actor as Professor Dumbledore. The following year, Rowling gave birth to her third child, Mackenzie, and in July book six, *Harry Potter and the Half-Blood Prince* was released, followed in November by the film version of *Goblet of Fire.*

Throughout 2006, Rowling was hard at work raising her children, supporting her charities, and finishing the last of the Harry Potter series. *Harry Potter and the Deathly Hallows* was completed at Edinburgh's Balmoral Hotel in January 2007 and published in July. Ten days previous, the release of *Order of the Phoenix* in theaters had broken all records for Harry Potter opening days.

Back in North America again, Rowling began her Open Book Tour in Los Angeles and traveled to New York and Toronto. About this time she penned seven copies of *The Tales of Beedle the Bard* and sold one at auction for charity. A documentary film, *J.K. Rowling, A Year in the Life*, aired on British television at the end of the year.

The Tales of Beedle the Bard was published for general distribution in 2008 at a children's tea party hosted by Rowling. Production began on *Half-Blood Prince* for release in 2009. Earlier in the year, Rowling had the title Knight of the Legion of Honour bestowed upon her by the French president. In response she apologized for giving her greatest villain, Voldemort, a French name.

Harry Potter and the Deathly Hallows will be released in two parts in 2010 and 2011. Rowling is said to be working on the monumental *Harry Potter Encyclopedia* with no definite publication date in sight. Beyond that, nothing is certain except that the Harry Potter books, films, and merchandise will go on far into the future as they drift into the realm of classics and join the ranks of the world's most beloved stories.

Bibliography

Conversations with J.K. Rowling, Lindsey Fraser. Scholastic, 2001.
J.K. Rowling: A Biography: The Genius Behind Harry Potter, Sean Smith. Arrow, 2002.
J.K. Rowling: The Wizard Behind Harry Potter, Marc Shapiro. St. Martin's Griffin, 2007.

Collecting Harry Potter

Collecting Harry Potter began on the day the first book, *Harry Potter and the Philosopher's Stone,* was published – June 26, 1997, according to Bloomsbury. Anyone who bought the book, read it, and decided to keep it had the potential to become a Harry Potter collector.

From that date until 2000, Harry Potter collectors had only early editions of the books to add to their collections. The ardent collector could have added magazine articles, newspaper clippings, or foreign language editions if they felt the need to expand their collections, but there was little else. The deluge of Harry Potter merchandise did not begin until Warner Bros. entered the picture as its contract with J.K. Rowling included control over merchandising.

It is well known that Rowling was not keen on handing control over to Warner Bros., but making films is expensive, and merchandising has become part and parcel of that industry. She did have some say, however, and in an interview with Jeremy Paxman (BBC Newsnight, June 19, 2003), she said, "Twice a year I sit down with Warner Brothers and we have conversations about merchandising...you should have seen some of the stuff that was stopped: Moaning Myrtle lavatory seat alarms and worse."

The early merchandise, released before the first film was completed, is easily discernable. Warner Bros.' resident artist, Fred Bode, did the majority of the artwork, and Harry Potter most frequently appeared with a red striped shirt under his black robes rather than the Gryffindor uniform he was to wear in the movies. The other characters as well bore only passing resemblances to the actors who would eventually appear on the screen. Though Bode images would reappear in later years, the majority of merchandise with what I term the "literary" version is pre-film items released in 2000 and 2001. Look for Warner Bros. © 2000 on the product to ensure it is an authorized item.

So, just how popular is Harry Potter? As reported in the June 1, 2009 issue of *License! Global Magazine* ("Warner Bros. and the Magic World of Harry Potter" by Tony Lisanto, editor-in-chief), since the release of the first Harry Potter film, Warner Bros. Consumer Products has become the world's third-largest licensor with $7 billion in total retail sales. This multi-faceted global strategy has expanded beyond the films to video games, museum exhibits, and, in 2010, a theme park attraction, The Wizarding World of Harry Potter, at Universal Orlando Resort in Orlando, Florida.

All of these present new merchandising opportunities, and as the films become darker and the characters older, the focus is shifting from children to an older audience who has grown up with Harry over the past decade. The most popular Harry Potter items after the books seem to be the video games (40 million sold worldwide) and DVDs (125 million sold worldwide).

Initially, for a short time, Harry Potter merchandise was available exclusively through Warner Bros. stores. In the first three years of the new millennium, the property experienced huge growth. This growth slowed midway through the decade when the gap between new releases of the books and movies widened. Still, the fan base is massive, and the general consensus is that Harry Potter merchandise has unlimited potential as it appeals to all age groups and all phases of the story. There is truly something for everyone.

With the continued expansion into international markets, growth has been predicted to double over the next few years. As well as Britain and North America, China, Russia, Japan, France, Germany, and Latin America all boast strong fan bases with collectors interested in adding to their collections. With this in mind, development is expanding in a direction that is faithful to the genre, particularly in adult collectibles that are movie-specific. It is probable that Harry Potter will continue long after the last of the movies is released.

What is to come? Despite the fact that J.K. Rowling has repeatedly stated that she has no desire to write an eighth Harry Potter book, it has been reported that she is working on the long awaited and highly anticipated *Harry Potter Encyclopedia*. When such a tome will be published is purely a matter of speculation as Rowling is under no deadline to complete the work and intends to take her time and enjoy the process. There are also currently no plans to expand into television, stage plays, or graphic novels, but one can not help but speculate on what the future might hold for this incredibly lucrative franchise.

A fond memory of reenacting favorite scenes from a much-loved book or movie is often a driving force behind collecting action figures. Considered cheap toys by some, the collector often sees them as a piece of their childhood, a small work of art, a topic of conversation, or a reflection of popular culture. Like all collectibles, the value of an action figure depends on how much someone is willing to pay for it. But it is also dependent as much on the way they are perceived as in their rarity or condition. As with most collectibles, there is profit to be made with action figures, but a collector should always follow the primary collecting rule: Collect what you like because you like it, not because you hope to make money off it.

A cross-collectible, action figures have been popular for many years, but the Harry Potter lines only became available in 2000 when Mattel released its Wizard Collection. Since then other manufacturers have entered the market with figures ranging from works of art to mediocre representations. It is important to know your subject. Details such as who the action figure portrays, when was it made, who made it, and how many were made can make the difference between spending a few dollars or hundreds of dollars to add to your collection.

How do you find out these details? All authorized Harry Potter action figures from the original Wizard Collection should have something like "™ and ©2000 Warner Bros." somewhere on the figure. Subsequent figures were marked in the same manner with different dates and sometimes will include the name of the manufacturer and the country where it was made, usually China. If the figure is still in its original package – a definite plus for value – the name of the character,

the manufacturer's name, date, retail value, and other details will often be available. Some characters will be more popular than others and produced in larger quantities. For example, Mattel produced numerous varieties of Harry Potter figures while making only one of the Richard Harrison portrayal of Headmaster Albus Dumbledore.

As Harry Potter action figures are relatively new to the market, there is not an overabundance of information available. This book was written to help fill that niche. More information can often be found at manufacturers' websites.

Condition is one of the most important variables in determining value. If the figure is in its original package, unmarked or undamaged in any way, it is considered mint in box condition (MIB) and will command a premium. The value of a loose figure as compared to one in its box is also dependent upon its rarity and whether or not it comes with all its original components. For example the Dumbledore figure mentioned above came with a Sorting Hat, a collectible casting stone, and a magic medallion trick.

The values listed for action figures in this book are based on an average of prices realized in various online auctions and prices charged in stores (both online and brick and mortar) over the past year. The price range is from loose figure to MIB figure and should be considered a guideline as prices fluctuate over time for a wide variety of reasons.

Mattel

Wizard Collection 2001

The latest sculpting technology was used by Mattel to reflect the actor's likeness when it designed the first lot of Harry Potter action figures. Based on the movie *Harry Potter and the Sorcerer's Stone*, the figures came with a casting stone for use in the Casting Stones Game, a wizard magic trick, and usually another accessory. The figures could also be used in the Electronic Powercasting Playset. The first figures were released in October 2001.

Gryffindor Harry†: Wearing a black robe and Gryffindor colors, the figure comes with a casting stone, magic trick, wand, and Hedwig (52664).......................................**$5-$15**

Gryffindor Hermione†: Wearing a black robe and Gryffindor colors, the figure comes with a casting stone, magic trick, wand, and three books (52670)...**$5-$15**

Gryffindor Ron†: Wearing a black robe and Gryffindor colors, the figure comes with a casting stone, magic trick, wand, and Scabbers (52665). ....**$5-$15**

†The variety that has caused the most controversy is the crest vs. no crest. The story goes that in the early days of producing the figures, Mattel was inconsistent with details on some of the figures, notably Gryffindor Harry, Gryffindor Ron, Gryffindor Hermione, Slytherin Malfoy, and Remembrall Malfoy. Some of these figures were produced with crests on the left sides of their chests, others without. Most that I have seen are without crests, but some sellers claim that the ones with the crests are the rare ones. The pictures of the figures on the package do not have crests, and therefore I assume this would be the correct variety. Until this debate has been decided, I suggest you take care in purchasing crest/no crest figures unless the seller can confirm the source of his information as to which is the rarity, if either.

Headmaster Dumbledore††: Wearing a red, burgundy, and gold robe, the white-bearded figure comes with a casting stone, magic trick, and Sorting Hat (52667)............**$30-$50**

Invisibility Cloak Harry: Cast in clear plastic, the figure wears a clear robe and comes with a casting stone and magic trick (52671). ...**$5-$15**

††There was some controversy when the Professor Dumbledore figure was released. It appeared that the figure had two right arms, and some people took advantage of this to sell the figure as a variety and charge an inflated price. According to Mattel, the figure was sculpted to hold the Sorting Hat in front with one arm while the other was to be behind his back. When the figure was posed in another manner, it would therefore appear that he had two right hands. The Dumbledore figure was a chase figure, meaning that there were a limited number of them sent to stores, and therefore it is not as numerous as some of the others. Adding to the value is the fact that the actor on whom this figure was based, Richard Harris, died after the filming of the second movie.

Lord Voldemort†††: Wearing dark green robes over a black suit (identical to Professor Quirrell), except his turban does not drape around his shoulder. He has a head that can be turned to have Voldemort's face on the other side and comes with a casting stone and magic trick (54877). ....**$30-$50**

Lord Voldemort††††: With garlic wreath and without casting stones and magic trick (56096). ....**$5-$15**

†††The Lord Voldemort action figure is considered the rarest of the Mattel figures. Apparently, in each box of 100 figures packed at Mattel, only one Voldemort was shipped. The packaging of He-who-must-not-be-named has the Powercaster ad on the top left and his face in dark green instead of white as described in the book and shown in the film.

††††The Voldemort figure with the wreath of garlic is the more common of the two and has a light green face compared to the dark green of the other version. It also has a brown turban instead of a purple turban and a dark brown robe. The picture is of Quirrell, not Voldemort, and there is no Powercaster ad in the top left of the package. There are also two versions of the backs of the packages as some have a factory placed sticker reading "not included" beside the words "Garlic necklace." This suggests that somewhere in production an error was made and not all packages received the necklace or some non-garlic figures were placed on garlic cards.

Professor Quirrell: Wearing dark green robes over a black suit, he has a purple turban that drapes around his right shoulder and comes with a casting stone and magic trick (52669). ....**$5-$15**

Professor Snape: Wearing a black robe, the figure comes with a casting stone, magic trick, wand, and potion bottles (52666)...........**$5-$15**

Quidditch Harry: Wearing a red Quidditch uniform, the figure comes with a casting stone, magic trick, Nimbus 2000 broom, Golden Snitch, and finger guide (52663). ....$5-$15

Remembrall Malfoy†: Wearing a black robe and Slytherin colors, this figure comes with a magic wand, Remembrall, casting stone, and magic trick. Available as a limited edition, this is one of the harder-to-find characters in the Harry Potter action figure series (52673). ....$20-$40

Slytherin Malfoy†: Wearing a black robe and Slytherin colors, the figure comes with a casting stone, magic trick, and wand (52668). ....$5-$15

Deluxe Creature Collection 2001

These figures differ from the other Mattel figures in that they are all non-human, larger, and more solid than the earlier figures in the series.

Fluffy: The three-headed dog comes with floorboards and a trapdoor that opens (52676). ....$12-$25

Mountain Troll: Wearing a vest and loin cloth, this ugly dude carries a club and comes with a break-apart sink (52675). ....$12-$25

Hagrid: Wearing a removable, full-length brown coat with bulging pockets over brown jacket, pants, and reddish brown shirt, the shaggy-bearded Hagrid carries a pink umbrella and a half-hatched baby Norbert (52674). ....$12-$25

Wizard Collection 2002

Photo courtesy Figure Realm

Cast-a-Spell Harry: Wearing a black robe and greenish-yellow pants, Harry comes with a wand casting red flame magic. There is supposedly a yellow flame variety of this figure, rarity factor unknown (56189). .... **$15-$17**

Cast-a-Spell Ron: Wearing black robes with a gray shirt and blue pants, Ron comes with a wand casting green flame magic (56191). .... **$15-$17**

Chamber of Secrets Harry: Wearing a black robe, Harry has blood on his face and hands and carries the Sword of Godric Gryffindor (56188). ....$14-$17

Dobby: Wearing a grubby pillowcase, the house elf comes with a lamp and iron with which to punish himself, and a cake and catapult to get Harry into trouble (56194). .... **$17-$25**

Hermione: Wearing a black robe and Gryffindor colors, she comes with a wand and potion bottle (B1511). .... **$15-$17**

Professor Flitwick: Wearing gold-trimmed black robes with a gold waistcoat and green pants, the diminutive professor stands on a book that turns and levitates him into the air; below his desk is a plethora of books (56193). .... **$10-$15**

Professor Lockhart: Wearing flamboyant gold robes, this vain professor comes with a wand and a cage that launches a Cornish pixie (56195). ....**$14-$17**

Photo courtesy Figure Realm

Professor Snape: Wearing black robes, Snape launches a green snake out of his cauldron (56192). ...... **$10-$15**

Seeker Harry: Wearing the red and yellow Gryffindor Quidditch team uniform, Harry comes with a broom, Golden Snitch, and flying cord guide (56187). .. **$10-$20**

Seeker Malfoy: Wearing the gray and green Slytherin Quidditch uniform, Malfoy comes with a Nimbus 2001 with flying cord guide (56190). .... **$10-$20**

Deluxe Creature Collection 2002

Aragog: The terror of the Forbidden Forest, this huge arachnid is completely poseable as his legs are fully articulated and his mandibles open and close (56128). .... **$20-$25**

Photo courtesy Figure Realm

Centaur: Not named but probably Firenze, this 8-3/4" figure moves at the waist, kicks his legs, and comes with a crossbow. His coloring is much darker than on the package (54882). .... **$20-$25**

Knight and horse (chess piece): The knight has an "exploding" feature: When his legs are squeezed together, the rider and his mount "explode" into pieces in imitation of what happened to Ron's knight in the climactic chess game in the first movie. The difference is that this chess piece has a knight wherein Ron was the rider in the film (55754). .... **$20-$25**

Norbert: Unless he is a full-grown dragon, Norbert – with a 20" wingspan – is way out of scale to the other figures (55299). ...... **$20-$25**

Playset Collection 2002

Harry Potter Web of Aragog Playset: Comes with a "grabbing action" Aragog, base, and an elastic spider web that can stretch to three feet to trap an unwary action figure (not included) (57607). .... **$10-$15**

Weasley Flying Car: Over 15" long, the blue Ford Anglia in pink box fits the 5" Harry Potter figures. Includes a small Hedwig "flying" with the car and disappearing luggage......................**$20-$30**

Basilisk Attack Playset: The monster's eyes flash yellow and its mouth flashes red as it hisses and bares its teeth. The Basilisk comes with a Chamber of Secrets background with a secret entrance and Sword of Gryffindor packaged in a box (54930). .... **$20-$25**

Quidditch Team Collection 2002

The Quidditch Team collection is amongst the hardest to find of the Harry Potter action figures. Of the three, Fred is the rarest on par with the Dumbledore figure, followed by George and Harry. Strangely enough, the only difference between the Weasley twins is the number and name on the package, therefore loose Fred and George figures are indistinguishable.

Quidditch Fred: Wearing the Gryffindor Quidditch uniform, he comes with a broom, bat, and bludger (55530). **$40-$50**

Quidditch George: Wearing the Gryffindor Quidditch uniform, he comes with a broom, bat, and bludger (54875)......................**$15-$20**

Quidditch Harry†: Wearing the Gryffindor Quidditch uniform, he comes with finger ring, broom, and Golden Snitch (56208). .... **$10-$15**

†This figure differs from the first Quidditch Harry (52663) in that there is no casting stone, and he comes in the package facing sideways, riding his broom, and holding the Snitch. Loose figures can be distinguished by Harry's glasses: They are black on the Quidditch Team Harry figure and gray on Quidditch Harry.

Slime Chamber Collection 2002

Griphook (The Gringotts Goblin): Wearing black pants, jacket, and green-spotted waistcoat, he comes with a cauldron, jewel cart, and bottle of purple slime (54879). .... **$15-$20**

Slime Chamber Fred: Wearing black robes, mustard pants, and green sweater, he comes with a cauldron and bottle of red slime (54876). ....**$10-$15**

Slime Chamber George: Wearing black robes, mustard pants, and green sweater, he comes with a cauldron and bottle of red slime (55529). ....**$10-$15**

Slime Chamber Harry: Wearing black robes with spider webs on them, he comes with a wand, cauldron, and bottle of blue slime (54870). ....**$10-$15**

Slime Chamber Malfoy: Wearing black robes splashed with green slime, he comes with a cauldron and bottle of green slime (54872). .... **$10-$15**

Slime Chamber Ron: Wearing black robes with slugs crawling on them, he comes with a cauldron and bottle of red slime (54871). .... **$10-$15**

Slime Chamber Playset: Features a basilisk head looking over a wall and base. When the head tilts, glow-in-the-dark slime pours out and onto a figure placed on the base below. Packaged in a box (54883). .... **$15-$20**

Slime Chamber Hermione: As she turns into a cat, Hermione sprouts ears, whiskers, and a tail. She is wearing black robes splashed with orange and comes with a cauldron, potion bottle, and bottle of orange slime (54873). ....**$13-$17**

Magical Minis Collection

The first part of the Magical Minis Collection was released early in 2002. The first five poseable figures came with an animal associated with that person and had a "magic motion feature" that would activate when you "wave the wand" or "wave the umbrella." The figures were representative of the first two books. The packaging comes in two kinds, the U.S. style with the name in large letters on a gold band on the front, and the international style with the name in small letters (in a dozen languages) in a gold band.

Series 1

U.S. style   International style

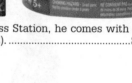

Albus Dumbledore: In the headmaster's office, he comes with a wand and Fawkes (47416). .... **$10-$15**

Harry Potter: At King's Cross Station, he comes with a wand and Hedwig in a cage (47412). ....**$10-$15**

Hermione Granger: In the Gryffindor Common Room, she comes with a wand and Crookshanks (47414). **$10-$15**

Ron Weasley: In his room at The Burrow, he comes with a wand, book, and Scabbers (47413). .... **$10-$15**

Rubeus Hagrid: Outside his hut, he comes with pink umbrella and Norbert (47415)........................ **$10-$15**

Series 2

The second series was released later in the year with the Chamber of Secrets movie. These three figures came with rubber stamps and ink pads.

U.S. style

International style

Hermione Granger: In the Potions classroom, she comes with cauldron and potion bottle (47418). .... **$10-$15**

Harry Potter: Over the Quidditch Pitch, he comes with broom and ball box (47417)...**$15-$20**

Ginny Weasley†: In the Gryffindor Common Room, she comes with book and quill in ink bottle (47419)........................**$10-$15**

†The figure of Ginny Weasley is known to exist with an all-white sweater instead of the correct sky-blue, red, purple, and white pattern. The box for this figure is also different. Rarity factor unknown, suggested price. ....$15-$20

Series 3

A third series was also released in which the figures moved when placed on a trunk. These are less common than the first two series.

Dumbledore: Comes with Fawkes (47464). ....$15-$20

Harry Potter: Comes with Dobby and cabinet (47462)...$15-$20

Ron Weasley: Comes with trunk, wand, Scabbers, and chess piece (47463). ....$15-$20

Dueling Club Collection 2003

Photo courtesy Figure Realm

Dueling Club Lockhart: Wearing flamboyant green and gold cloth robes, he twists at the waist to duel and comes with a wand and collectible holo-tile (57602). ....**$15-$20**

Dueling Club Malfoy: Wearing black robes and Slytherin colors, Draco twists at the waist and comes with a wand and collectible holo-tile (57604). ....**$15-$20**

Dueling Club Harry: Wearing black robes and Gryffindor colors, Harry twists at the waist and comes with a wand and collectible holo-tile (57601). ....**$15-$20**

Tom Riddle: Wearing black robes and Slytherin colors, young Tom carries the diary with which he bewitched Ginny Weasley, and he glows in the dark (56196). ....**$15-$20**

Deluxe Wizard Collection 2004

These are very nice figures though oversized and not in scale with most previous Mattel Harry Potter lines. They are highly articulated and based on characters as seen in *Harry Potter and the Prisoner of Azkaban*.

Albus Dumbledore: 8" tall, based on Michael Gambon playing Dumbledore, includes wand and spell blast effect. ....**$20-$25**

Azkaban Dementor: Ten inches tall wearing black cloth robes over skeleton frame, moves on rolling base (C3149). ....**$15-$20**

Expecto Patronus Harry: Wearing black robes and Gryffindor colors, Harry casts three spells, none of which resembles a patronus! C3145). ....**$10-$15**

Extreme Quidditch Harry Potter: 8" tall in full Quidditch Gryffindor uniform, he comes with broom, display stand, and magnet grip to hold Snitch (C3144). ....**$10-$15**

Lupin/Werewolf: Transforms from Professor Lupin into werewolf in three easy steps (C3147). ....**$15-$20**

Harry Potter and the Prisoner of Azkaban Mini Collection 2004

Draco Malfoy, Harry Potter, Buckbeak, and Buckbeak's tether: Series 1, 1 of 4 (C3154), 2-1/2" x 3" figures. ....**$10-$15**

Harry Potter Knight Bus Playset: Designed as a carrying case, the bus holds eight mini figures and can be used as a playset. The bus is 10" long and 10-3/4" high and comes with a unique Harry Potter figure...**$10-$15**

Crookshanks, Hermione, Scabbers, Ron, and Harry: in robes. Series 1, 4 of 4 (C3157).....**$10-$15**

Hermione, Ron, and Harry: at Hogsmeade in casual clothes. Series 2, 1 of 3.................**$10-$15**

Professor Snape, Harry, and Dumbledore: In robes, with broomstick, potion bottle, and walking stick. Series 2, 2 of 3 (C3162). ....**$10-$15**

Magical Creatures Playset: Harry and Hagrid in Hagrid's Hut with assorted creatures. ....**$15-$20**

Potions Class Playset: Harry and Snape in Potions classroom with various cauldrons, skeletons, break-away walls, etc. ....**$15-$20**

Quidditch Draco, Harry, and Oliver Wood: Dressed in Quidditch uniforms; with Snitch, broom, and Quidditch case. Series 2, 3 of 3. ....**$10-$15**

Remus Lupin, Harry in robes with patronus, Lupin as werewolf: Comes with Marauder's Map. Series 1, 3 of 4 (C3157). ....$10-$15

Dementor, Harry in casual clothes, Black as Snuffles, Sirius Black: Series 1, 2 of 4 (C3155). ....$10-$15

NECA, Inc.

With the last of the Mattel figures in 2004, there was a three-year drought before any more Harry Potter figures appeared on the market. In July 2006 Warner Bros. signed an agreement with NECA, Inc. (National Entertainment Collectibles Association) for a new line of figures based on *Harry Potter and the Goblet of Fire* and *Harry Potter and the Order of the Phoenix*. The first part of the new line was scheduled to hit the stores in early March 2007 with the last four figures in May. The 7" figures were released first, followed by the 4" figures in May. They are virtually identical except in size. All photos of NECA, Inc. figurines are courtesy of Figure Realm.

Harry Potter: Exclusive 2007 San Diego Comic-Con Harry Potter 7" Action Figure dressed in Gryffindor colors; it comes with unique flying Hedwig (60542)...**$15-$20**

Goblet of Fire – Series 1, 7" Figures

Death Eater 1: Wearing black mask and robes, it comes with base and wand (49102). ....**$10-$15**

Death Eater 2: Wearing black mask and robes, it comes with base, torch, and wand (49103). ....**$10-$15**

Dementor: Wearing black robes, it comes with base (49104). ....**$15-$20**

Harry Potter: Wearing Gryffindor colors without robe, he comes with base and wand (60008)..**$10-$15**

Hermione Granger: Wearing Gryffindor colors without robe, she comes with base and wand (60015). ....**$15-$20**

Lord Voldemort: Wearing black robes, he comes with base and wand (49105)...**$15-$20**

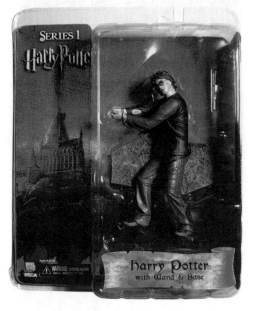

Triwizard Harry Potter: Wearing the red and black shirt he wore into the maze in Goblet of Fire, he comes with base and wand (49101). ....**$5-$10**

Order of the Phoenix – Series 1, 4" Figures

Harry Potter†: Wearing Gryffindor colors without robes, comes with base and wand (60031). .... **$5-$10**

Fred and George Weasley: Two-pack. .... **$10-$15**

Hermione Granger†: Wearing Gryffindor colors without robes, comes with base and wand (60014). .... **$5-$10**

Ron Weasley†: Wearing Gryffindor colors without robes, shirt out, comes with base and wand (60022). .... **$5-$10**

Sirius Black: Wearing brown coat, comes with base and wand (60032)................ **$8-$12**

†Harry, Ron, and Hermione come with an extra piece that can be used with the others to build a "Dummy Death Eater" figure.

Order of the Phoenix – Series 2, 7" Figures
Released September 2007

Albus Dumbledore: Wearing purple and gray robes, comes with base and wand (60536). .... **$10-$15**

Death Eater A: Wearing black robes and green mask, comes with base and wand (60537). .... **$10-$15**

Death Eater B: Wearing black robes and silver mask, comes with base and wand (60538). .... **$10-$15**

Harry Potter: Wearing Gryffindor colors without robe, open sweater, comes with base and wand (60535).................................. **$5-$10**

Severus Snape: Wearing black robes, comes with base and wand (60539)..**$10-$15**

Order of the Phoenix – Series 3, 7" Figures
Released January 2008

Bellatrix Lestrange: Wearing black outfit comes with base and wand (49157)...........**$10-$15**

Casual Harry Potter: Wearing gray sweater, red shirt, and blue pants, comes with base, prophecy orb, and wand (49155). ....**$5-$10**

Lucius Malfoy: Wearing black robes, comes with base, cane, mask, and wand (49156). .... **$10-$15**

Boxed Sets

Harry Potter and Headmaster Albus Dumbledore: 7" two-pack featuring the original Dumbledore and Harry in robes. The pack also comes with Fawkes on his perch, the sword of Gryffindor, and the Sorting Hat, released in July 2008 (60561). .... **$25-$35**

Harry Potter vs. Voldemort Boxed set: 7" Harry and He-Who-Must-Not-Be-Named in the cemetery with a statue (same figures as above with statue base added), 19" x 16", released in 2007 (60448). .... **$35-$40**

Harry Potter, Ginny Weasley, Draco Malfoy and Mad-Eye Moody: Released in September 2009 (49167). .... **$30-$40**

Order of the Phoenix – Defensive Magic 4-Pack: This 4" set includes Harry, Neville Longbottom, Hermione, and Cho Chang, along with a Death Eater Dummy with an exploding feature to use for spell practice. .... **$40-$50**

Deluxe Action Figures

Hagrid Deluxe Action Figure: 9-3/4" with Fang, Norbert, dead ferrets, umbrella, and lantern; "Push Button Sound," speaks 10 phrases, released in 2007 (60013). .....**$25-$30**

Hermione Granger: 12" action figure with "Push Button Sound," similar to 7" figure, released in September 2007 (60523). .**$25-$30**

Harry Potter: 12" action figure with "Push Button Sound," similar to 7" figure, released in May 2007 (49106). ....**$20-$25**

Harry Potter: 18" action figure with "Push Button Sound," similar to 7" figure, released in May 2007 (49167). ....**$20-$25**

Ron Weasley: 12" action figure with "Push Button Sound," similar to 7" figure, released in September 2007 (60524)..................**$25-$30**

Half Blood Prince – Series 1, 4" Figures†
Released April 2009

Draco Malfoy: with stand and wand..$7-$12

Ginny Weasley: with stand and wand..$7-$12

Harry Potter: with stand and wand. ....$7-$12

Lord Voldemort: with stand and wand...$7-$12

Mad-Eye Moody: with stand, staff, and wand...$7-$10

† Same as 7" figures in detail but not size.

Half Blood Prince – Series 1, 7" Figures
Released April 2009

Draco Malfoy: Wearing Slytherin colors, comes with wand and base (60572)... **$10-$15**

Ginny Weasley: Wearing Gryffindor colors, comes with wand and base (60570)... **$10-$15**

Harry Potter: Wearing burgundy jacket, gray shirt, and blue pants, comes with wand and base (60573)... **$10-$15**

Mad-Eye Moody: Wearing brown coat, black clothes, comes with staff and base (60587). .... **$10-$15**

When the Warner Bros. Studio Stores were closed in 2001, one part of the business was deemed worthy to continue. The animation art department, Gallery License, with its Looney Tunes, Hanna Barbera, and Harry Potter properties, was awarded to Clampett Studio Collections.

Ruth Clampett, daughter of famed Warner Bros. animator and director Bob Clampett and Warner Bros. Studio Store executive, opened the business in September 2001. The agreement with Warner Bros. gave Clampett Studio Collections the inventory from the Warner Bros. stores along with the rights to publish art from the Time Warner Library and the position as the licensing agent representing Warner Bros. properties for other companies. Among these are the works by various artists with a Harry Potter theme:

Art by Fred Bode

An artist for Warner Bros., Fred Bode created the style guides for all the early Harry Potter merchandise. His work with Looney Tunes is in sharp contrast to the more subdued renderings of his Harry Potter work. He is presently director of character art at Warner Bros.

Art by Mary GrandPre

Mary GrandPre illustrated all of the Harry Potter books published by Scholastic. Her preferred medium is pastels, and her favorite subjects are children's books, though she also does advertising and corporate art. She was featured on the cover of *Time* magazine for her work with the Harry Potter series.

Art by Jim Salvati

Jim Salvati was surrounded by the arts as he grew up in Southern California. During his career he worked at most of the movie studios and continues with Disney and Warner Bros.

Counting the Days by Mary GrandPre

All photographs in this chapter are courtesy of Clampett Studio Collections — ClampettStudio.com and WildsvilleGallery.com.

Art by Fred Bode

The Harry Potter Portfolio: Set of six giclée prints of original drawings used in the early development of art for the Harry Potter program. Released in 2000; edition of 250... **$650-$700**

The process of making fine art prints from a digital source using ink-jet printing is known as giclée.

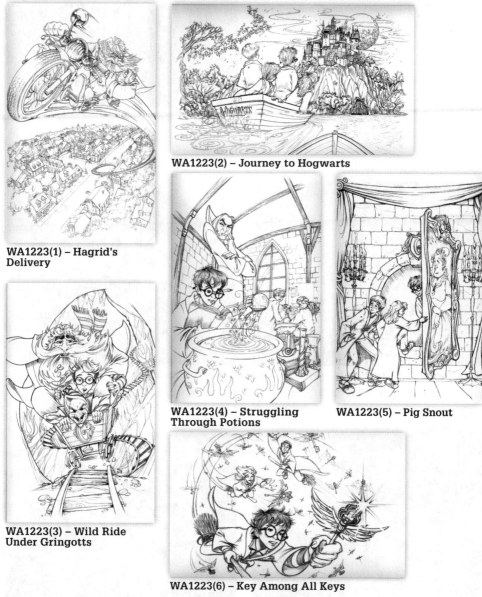

WA1223(1) – Hagrid's Delivery

WA1223(2) – Journey to Hogwarts

WA1223(4) – Struggling Through Potions

WA1223(5) – Pig Snout

WA1223(3) – Wild Ride Under Gringotts

WA1223(6) – Key Among All Keys

Struggling Through Potions
Edition size: 100. Size: 21" x 29". Fine art giclée on canvas, unframed, signed by Fred Bode.
....**$600-$625**
Key Among All Keys, The
Edition size: 250. Size: 32" x 23". Fine art giclée on canvas, unframed, signed by Fred Bode.
....**$600-$625**

Art by Mary GrandPre

Created from GrandPre's original pastels, each print is hand signed by the artist. The price is for unframed art.

Battle With the Dragon
Edition size: 250. Size: 11" x 14". Giclée on paper..**$200-$250**

Christmas in the Great Hall
Edition size: 250. Size: 11" x 14". Giclée on paper..**$200-$250**

Cloak of Invisibility, The
Edition size: 250. Image size: 9-3/8" x 11-3/4". Print size: 11" x 14". Fine art giclée print on paper..**$200-$250**

Counting the Days
Edition size: 250. Image size: 9-3/8" x 11-3/4". Print size: 11" x 14". Fine art giclée print on paper..**$200-$250**

Diagon Alley
Edition size: 250. Image size: 9-3/8" x 11-3/4". Fine art giclée print on paper. ....**$200-$250**

Ducling Wizards

Edition size: 250. Image size: 9-3/8" x 11-3/4". Print size: 11" x 14". Fine art giclée print on paper. Battle in the Ministry of Magic from *Harry Potter and the Order of the Phoenix*............... **$200-$250**

Enchanted Car, The

Edition size: 250. Size: 11" x 14". Giclée on paper...**$200-$225**

Expelliarmus!

Edition size: 250. Image size: 11" x 14". Fine art giclée print on paper..................**$200-$250**

Flying Keys

Bonus print, available only when entire portfolio was purchased. Edition size: 250. Size: 11" x 14". Giclée on paper........**$200-$250**

Golden Web, The

Edition size: 150. Size: 11" x 14". Giclée on paper...**$300-$350**

Harry Potter and the Prisoner of Azkaban (2004) Rescue of Sirius
Edition size: 250. Giclée on paper.
Deluxe: 21-1/2" x 26" ....**$325-$350**
Small: 11" x 14"...............................**$200-$250**

Harry Potter and the Sorcerer's Stone (2001)
Quidditch
Edition size: 250. Giclée on paper.
Deluxe: 21-1/2" x 26" ....**$325-$350**
Small: 11" x 14"..................................**$200-$250**

Mirror of Erised
Edition size: 250. Image size: 9-3/8" x 11-3/4".
Print size: 9" x 11". ....**$200-$250**

Pixie Mayhem
Edition size: 250. Image size: 9-3/8" x 11-3/4".
Print size: 11" x 14". Fine art giclée print on
paper..**$200-$250**

Three Friends
Edition size: 250. Size: 11" x 14". Giclée on
paper..**$200-$250**

The Harry Potter Book Cover Art Series

Set of seven in an edition size of 500; includes a bonus print. These 15" x 29" fine art giclée prints are signed by Mary GrandPre. ....**$425-$450**

Harry Potter and the Sorcerer's Stone

Harry Potter and the Chamber of Secrets

Harry Potter and the Prisoner of Azkaban

Harry Potter and the Goblet of Fire

Harry Potter and the Order of the Phoenix

Harry Potter and the Half-Blood Prince

Harry Potter and the Deathly Hallows

Harry Potter and the Half-Blood Prince Bonus Print
Available only when entire portfolio of seven is purchased.

Escape From Gringotts
Edition size: 500, same format as above.. $425-$450
Same printed on canvas. Edition size: 50.. $800-$850

Book Cover Lithographs

Harry Potter and the Chamber of Secrets
Edition size: 2,500. Print size: 20" x 16"..$95-$110

Harry Potter and the Prisoner of Azkaban
Edition size: 2,500. Print size: 20" x 16"..$95-$110

Harry Potter and the Sorcerer's Stone
Edition size: 2,500. Print size: 20" x 16"...$95-$110

Art by Jim Salvati

Full Moon at Hogwarts

Edition size: 250. Size: 17" x 20-1/2". Giclée on paper of Hogwarts under a full moon, signed by Jim Salvati ....**$225-$250**

Same printed on canvas. Edition size: 100. Size: 21-3/4" x 25-3/4". ....**$550-$575**

Harry and Hedwig

Edition size: 250. Size: 17" x 22-1/4". Giclée on paper, signed by Jim Salvati. ....**$275-$300**

Same printed on canvas. Edition size: 100. Size: 21-3/4" x 25-3/4". ....**$600-$625**

Harry Potter and the Goblet of Fire, "Harry and the Golden Snitch"

Edition size: 250. Size: 14-1/2" x 20-5/8". Giclée on canvas. Harry pursues the Golden Snitch. ......**$275-$300**

Same printed on canvas. Edition size: 100. Size: 21-3/4" x 25-3/4". ...**$600-$625**

Harry Potter Hogwarts Express

Edition size: 250. Size: 17" x 22-1/4". Giclée on paper, signed by Jim Salvati. ....**$225-$250**

Same printed on canvas. Edition size: 100. Size: 30-1/2" x 20-1/2"....**$550-$575**

Movie Art
The Witches and Wizards of Harry Potter Collection

This collection of 10 is reproduced in the fine art giclée process on archival paper in a numbered limited edition of 700. The images have been taken from production stills from the Harry Potter movies and include one large picture of a character on the left and five small images of scenes from the films on the right. The prints are presented in a black mat with the Harry Potter name logo in gold and designed to fit a standard 11" x 14" frame.
....**$50-$70 each**

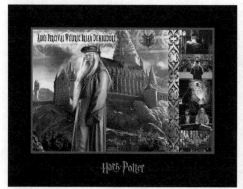

Albus Percival Wulfric Brian Dumbledore, the headmaster (actor Michael Gambon) in front of Hogwarts.

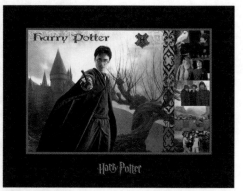

Harry Potter in front of Hogwarts and the Whomping Willow.

Rubeus Hagrid standing in front of his hut.

Hermione Granger in front of field with Hogwarts in distance.

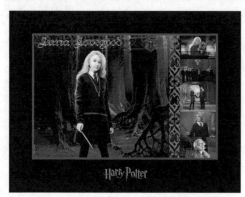

Luna Lovegood in front of Forbidden Forest.

Ronald Weasley in front of Hogwarts.

Remus Lupin in Shrieking Shack.

Sirius Black in Hogsmeade at night.

Minerva McGonagall inside Hogwarts.

Severus Snape in front of Hogwarts in winter.

Board Games

Harry Potter board games are reasonably easy to find online and in stores. Having been available for little more than 10 years, they are not considered vintage games and therefore do not command the higher prices of board games from the 1950s and earlier.

Character games, whether Harry Potter, a superhero, or a cartoon character, are among the most popular and a cross-collectible sought after by both general game collectors and those looking for specific character games.

I have play tested some of the Harry Potter games with my grandson and found them to be quite enjoyable. Like the action figures, they give players an opportunity to relive exciting scenes from the books or movies. The Harry Potter chess game is the perfect opportunity to introduce youngsters to one of the world's oldest board games.

Like all collectibles, condition is of primary concern to board game collectors. Games in excellent condition, with the boxes, boards, and all playing pieces intact, are preferable. Most games have a list of contents in the rules booklet, and it is wise to check this before purchasing. If buying from online auctions, contact the seller for confirmation that the game is complete and for permission to return it if it is not. The first thing to look at when examining for condition are the box corners; make sure they are crisp and sharp. A damaged box will seldom have pristine components inside. Unopened games will command a premium but are rare as most people want to play their games. If you want to play the games as well as collect them, use care when opening and closing the boxes and carefully store the rules booklet and pieces. Keep the games in a clean, warm, dry place, flat on a shelf. Extra care should be taken with the Scene It? games that include DVDs. Take precautions to keep the discs free of dust and scratches and examine them carefully before purchasing a used game.

It is also a wise precaution to store the smaller pieces in small plastic bags to prevent damage or loss. The cards that come with most games are also easily damaged, so card protectors such as those used for storing collectible cards can be used to maintain pristine condition.

Hallmark

Harry Potter Magnetic Quidditch Game (15012-62621): This metal board game comes with 13 magnetic figures, flags, and balls to be thrown at the 13-1/2" x 9-1/2" tasseled board, which can be hung on the wall or used to make scenes of a Quidditch game. .... $5-$10

Mattel
Harry Potter Chapter Games

Six Harry Potter Chapter Games were released in 2001. These games came in plastic carrying cases shaped like books that fold open to reveal the board and playing pieces. Diagon Alley, Halloween, Quidditch, and Through the Trapdoor are based on *Philosopher's Stone,* and Aragog and Heir of Slytherin are based on *Chamber of Secrets.* They came in blister packs.

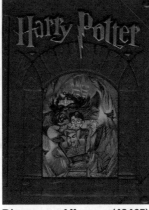

Diagon Alley (43465): Players shop for school supplies in Diagon Alley at Gringotts, Ollivanders, Madam Malkin's, Eeylops Owl Emporium, Flourish and Botts, Apothecary; avoid Malfoy; and return to the Leaky Cauldron to win. ....**$10-$15**

Quidditch (43467): Let's play Quidditch! Players must score 300 points or be the first to catch the Golden Snitch in this three-dimensional version of the wizards' game. .... **$10-$15**

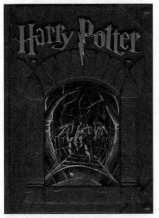

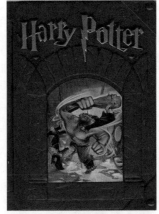

Aragog (47407): This three-dimensional game pits the players against Aragog as they make their way through the web maze to escape in the Weasleys' Ford Anglia. .... **$10-$15**

Halloween (43516): Players must battle a mountain troll, knock him out, and rescue Hermione................... **$10-$15**

Heir of Slytherin: Players take on the basilisk armed with the Sword of Gryffindor and fang cards. .... **$15-$20**

Through the Trapdoor (43466): Players must negotiate their way across the perils of the board to reach the Sorcerer's Stone. .... **$10-$15**

Other Mattel Board Games

3-D Mini Game—Capture the Pixies (47437): Released in 2007, this Defense Against the Dark Arts class unfolds into a three-dimensional game board. Players race to capture the most pixies. .... **$5-$10**

3-D Mini Game—Escape the Dursleys' (47438): Released in 2007, the Dursleys' house at Number 4 Privet Drive unfolds into a three-dimensional game board, which includes the only Uncle Vernon figure made. Players must avoid Uncle Vernon and escape in the Ford Anglia before he catches them. .... **$5-$10**

Dicers (43020): Released in 2002, this is another collectible pieces game of "fantastic characters and rolling magic." Each dicer has five clear sides and a Harry Potter-related figure inside. The sixth side has information regarding the character, such as name, number, casting ability, and affiliations. The first starter pack dicers released were #1-6, then #7-18 were released in individual blister packs, followed by the second starter pack of #19-24, and then #25-36 individually. Originally 54 different dicers were to be released, but only 36 actually appeared.

Collectible dice game starter kit .... **$5-$10**

Booster pack .... **$5-$8**

   Prices for individual dicers depends primarily upon the popularity of the character and range from 25 cents to $5 (detailed pricing of individual dicers is beyond the scope of this guide).

Front

Singles

Back

Dicers Checklist

1	Malfoy
2	Hagrid
3	Harry Potter #1 (standing with wand)
4	Hermione
5	Snape
6	Sorting Hat
7	Crabbe
8	Dumbledore
9	Firenze
10	Fluffy
11	Goyle
12	Hedwig
13	Mirror of Erised
14	Troll
15	Norbert
16	Quirrell
17	Ron
18	Sorcerer's Stone
19	Fred & George
20	Harry Potter #2 (playing Quidditch)
21	McGonagall
22	Nimbus 2000
23	Oliver Wood
24	Golden Snitch
25	Aragog
26	Bludger
27	Dobby
28	Fawkes
29	Flying Car
30	Garden Gnome
31	Mandrake
32	Mrs. Norris
33	Polyjuice Potion
34	Scabbers
35	Voldemort
36	Whomping Willow

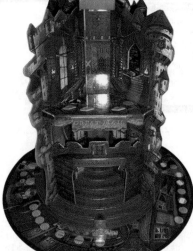

Harry Potter Adventures Through Hogwarts Electronic 3-D Game (42908): Released in 2001, this electronic game challenges problem-solving skills as the players journey through Hogwarts' 11 rooms seeking the Sorcerer's Stone. .... **$15-$20**

Harry Potter and the Chamber of Secrets Trivia (43452): Released in 2002, this game features Quidditch-style play and questions from Harry Potter and the Chamber of Secrets. .... **$12-$17**

Harry Potter and the Goblet of Fire Quidditch Dice Game (H6496): Released in 2005, this game comes in a Quidditch ball trunk-shaped carrying case with nine dice (quaffle, bludger, Snitch, keeper, and goal dice) and scoring markers... **$5-$10**

Harry Potter and the Sorcerer's Stone Quidditch: This is a slot race game with two remote-controlled collector-quality figures (in Gryffindor and Slytherin uniforms) racing over 15 feet of track around an authentic looking Quidditch field. .... **$50-$75**

Harry Potter and the Sorcerer's Stone Trivia Game (42748): Released in 2001, this game resembles Trivial Pursuit. Players move around a circular track, answering questions, avoiding curses, and collecting charms. .... **$10-$15**

Harry Potter and the Sorcerer's Stone Trivia Game Prefects Edition (42749): Same as above with different box, slip cover, and fancier components. .... **$12-$17**

Harry Potter Casting Stones Game (42750): The Starter Game comes with a fabric game board that doubles as a carrying pouch, 12 casting stones, two casting cards, 12 turret gems, and the instructions. It is basically a rock-paper-scissors game with visual appeal. Additional casting stones can be purchased separately and are listed below. Some of the casting stones were only available with the action figures, in starter sets, and Powercaster Sets.

Starter Game...$10-$15

Harry Potter Championship Quidditch Game (B8504): Released in 2004, this game features Harry Potter and Draco Malfoy facing off in a fast-paced Quidditch game based more on luck than skill in shooting. It includes an electronic timer and scoring feature......................$15-$20

Harry Potter Diagon Alley Board Game (43184): Released in 2002, this game challenges players to gather the items they need from the shops in Diagon Alley with dice, spell cards, and floo powder...$15-$20

Harry Potter: Halls of Hogwarts (43595): Released in 2003, this unique game never plays the same twice as players try to make their way through Hogwarts over ever-changing staircases............................ **$10-$15**

Harry Potter Hogwarts Dueling Club Game (C1895): Released in 2004, players move about the Hogwarts board, learning spells for dueling.. **$10-$15**

Harry Potter Levitating Challenge Game (42907): Released in 2001, this electronic game uses a fan and lightweight foam ball to create the illusion of levitation as the player maneuvers the ball through a maze... **$10-$15**

Harry Potter Mystery at Hogwarts Game (42754): Released in 2001, this game is similar to the Parker Brothers Clue game. A few new twists have been added, like the roaming ghost that sends you back to the beginning, and emblems that allow you to peek at your opponent's cards. .... **$10-$15**

Harry Potter Rescue at Hogwarts Game (C5555): Released in 2003, this three-dimensional board game is based on Harry Potter and the Prisoner of Azkaban. Players work together to repel dementors, free Buckbeak, and rescue Sirius Black before time runs out. .... **$20-$25**

Harry Potter Whomping Willow Game (43468): This game was previewed at the American International Toy Fair in February 2002. The electronic willow challenges players to gather up their lost possessions in easy or difficult mode and in three different methods of play. .... **$15-$20**

Harry Potter Wizard's Chess (43533): Released in 2002, this chess set closely resembles the game as it was presented in Harry Potter and the Philosopher's/Sorcerer's Stone as the pieces were based on the same sketches used by Warner Bros. for the film. There are two different boxes, one with the kids who are on the back of the box also in a box on the front, the other with no kids on the front. The later seems to be the more common............................. **$50-$75**

Powercaster Electronic Spell-Casting Game (50697): Unveiled at the International Toy Fair in New York in February 2001, this game can be used with the Wizard Collection figures listed previously. Figures include two chipboard characters for use until the wizard figures can be purchased. Also included are six casting stones. Two casting stones are placed on the designated places on the playset and a spell is cast, causing the weakest of the two spells to be ejected from the playset. The casting stones and their equivalent cards are listed below. .... **$30-$45**

Harry Potter Triwizard Maze Game (H1314): Released in 2005, this game focuses on journeying through the maze and capturing the Triwaizard Cup. It comes with figures of the four tournament champions, dice, and cards. .... **$10-$15**

Casting Cards Checklist
1 A Simple Potion
2 Albus Dumbledore
3 Alohomora
4 An Ounce of Light
5 Animals
6 Bertie Bott's Every Flavor Beans
7 Bell Flames
8 Body-Bind
9 Centaurs
10 Charms
11 Chocolate Frogs
12 Christmas
13 Countercurse
14 Cure for Boils
15 Curse of the Bogies
16 Devil's Snare
17 Diagon Alley
18 Double Potions
19 Draco Malfoy
20 Dragon Egg
21 Draught of the Living Death
22 Elixir of Life
23 Family
24 First Year
25 Fluffy
26 Forbidden Forest
27 Gringotts
28 Gryffindors Score
29 Guarding the Stone
30 Harry Potter
31 Head of Gryffindor
32 Herbology
33 Hermione Granger
34 History of Magic
35 House Cup
36 Inside the Mirror
37 Invisibility Cloak
38 Jinx
39 Keeper of the Keys
40 Leg Locker
41 Love
42 Man With Two Faces
43 Mirror of Erised
44 Mountain Troll
45 Neville Longbottom
46 Nicolas Flamel
47 No More Dragon
48 Norbert
49 Ollivanders
50 Poltergeist
51 Potions Lesson
52 Potions Master
53 Professor Quirrell
54 Put-Outer
55 Ron Weasley
56 Small Fortune
57 Sorting Ceremony
58 Sorting Ceremony- Gryffindor
59 Sorting Ceremony- Hufflepuff
60 Sorting Ceremony- Ravenclaw
61 Sorting Ceremony- Slytherin
62 Start of Term Banquet
63 Teachers
64 The Boy Who Lived
65 Transfiguration
66 Wingardium Leviosa
67 Winged Keys
68 Wizard Chess
69 Wizard's Duel
70 You-Know-Who

Casting Stones Checklist 1st Edition
1 Fawkes
2 Basilisk
2 Earmuffs
3 Mandrake
4 Sword of Gryffindor
5 Chamber of Secrets
6 Whomping Willow
7 Riddle's Diary
8 Aragog
9 Quidditch Cup
10 Fred Weasley
11 George Weasley
12 Tom Riddle
13 Ginny Weasley
14 Gilderoy Lockhart
15 Fat Friar
16 Nearly Headless Nick
17 Dobby
18 Moaning Myrtle
19 Sir Patrick Delaney- Podmore
20 Oliver Wood
21 Filch
22 Mrs. Norris
23 Harry Potter-2nd Year
24 Ron Weasley-2nd Year
25 Hermione Granger-2nd Year
26 Draco Malfoy-2nd Year
27 Dumbledore-2nd Year
28 Hagrid-2nd Year
29 Crabbe-2nd Year
30 Goyle-2nd Year
31 Godrick Gryffindor
32 Helga Hufflepuff
33 Rowena Ravenclaw
34 Salazar Slytherin
35 Lucius Malfoy
36 Seamus Finnigan
37 Madam Hooch
38 Penelope Clearwater
39 Mr. Borgin
40 Marcus Flint
41 Colin Creevey
42 Justin Finch-Fletchley
43 Millicent Bulstrode
44 Ron's Wand
45 Hermione's Wand
46 Phoenix Tears
47 Hand of Glory
48 Ghoul
49 Errol the Owl
50 Crossbow
52 Pipes
53 Quaffle
54 Bludger
55 Cleansweep Five
56 Chains and Manacles
57 Kwikspell
58 Forbidden Forest
59 Pillowcase
60 Cupboard
61 Draco's Wand
62 Fireplace
63 Moste Potente Potions
64 Filibuster Fireworks
65 Pudding
66 Weasley Car
67 Sock
68 Dumbledore's Spectacles
69 Camera
70 Gilderoy Lockhart's Guide to Household Pests
71 Flying with the Cannons
72 Howler
73 Garden Gnome
74 Dwarfs (with Wings & Harps)
75 Headless Hunt
76 Heir of Slytherin
77 Sirius Black's Motorcycle
78 Dueling Club
79 Snape's Wand
80 Egg
81 Toad
82 Harry's Scar
83 Phoenix Flames
84 Phoenix Ashes
85 Flesh-Eating Slug Repellent
86 Loyalty
87 Polyjuice Potion
88 Tarantallegra
89 Skele-Gro
90 Expelliarmus
91 Floo Powder
92 Snitch Catch
93 Human Fingernails
94 Nimbus Two Thousand and One

95 Salamander
96 Boomslang Skin
97 Serpensortia
98 Parseltongue
99 Keeper
100 Courage
101 Detention
102 Freedom
103 Spider Web
104 Seeker
105 Spellotape
106 Beater
107 Deepest Fears & Darkest Secrets
108 Logic
109 Scarlet Light
110 Scream
111 Snake Skin
112 Death
113 Privet Drive
114 Basilisk Gaze
115 Bicorn Horn
116 Black Spiders
117 Finite Incantatem
118 Rictusempra
119 Hogwarts Express
120 Rooster
121 Chaser
122 Bloody Playing Cards
123 Glass Eye
124 Rat Intestines
125 Frog Brains

Casting Stones Checklist
2nd Edition
1 Dumbledore
2 Mirror of Erised
3 Dragon's Blood
4 Dumbledore's Wand
5 Lemon Drops
6 Voldemort
7 Voldemort's Wand
8 Unicorn Blood
9 Put-Outer
10 Light
11 Harry Potter
12 Harry's Wand
13 Hedwig (Owl)
14 Flute
15 Phoenix Feather
16 Professor Quirrell
17 Turban
18 Garlic
19 Dragon Egg
20 The Dark Forces

21 Draco Malfoy
22 Eagle Owl
23 Ron Weasley
24 Scabbers (Rat)
25 Black Knight
26 Hermione Granger
27 Bell Flame
28 Alohomora (Opening)
29 Hagrid
30 Pink Umbrella
31 Norbert
32 Fang
33 Violet Light
34 Neville Longbottom
35 Remembrall
36 Trevor (Toad)
37 Professor Snape
38 Horned Slugs
39 Porcupines' Quills
40 Root of Asphodel
41 Infusion of Wormwood
42 Bezoar
43 Goyle
44 Dried Nettles
45 Crushed Snake Fangs
46 Cauldron
47 Magical Drafts and Potions
48 Professor McGonagall
49 White Queen
50 Snuff Box
51 Needle
52 A Beginner's Guide to Transfiguration
53 Professor Binns
54 A History of Magic
55 Professor Sprout
56 Fungi
57 1,001 Magical Herbs and Fungi
58 Bloody Baron
59 Peeves
60 Crabbe
61 Lily Potter
62 Lily's Wand
63 James Potter
64 James Potter's Wand
65 Nicolas Flamel
66 Shield Gryffindor
67 Shield Slytherin
68 Shield Hufflepuff
69 Shield Ravenclaw
70 Music
71 Love
72 Ptolemy

73 Merlin
74 Grindelwald
75 Professor Flitwick
76 Emeric the Evil
77 Uric the Oddball
78 Ronan
79 Bane
80 Firenze
81 Mars
82 Telescope
83 Elixir of Life
84 Dittany
85 Black Flames
86 Fire
87 Locomotor Mortis
88 Petrificus Totalus
89 Brass Scales
90 Crystal Phials
91 Devil's Snare
92 Galleon
93 Knut
94 Griphook
95 Parchment
96 Potion Bottles
97 Quills
98 Sickle
99 Standard Book of Spells
100 Mouse
101 Bat Spleen
102 Beetles Eyes
103 Curse of the Bogies
104 Snitch
105 Dragon Liver
106 Weasley Sweater
107 Eels Eyes
108 Fangs
109 Gold
110 Feather
111 Holly
112 Cat
113 Mistletoe
114 Troll
115 Flying Keys
116 Silver
117 Wingardium Leviosa
118 Snarled Claws
119 Spine of Lionfish
120 Unicorn Hair
121 Scorcerer's Stone
122 Sorting Hat
123 Cloak of Invisibility
124 Nimbus 2000
125 Fluffy

Prices for individual casting stones range from **25 cents to $5** (detailed pricing of individual stones is beyond the scope of this guide). The five rare chaser stones were found only in Casting Stones Booster Packs (42875) and included Sorcerer's Stone, Sorting Hat, Cloak of Invisibility, Nimbus 2000, and Fluffy. ....**$15-$20**

NECA, Inc.

Harry Potter Checkers Set: A standard checkers game with a Hogwarts theme on the board and pieces. ....**$20-$25**

Harry Potter Hogwarts House Cup Challenge Adventure Board Game (60551): Players portray Harry, Ron, Hermione, and Neville in their increasingly difficult quest to win the House Cup for Gryffindor. ....**$25-$30**

Harry Potter Wizard Chess: Based on the board in Sorcerer's Stone.....................**$35-$40**

Noble Collection

Harry Potter Final Challenge Chess Set (NN7979): Released in 2004, this chess set re-creates the board and pieces from the *Philosopher's Stone/Sorcerer's Stone* film. The pieces are die-cast in zinc and play on a 20" x 20" Plexiglas board..........................**$375-$400**

Harry Potter Hogwarts Houses Quidditch Chess Set (NN7109): This chess set features four sets of die-cast and enameled pieces, a set for each Hogwarts House, on a 12" x 12" x 3" hardwood board with 24 karat gold-plated attachments. ....**$275-$300**

Parker Brothers

Clue: Harry Potter Edition (40614): Released in 2008, this edition adds a Hogwarts twist to the original Clue game. Players are Harry, Ron, Hermione, Ginny, Luna, or Neville and move about the castle where secret passages and hidden staircases are revealed when wheels on the board move..**$20-$25**

Screenlife

Harry Potter Scene It? DVD Game (21410): This interactive DVD board game in the popular Scene It? series has clips from the first four Harry Potter films. Includes flextime board, dice, four themed metal movers, 160 trivia cards, house cards, and a DVD............. **$15-$20**

Harry Potter Scene It? DVD Game 2nd Edition (25606): Includes new questions and is updated to include scenes from the first five Harry Potter films. Includes flextime board, dice, themed metal movers, trivia cards, buzz cards, DVD, and four exclusive trading cards...............**$15-$20**

Scene It? Deluxe Harry Potter Edition (HPT05): In addition to the items in the regular edition, the deluxe edition includes a collectible metal tin, two extra metal movers, 200 question cards, and exclusive collectible trading cards. ....**$25-$30**

Scene It? Deluxe Harry Potter 2nd Edition (25606): In addition to the items in the regular second edition and the deluxe second edition, this game includes a collectible metal tin and exclusive collectible trading cards as well as scenes and questions from *Order of the Phoenix*..**$25-$30**

University Games

Harry Potter and the Sorcerer's Stone—The Game (1351): Consists of 6-3/4 mini-games based on the challenges faced in the finale of *Harry Potter and the Sorcerer's Stone.* ....**$10-$15**

Quidditch The Game: One of the most detailed games based on a Quidditch match with a Quidditch pitch for a board, three different kinds of balls, seekers, beaters, chasers, and keepers for up to 14 players. ....**$15-$20**

Books

Harry Potter is first and foremost about the books. The first edition of *Harry Potter and the Philosopher's Stone* was released on June 26, 1997 with a print run of 500 books. Since then the series has sold over 400 million copies and been published in 67 languages (including Latin and ancient Greek). For the purposes of this guide, only three major publishers, Bloomsbury (Great Britain), Raincoast (Canada), and Scholastic (United States) will be considered.

A first edition of *Harry Potter and the Philosopher's Stone* is one of the most coveted collectibles in Potterdom. Only 500 were printed, and of those, 300 went to British libraries. An autographed first edition would be the Holy Grail of Potter collecting. How then does one know whether or not they have a first edition? Quite simply by checking the back of the title page. A first edition will have the complete number sequence – 10 9 8 7 6 5 4 3 2 1 (the last number on the right indicates the edition), and the names of the author as "Joanne Rowling" and the cover artist "Thomas Taylor1997" (no space before year). It was also issued without a dust jacket until the third printing.

Heritage Auction Galleries of Dallas recently sold a first edition soft cover of this book. A card featuring the front cover art and signed by J. K. Rowling was mounted inside the back cover. Heritage placed an estimate of $8,000-$12,000 on the book, which sold for $19,120.

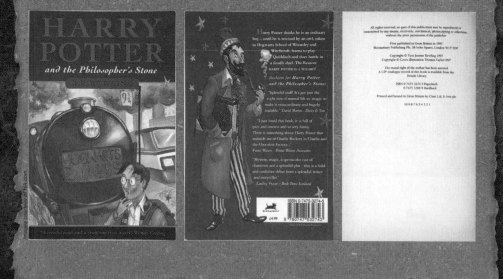

A first edition hardcover (unsigned) with a starting bid of $25,000 sold for $29,875. In the same auction (June 2009), a complete set of Harry Potter books 1-7, all signed, all first editions (*Philosopher's Stone* was a first edition, third printing, the first to have a dust jacket) sold for $9,560. The highest known price paid to date for a *Philosopher's Stone* first edition was by a person on the West Coast of the United States who paid $37,000 through AbeBooks.com.

Generally, second and third editions are not desirable to collectors because they're not first editions and they're not as rare — there are simply more of them out there. Also, first print runs are usually much smaller, and often happen when the general public has no idea about a book, its author, etc., and well before the book becomes anything close to popular. Therefore, when Bloomsbury printed the first 500 Harry Potter books, very few people in the world knew who J. K. Rowling was. By the time the third edition was printed, millions knew. So, therefore, collectors sought out the first 500, which is a small number to begin with, and even smaller when compared to the number of people who now want the book and the number of people aware of the book and the number of books printed in the subsequent editions. A book's value is based on several factors, not all of which apply to every book, but most apply to most books. Basically, a book's value is determined by its rarity, condition, completeness, importance, reputation, and uniqueness (i.e., signed first editions vs. unsigned). And yes, ultimately, what someone is willing to pay for it at any given time.[1]

In 1998, Scholastic released 30,000 copies of the book in the United States with the altered title of *Harry Potter and the Sorcerer's Stone* and some of the text Americanized. First editions have the line, "Printed in the U.S.A.23," the full number line (1 3 5 7 9 10 8 6 4 2 8 9/9 0/0 01 02), and "First American edition, October 1998." The dust jacket was done by Mary GrandPre, and the back has a blurb from *The Guardian*, whereas subsequent editions have a blurb from *Publisher's Weekly*. Autographed copies are available, as Rowling's first U.S. book tour coincided with the release of *Sorcerer's Stone*. A first American edition, first printing sold at auction in October 2009 for $1,792.50.

When *Harry Potter and the Chamber of Secrets* was issued in 1998, Rowling was very much into book tours and signings, so more signed first editions are available. Therefore, a hardcover

Joe Fay, Heritage Auction Galleries, HA.com (with permission).

first edition will generally go for around $9,000 while soft covers will command three figures. Many ardent American fans bought these editions online when they could not wait for the U.S. version to be released in 1999. The first edition has the full number line down to "1" on the copyright page. It was issued with a dust jacket illustrated by Cliff Wright. This book has covers illustrations matching those on the dust jacket. A signed first edition is worth $1,500-$1,800.

Scholastic published 250,000 copies of *Chamber of Secrets* in June 1999. The trade edition first printing has purple-blue covers with an embossed diamond pattern. Watch for the full number line, however, as subsequent editions retained the "First American Edition" line. The dust jacket was again the work of Mary GrandPre (she did the art for all of the books), and the first edition does not have a number on the spine. A signed copy was sold at auction in October for $956.

The prize to watch for in the hardcover first editions of *Harry Potter and the Prisoner of Azkaban* is the name "Joanne Rowling" appearing on the copyright page. Apparently, when this was discovered, the run was stopped and the name changed to J. K. Rowling before the 500,000 run was finished. Signed copies of this gem have gone for $12,000. The first edition has the full number line down to "1" on the copyright page. It has a dust jacket illustrated by Cliff Wright. The covers match the illustration on the dust jacket. A deluxe edition was issued simultaneously with the trade edition. The author was still doing a lot of tours and signings at this time, and an autographed copy recently sold for $2,100, while a signed first edition deluxe edition copy went for $900.

Rowling did a three-week tour of the United States in October 1999, shortly after the release of the American edition. The first edition of the U.S. trade edition had green covers with an embossed diamond pattern, full number line, "First

American Edition," "October 1999," and "Printed in the USA 37." Reportedly, Scholastic printed 500,000 copies. As before, the "First American Edition" line remained on later editions. Although the edition date is stated as October 1999, the book was actually released in September; the date was pushed up when impatient fans started buying the British version online instead of waiting for the U.S. version to be released. A signed first edition was recently sold for $932 by Heritage Auction.

Advanced reading copies (ARC) are books sent out to reviewers, bookstores, and magazines three to six months before the official release of the book. These often do not have the final dust cover, format, or binding of the finished book, and the text may also differ. These are not meant for sale and are produced in limited quantities. *Harry Potter and*

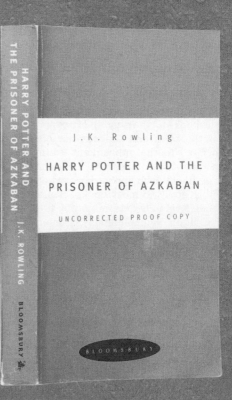

the *Prisoner of Azkaban* was the last of the books to be released with an ARC in order to protect the secrecy of the following books. A set of the first three was auctioned by Heritage Auction in October 2009 and sold for $956. These were marked "Uncorrected Proofs – Not For Sale" on the back cover and contained a letter from the publisher. A single ARC of *Sorcerer's Stone* sold for $597 and an ARC of *Prisoner of Azkaban* sold for $478 at the same auction in October.

By the time *Harry Potter and the Goblet of Fire* was published in 2000, Rowling did only a four-day tour of England and, therefore, fewer signed books are available. This drives up the price of autographed copies. Although first editions of *Goblet of Fire* run to over five million copies, signed copies command a premium. The initial print run was split between two printers, Clays Ltd. and Omnia Press in Scotland. All of the first printings state "First Edition" with no number line on the copyright page. The copyright holder is listed as J. K. Rowling. The book was issued with illustrated covers by Giles Greenfield and a matching dust jacket.

Scholastic learned its lesson this time and released the U.S. version at the same time as the U.K. version. The covers were maroon with an embossed diamond pattern and had a full number line, "First American Edition," "July 2000," and "Printed in the USA 56" on the copyright page.

Finally, in June 2003, book five was released in the United Kingdom and the United States. With an initial print run of almost 6.5 million copies in the United States alone, *Harry Potter and the Order of the Phoenix* tops them all for length with 870 pages. It was issued with illustrated covers by Jason Cockcroft, matching the dust jacket. The major signing event was in Edinburgh in 2003, and books from that time are valued in the four-figure range.

By July 2005 and the release of *Harry Potter and the Half-Blood Prince*, signings were rare, and the few available signed books sell for around $5,000. The print run of over 10 million copies assures that editions of this book will never be of great monetary value. The book was issued with illustrated covers by Jason Cockcroft, matching the dust jacket. Book sales set a record as nine million copies sold in the first day. The hardcover version from Scholastic has a text change that did not occur in the United Kingdom or paperback versions. It occurs in Chapter 27 and deals with a conversation between Draco and Dumbledore.

The last book in the series, *Harry Potter and the Deathly Hallows* was released in July 2007, and every book signed by J. K. Rowling has a holographic sticker of authenticity attached. Again, a huge print run makes this book easily available, with the exception of the hard-to-find signed editions. The Scholastic deluxe edition is a treat for collectors as it includes reproductions of Mary GrandPre's art, a foil-stamped slipcase, and full-color endpapers with art from the trade edition. In October 2007, after a seven-year absence, Rowling made another North American tour. The all-time record for sales was broken by this book when 15 million copies were sold the first day.

While the Scholastic books had different covers, chapter head illustrations, and a variety of language differences from the Bloomsbury editions, Raincoast Books were almost identical. The only differences were on the spine with the addition of the Raincoast name and logo; on the back with an additional ISBN number, name, logo, and website of Raincoast, Canadian price, blurbs from Canadian magazines, and on *Philosopher's Stone* the wording "Ancient Forest Friendly: Printed on 100% Recycled (40% post-consumer) Paper"; and on the inside with the Raincoast name and logo on the title page and Canadian printing data on the back of the title page. Later editions would have listings of other Harry Potter books available on the end pages and the word "Bloomsbury" omitted from the front cover.

Since the original hardcover and paperback versions were published, various other editions have been released of all seven books. These include adult editions in hardcover and paperback, large print editions, celebratory editions, and deluxe editions. Scholastic's celebratory edition was published on the 10th anniversary of the book and has a different cover; its deluxe editions were specially bound books with colored harlequin cloth covers, gilt edges, and a bound-in silk bookmark. The trade copy cover illustration is embossed on the front cover with J. K. Rowling's signature in gold.

Harry Potter and the Prisoner of Azkaban was the first to be released in a deluxe edition.

Scholastic did not publish adult editions but did publish a special school edition. A collector's edition of *Sorcerer's Stone* with a reputed run of 100,000 was released in November 2000 with gilt writing and embossed stamping on the dark green leatherette cover.

Two small textbooks were published in March 2001: *Quidditch Through the Ages* and *Fantastic Beasts and Where to Find Them.* The books were written to benefit Comic Relief, and 80 percent of the cover price went to the charity, amounting to over £15 million ($24.4 million). The books were published under the pseudonyms Kennilworthy Whisp and Newt Scamander.

A third textbook, *The Tales of Beedle the Bard*, was published in December 2008. Originally, the book was produced in a limited edition of only seven copies. These were handwritten and illustrated by Joanne Rowling. Six of the copies were uniquely dedicated and given to people most responsible for the success of the Harry Potter books. The seventh copy, distinguished from the others by its moonstone cover, was offered through Sotheby's auction in late 2007 and was bought by Amazon.com for £1.95 million ($3.98 million). Proceeds went to The Children's Voice charity. A year later Amazon released the book to the general public, with proceeds going to the Children's High Level Group. This exclusive edition is a reproduction of Rowling's book with 10 additional illustrations not found in the other versions. A standard edition was later released by Bloomsbury.

All of the Harry Potter books are available from the publisher or your favorite bookstore. Later editions are easily obtainable and therefore not highly valued above the original cover price. Traditionally, used books sell at half the cover price or less, dependent on condition.

Following is a cross section of many of the editions that were published. New book prices are taken from the publisher's websites and converted to approximate U.S. dollars. Out-of-print books have a price range.

Bloomsbury

Photos of Bloomsbury books are courtesy of Bloomsbury Publishing, LLC.

Harry Potter and the Philosopher's Stone

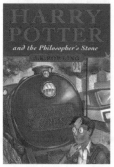  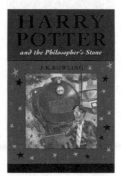 

Paperback............$11
Hardcover............$28

Adult edition
paperback............$13
Adult edition
hardcover $20

Celebratory edition
paperback............$11
Large print
hardcover $27

Deluxe edition.....$35

Harry Potter and the Chamber of Secrets

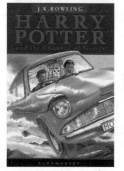 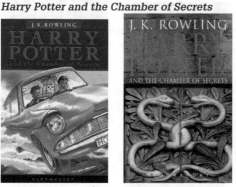 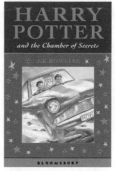 

Paperback............$11
Hardcover............$28

Adult edition
paperback............$13
Adult edition
hardcover $20

Celebratory edition
paperback............$11
Large print
hardcover $30

Deluxe edition.....$35

Harry Potter and the Prisoner of Azkaban

 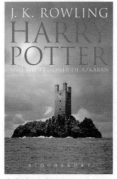  

Paperback............$11
Hardcover............$20

Adult edition
paperback............$13
Adult edition
hardcover $20

Celebratory edition
paperback............$11
Large print
hardcover $32

Deluxe edition.....$35

Harry Potter and the Goblet of Fire

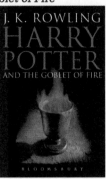
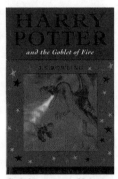
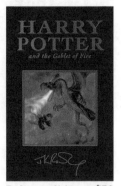

Paperback............**$14**
Hardcover............**$28**

Adult edition
paperback............**$11**
Adult edition
hardcover **$28**

Celebratory edition
paperback............**$14**
Large print
hardcover **$40**

Deluxe edition.....**$50**

Harry Potter and the Order of the Phoenix

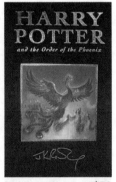

Paperback............**$14**
Hardcover............**$28**

Adult edition
paperback............**$11**
Adult edition
hardcover **$28**

Celebratory edition
paperback............**$14**
Large print
hardcover **$40**

Deluxe edition.....**$50**

Harry Potter and the Half-Blood Prince

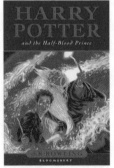

Paperback............**$14**
Hardcover............**$27**

Adult edition
paperback............**$14**
Adult edition
hardcover **$27**

Celebratory edition
paperback............**$11**
Large print
hardcover **$48**

Deluxe edition.....**$50**

Harry Potter and the Deathly Hallows

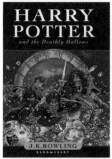

Paperback............**$14**
Hardcover............**$28**

Adult edition
paperback   **$14**
Adult edition
hardcover **$28**

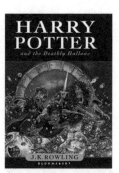

Celebratory edition
paperback............**$11**
Large print
hardcover **$64**

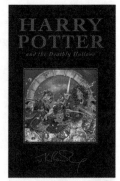

Deluxe edition.....**$56**

Fantastic Beasts & Where to Find Them

Original   paperback
...........................**$2-$6**

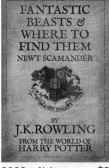

2009 edition **$8**

Quidditch Through the Ages

Original   paperback
...........................**$2-$6**

2009 edition **$8**

The Tales of Beedle the Bard

Hardcover............**$11**

Boxed Sets

Hardcover boxed set of seven...**$167**
Adult paperback boxed set of seven...............................**$96**
Adult hardcover boxed set of seven.................................**$183**

Special edition
boxed set of seven
...........................**$295**

Textbook Boxed Set
Hardcover boxed set
of two, *Harry Potter's
School Books*.......**$16**

Raincoast

Photos of Raincoast books are courtesy of Raincoast Books.

Harry Potter and the Philosopher's Stone

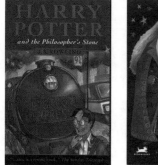  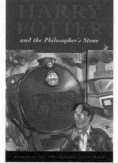 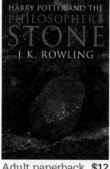

Paperback......................................$12	Hardcover............$20 Deluxe gift edition ....$43 Large print hardcover $37	Adult paperback $12 Adult hardcover .$20 A-format ....$10 Celebratory edition – paperback........$13

Harry Potter and the Chamber of Secrets

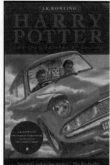 

Paperback............$12
Hardcover............$20
Deluxe gift edition
............................$43

Adult paperback .$12
Adult hardcover..$20
A-format $10
Large print
hardcover $40

Harry Potter and the Prisoner of Azkaban

Paperback............$13
Hardcover............$20
Deluxe gift edition
............................$43

Adult paperback .$13
Adult hardcover..$20
A-format $11
Large print
hardcover $43

Harry Potter and the Goblet of Fire

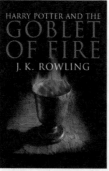

Paperback............$19
Hardcover............$35
Deluxe gift edition
............................$50

Adult paperback .$19
Adult hardcover..$35
A-format $15
Large print
hardcover $54

Harry Potter and the Order of the Phoenix

Paperback............$19
Hardcover............$43
Deluxe gift edition
............................$70

Adult paperback .$19
Adult hardcover..$43
A-format $15
Large print
hardcover $65

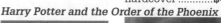

Harry Potter and the Order of the Phoenix

Paperback............**$19**	Adult paperback.**$19**
Hardcover............**$43**	Adult hardcover..**$43**
Deluxe gift edition	A-format **$15**
..............................**$70**	Large print hardcover **$65**

Harry Potter and the Half-Blood Prince

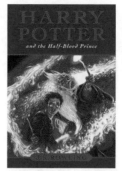

Paperback............**$17**	Adult paperback **$17**
Hardcover............**$41**	Adult hardcover .**$41**
Deluxe gift edition	A-format **$15**
..............................**$65**	Large print hardcover **$65**

Harry Potter and the Deathly Hallows

Hardcover..**$45**

Paperback............**$19**

Adult paperback **$19**
Adult hardcover **$45**
A-format **$16**
Large print hardcover **$75**

Deluxe gift edition
..............................**$80**

Boxed Sets

Paperback boxed set of seven...**$111**
Hardcover boxed set of seven...**$224**
Adult paperback boxed set of seven **$110**
Adult hardcover boxed set of seven **$224**
Deluxe gift edition boxed set of seven **$394**
A-format boxed set of seven **$92**

Scholastic

Photos of Scholastic books are courtesy of Scholastic, Inc.

Harry Potter and the Sorcerer's Stone

Paperback..............$6
Hardcover............$20
Tenth anniversary
edition $24
Large print
hardcover $14
Deluxe edition...$100

School edition $6

Harry Potter and the Chamber of Secrets

Paperback..............$9
Hardcover............$20
Deluxe edition.....$75
Large print
paperback............$14
School edition $9

Harry Potter and the Prisoner of Azkaban

Paperback..............$9
Hardcover............$20
Large print
paperback............$14
Large print
hardcover $25
Deluxe edition.....$75
School edition $9
Advanced reading
copy ....$90-$100

Harry Potter and the Goblet of Fire

Paperback............$12
Hardcover............$30
Deluxe edition.....$60
School edition $12
Large print
paperback............$15
Library edition....$35

Harry Potter and the Order of the Phoenix

Paperback...........$13
Hardcover $30
Deluxe edition....$66
Large print
hardcover............$33
School edition $13

Harry Potter and the Half-Blood Prince

Paperback $13
Hardcover $30
Large print
paperback...........$15
Large print
hardcover............$30
School edition $13
Deluxe edition....$60
Library edition...$35

Harry Potter and the Deathly Hallows

Paperback $15
Hardcover $35
Deluxe edition....$65
Large print
paperback...........$15
Large print
hardcover............$35
School edition $15
Library edition...$40

Fantastic Beasts & Where to Find Them
Paperback..$4-$5
Hardcover..$6-$8

Quidditch Through the Ages
Paperback..$4-$5
Hardcover..$6-$8

The Tales of Beedle the Bard
Hardcover...$13
Library Binding...$17

Boxed Sets

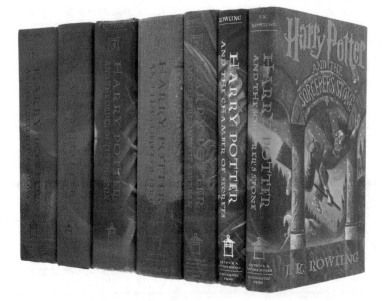

Paperback boxed set
of seven **$56**
Hardcover boxed set
of seven **$126**

Textbook Boxed Set
Paperback boxed set
of two.................. **$10**
Hardcover boxed set
of two.................. **$15**

Amazon.com

Photos of Amazon.com books are from the collection of Megan Barrow.

The Tales of Beedle the Bard

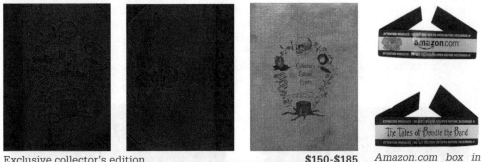

Exclusive collector's edition.. **$150-$185**

Amazon.com box in
which the exclusive
edition was shipped.

Sotheby's auction catalog .... **$16-$20**

National Braille Press

All of the Harry Potter books are also available in Braille from National Braille Press, a non-profit Braille printer and publisher. I have seen these offered at overly inflated prices on assorted auction sites, but they can be purchased at very reasonable prices directly from the publisher, and the prices given reflect that fact.

The books are available in both Braille and Portabook, a Braille file on disk designed to be read on a portable Braille reading device.

Harry Potter and the Sorcerer's Stone: Four volumes in Braille or Portabook ....$5-$7

Harry Potter and the Chamber of Secrets: Five volumes in Braille or Portabook ....$5-$7

Harry Potter and the Prisoner of Azkaban: Six volumes in Braille or Portabook ....$6-$8

Harry Potter and the Goblet of Fire: Ten volumes in Braille or Portabook ....$7-$9

Harry Potter and the Order of the Phoenix: Fourteen volumes in Braille or Portabook ....$8-$10

Harry Potter and the Half-Blood Prince: Ten volumes in Braille or Portabook ....$8-$10

Harry Potter and the Deathly Hallows: Twelve volumes in Braille or Portabook ....$13-$15

Set of seven Harry Potter books: in Braille or Portabook ....$50-$60

Tales of Beedle the Bard: One volume in Braille or Portabook ....$11-$13

Waterstone's

In May 2008, J. K. Rowling announced that she was writing a short story prequel to the Harry Potter series in support of English PEN and Dyslexia Action. The story was handwritten on a card and signed and auctioned with 13 similar card stories by a variety of authors. At Waterstone's "What's Your Story?" Auction, the card sold for £25,000 ($40,600 U.S.) to a buyer from Tokyo. The stories were later published in a postcard-sized book, and the proceeds went to charity.

Photos of Waterstone's books are from the collection of Megan Barrow.

What's Your Story? paperback postcard book ....$10-$20

Other Books
Scholastic
Coloring Books

Photo from the collection of Megan Barrow

Harry Potter and the Sorcerer's Stone Deluxe Coloring Kit: Includes seven Magic Markers. .... **$3-$5**

Harry Potter and the Sorcerer's Stone Coloring Adventures – Learning to Fly: Comes with three lightning bolt crayons, ISBN 0-439-28616-6. .... **$3-$5**

Harry Potter and the Sorcerer's Stone Coloring Adventures – Sorting Hat Ceremony: Comes with sticker sheet, ISBN 0-439-28617-4. .... **$3-$5**

Harry Potter and the Sorcerer's Stone Coloring Adventures – Hogwarts School: Comes with a glow-in-the-dark magic wand, ISBN 0-439-28619-0. .... **$4-$6**

Harry Potter and the Sorcerer's Stone Coloring Adventures – Adventures with Hagrid: Comes with a tattoo sheet, ISBN 0-439-28620-4. ...... **$3-$5**

Harry Potter and the Sorcerer's Stone Coloring Adventures – Hogwarts Express: Comes with eight-color paint tray, ISBN 0-439-28618-2. ...... **$3-$5**

Harry Potter and the Sorcerer's Stone Coloring Adventures – Friendship: Comes with two glitter tubes, ISBN 0-439-28621-2. .... **$3-$5**

Harry Potter Deluxe Coloring Kit – The Creatures of Harry Potter and the Sorcerer's Stone: Comes with five markers and a metallic gel pen, ISBN 0-439-28625-5. .... **$4-$6**

Harry Potter Deluxe Coloring Kit – The Magic of Harry Potter and the Sorcerer's Stone: Comes with five markers and a metallic gel pen, ISBN 0-439-28977-7. .... **$4-$6**

Harry Potter Stained Glass Coloring Book – The Characters of Harry Potter and the Sorcerer's Stone: ISBN 0-439-28632-8. .... **$3-$5**

Harry Potter Stained Glass Coloring Book – Scenes from Harry Potter and the Sorcerer's Stone: ISBN 0-439-28633-6. .... **$3-$5**

Harry Potter Invisible Image Coloring Book – The Mysteries of Harry Potter and the Sorcerer's Stone: Comes with "magic ink pen," ISBN 0-439-28615-8. .... **$3-$5**

Harry Potter and the Chamber of Secrets Art Coloring Book – Trace a Scene: Comes with tracing paper, ISBN 0-439-42525-5. .... **$3-$5**

Harry Potter and the Chamber of Secrets Art Coloring Book – Sticker Scenes: Comes with four-color stickers, ISBN 0-439-42526-3. .... **$3-$5**

Harry Potter and the Chamber of Secrets Art Coloring Book – Stencil Art: Comes with cardboard stencils, ISBN 0-439-41897-6. .... **$5-$7**

Harry Potter and the Chamber of Secrets Art Coloring Book – Scene for Scene: Comes with an eight-page full-color insert, ISBN 0-439-41898-4. .... **$5-$7**

Harry Potter and the Prisoner of Azkaban – Coloring and Sticker Book: Comes with two pages of stickers, ISBN 0-439-62561-0. .... **$5-$7**

Harry Potter and the Goblet of Fire – Coloring Book: ISBN 0-439-63295-1. .. **$3-$5**

Harry Potter and the Goblet of Fire – Book of Creatures – Create and Trace: ISBN 0-439-63296-X.................**$3-$5**

Harry Potter Deluxe Coloring Book: 275 pages from all five movies, ISBN 0-439-02488-9. ....**$5-$7**

Harry Potter and the Half-Blood Prince Deluxe Coloring Book: "Over 300 pages of coloring fun!", ISBN 0-545-08215-3, 2009................**$5-$7**

Flip Book

Harry Potter Flip Book (Order of the Phoenix): ISBN 0-439-02489-7, 2007, cover. .... **$3-$5**

Literature Guides

Harry Potter and the Sorcerer's Stone Literature Guide ....**$4-$6**

Harry Potter and the Chamber of Secrets Literature Guide ....**$4-$6**

Harry Potter and the Prisoner of Azkaban Literature Guide ....**$4-$6**

Harry Potter and the Goblet of Fire Literature Guide ....**$4-$6**

Pop-Up Books

Hogwarts School – "A Magical 3-D Carousel Pop-Up,":
ISBN 0-439-28611-5....................................**$20-$25**

Harry Potter and the Sorcerer's Stone Deluxe Pop-Up Book:
ISBN 0-439-29482-7.......................................**$20-$25**

Harry Potter and the Chamber of Secrets Deluxe Pop-Up Book:
ISBN 0-439-45193-0. ....**$20-$25**

Poster Books

Harry Potter and the Sorcerer's Stone Poster Book:
ISBN 0-439-28623-9. .... **$5-$7**

Harry Potter and the Chamber of Secrets Poster Book: ISBN 0-439-42523-9.
....**$5-$7**

Harry Potter and the Prisoner of Azkaban – Movie Poster Book: ISBN 0-439-62558-0 ....**$5-$7**

Harry Potter and the Prisoner of Azkaban Harry Potter Lenticular Poster Book.....**$6-$8**

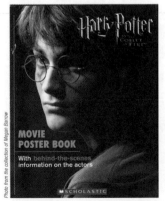

Harry Potter and the Goblet of Fire Movie Poster Book:
ISBN 0-439-633298-6... **$5-$7**

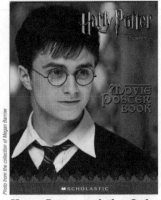

Harry Potter and the Order of the Phoenix Movie Poster Book: ISBN 0-439-02491-9.
....**$5-$7**

Hogwarts Through the Years Poster Book: ISBN 0-439-02490-0, 2007................**$6-$7**

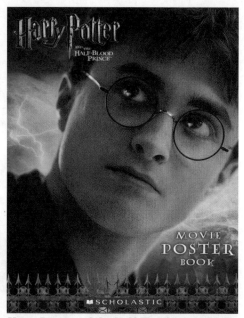

Harry Potter Poster Book: Hogwarts and Beyond: ISBN 0-545-08218-8, 2009, hardcover. ....**$8-$10**

Harry Potter and the Half-Blood Prince Movie Poster Book: ISBN 0-545-08217-X, 2009, 30 full-sized portraits of the actors from the Potter films................................**$5-$7**

Sticker Books

Harry Potter Sticker Books – Mysterious Halls of Hogwarts: includes four sheets of reusable stickers, ISBN 0-439-28634-4. ....**$6-$8**

Other Books

Conversations With J. K. Rowling: Lindsay Fraser, Scholastic Inc., 2001.....**$4-$6**

Harry Potter Sticker Book – Flying at Hogwarts: Includes four sheets of reusable stickers, ISBN 0-439-28635-2. ....**$6-$8**

Harry Potter and the Half-Blood Prince Collector's Sticker Book: Comes with more than 75 stickers, ISBN 0-545-08300-1, 2009. ....**$6-$8**

Unauthorized Harry Potter Books

Dozens of books have been published about Harry Potter, J. K. Rowling, the world she created, and the influence of the books and films on today's society. These books are unauthorized and beyond the scope of this guide. However, I have included a cross section of some of them without prices for the sake of interest.

An Interview with J. K. Rowling: Lindsay Fraser, Mammoth, London, 2000

Charmed Knits: Projects for Fans of Harry Potter: Alison Hansel

Collector's Value Guide: Harry Potter Collectibles: CheckerBee Publishing, 2000

Deathly Hallows Lectures, The: The Hogwarts Professor Explains the Final Harry Potter Adventure: John Granger, Zossima Press, 2008

Definitive Harry Potter Guide Book Series, The: Francisca and Jason Swist, Suggitt Group Ltd., 2001

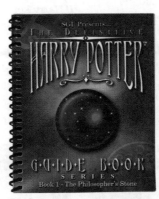

Book 1:
The Philosopher's Stone

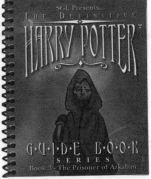

Book 3:
The Prisoner of Azkaban

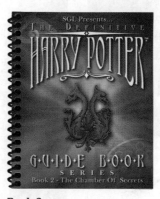

Book 2:
The Chamber of Secrets

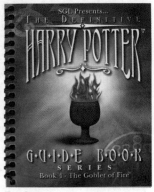

Book 4:
The Goblet of Fire

Does Harry Potter Tickle Sleeping Dragons?: Nancy Solon Villaluz, Ramance Press, 2008

End of Harry Potter, The: David Langford, McArthur & Company, 2006, St. Martin's Press, 2007

Fact, Fiction, and Folklore in Harry Potter's World: An Unofficial Guide: George Beahm, Hampton Roads Pub.

God, the Devil and Harry Potter: John Killinger, St. Martin's Griffin, 2004

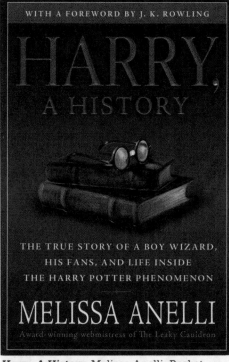

Harry, A History: Melissa Anelli, Pocket Books, 2008

Harry Potter & Imagination: The Way Between Two Worlds: Travis Prinzi, Zossima Press, 2009

Harry Potter's Bookshelf: The Great Books Behind the Hogwarts Adventures: John Granger, Penguin/Berkeley, 2009

Harry Potter Strategy Guide: Wizards of the Coast, 2001

Hidden Myths in Harry Potter, The: Spellbinding Map and Book of Secrets: David Colbert and David Maine, St.

Hocus Pocus! Yet Another Book about the Harry Potter Movies for Your Collection: Jason Hayes, Xlibris Corporation, 2008

How Harry Cast His Spell: The Meaning Behind the Mania for J. K. Rowling's Bestselling Books: John Granger, Tyndale, 2008 (previously titled Hidden Key to Harry Potter: Zossima Press, 2002; Looking for God in Harry Potter: Tyndale, 2004, 2006)

If Harry Potter Ran General Electric: Leadership Wisdom from the World of the Wizards: Tom Morris, Bantam Dell Pub Group, 2006

In Search of Harry Potter: Steve Vander Ark, Methuen Publishing Ltd., 2008

J. K. Rowling: A Biography: The Genius Behind Harry Potter: Sean Smith, Arrow, 2002

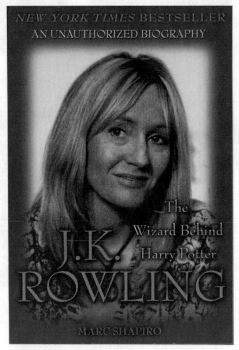

J. K. Rowling: The Wizard Behind Harry Potter: Marc Shapiro, St. Martin's Press, 2001, 2004, 2007

Kids' Letters to Harry Potter From Around the World: Running Press, 2002

Lexicon, The: Steve Vander Ark, RDR Books, 2009

Magical Worlds of Harry Potter, The: David Colbert, McArthur & Company, 2001

Mugglenet.com's What Will Happen in Harry Potter 7: Who Lives, Who Dies, Who Falls in Love and How Will the Adventure Finally End: Ben Schoen, Ulysses Press, 2006

Muggles and Magic: An Unofficial Guide to J. K. Rowling and the Harry Potter Phenomenon: George Beahm, Hampton Roads Pub., 2004

Psychology of Harry Potter, The: An Unauthorized Examination of the Boy Who Lived: Neil Mulholland (Editor), Benbella Books, 2007

Mythmaker: J. K. Rowling: Charles J. Shields, Chelsea House, 2002

My Year With Harry Potter: Ben Buchanan, Lantern Books, 2001

Repotting Harry Potter: A Professor's Book-by-Book Guide for the Serious Re-Reader: James W. Thomas, Zossima Press, 2009

Sorcerer's Companion, The: A Guide to the Magical World of Harry Potter: Allan Zola Kronzek and Elizabeth Kronzek, Broadway, 2004

Ultimate Unofficial Guide to the Mysteries of Harry Potter: Analysis of Book 6: Galadriel Waters, E. L. Fossa, Astre Mithandir, Wizarding World Press, 2007

Unlocking Harry Potter: Five Keys for the Serious Reader: John Granger, Zossima Press, 2007

We Love Harry Potter!: Sharon Moore, St. Martin's Press, 1999

Who Killed Albus Dumbledore? What Really Happened in Harry Potter and the Half-Blood Prince? Six Expert Harry Potter Detectives Examine the Evidence: John Granger (editor), Zossima Press, 2006

Calendars

Calendars with images of the Harry Potter characters or scenes from the books issued before the movies were made are very popular with collectors. As they are recently printed, most Harry Potter calendars are easy to find in good condition, meaning that they are free from tears, folds, or writing. Calendars still wrapped in original packaging command a small premium.

The first thing most calendar collectors look for is the illustration. Often these are works of art and, in the case of Harry Potter calendars, can depict a favorite character or scene from a book or film. The calendars listed here as "literary" are the most sought-after as the artwork was done before anyone knew what the characters would look like in the films, and they tend to reflect the characters more as J. K. Rowling depicted them. In the world of Harry Potter, the older calendars are the most difficult to find because they are not as readily available due to being discarded and not considered collectibles at the time. Many calendars serve a utilitarian purpose and are discarded after the year is over.

Harry Potter fans who enjoy the artwork will often put aside the calendars and add them to their general Potter collection. In time most calendars will become collectibles due to illustrations or date association. Collectibles featuring famous characters will often hold their value beyond those with generic dogs or cats. Pop icons such as Harry Potter will become more popular as time goes on, and people will want to have them for nostalgic reasons.

Literary calendars show the characters before they appeared in the movies and are often more in keeping with J. K. Rowling's original concept. These pages are from the 2003 literary calendar *Harry Potter and the Chamber of Secrets*.

Unless otherwise noted, photographs in this chapter are courtesy of Andrews McMeel Publishing.

Andrews McMeel Publishing

Though out-of-date calendars are useless for finding out the current date, they are highly collectible for the artwork they contain. The early ones from 2001 have artwork provided by Warner Bros. artists and later issues have fantastic color montages and images from the films. My favorites are the day-to-day calendars with numerous scenes from the movies and the "magical image" holographic stand.

Photo from the collection of Megan Barrow

Day-to-Day Calendars

2001 – Harry Potter and the Sorcerer's Stone: literary .... **$12-$15**

2002 – Harry Potter and the Sorcerer's Stone: .... **$12-$15**

2003 – Harry Potter and the Chamber of Secrets: literary .... **$12-$15**

Day-to-Day Calendars with "Magical Image"

2003 – Harry Potter and the Chamber of Secrets .... **$15-$20**

2004 – Sorcerer's Stone and Chamber of Secrets .... **$15-$20**

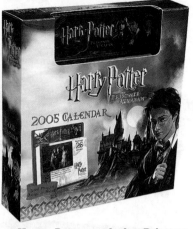

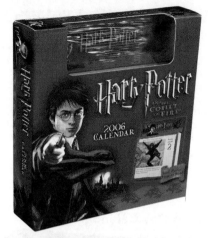

2005 – Harry Potter and the Prisoner of
Azkaban...$15-$20

2006 – Harry Potter and the Goblet of Fire
....$15-$20

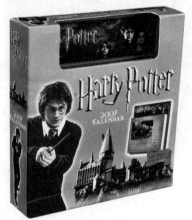

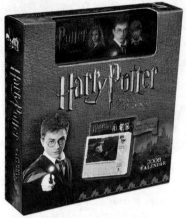

2007 – Harry Potter (scenes from first four
films)..$15-$20

2008 – Harry Potter and the Order of the
Phoenix...$15-$20

2009 – Not produced

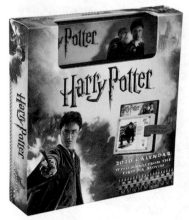

2010 – The World of Harry Potter (scenes
from the first six films).......................$15-$20

Hardbound Desk Calendars
(Weekly journal pages, hardbound, textured cover.)

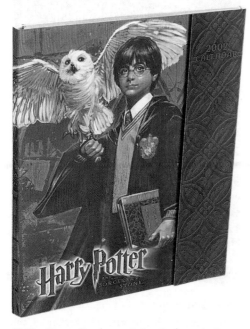

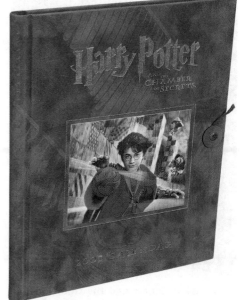

2002 – Harry Potter and the Sorcerer's Stone ....$18-$20

2003 – Harry Potter and the Chamber of Secrets..$18-$20

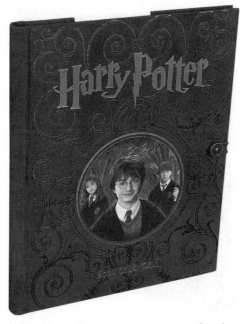

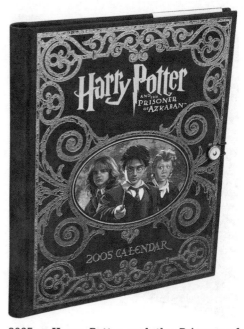

2004 – Harry Potter ....$18-$20

2005 – Harry Potter and the Prisoner of Azkaban...$18-$20

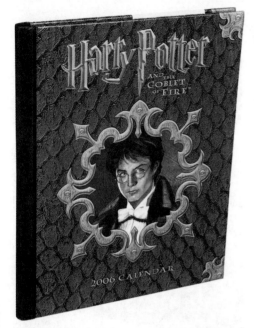

2006 – Harry Potter and the Goblet of Fire ....$18-$20

2007 – Harry Potter ....$18-$20

2008 – Harry Potter and the Order of the Phoenix...$18-$20

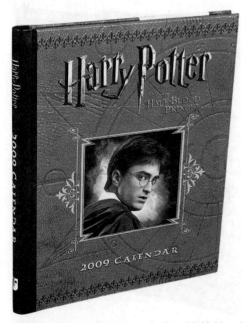

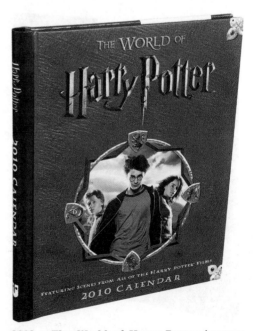

2009 – Harry Potter and the Half-Blood Prince ....$18-$20

2010 – The World of Harry Potter (scenes from the first six films).......................$18-$20

Mini Wall Calendars (7" x 7")

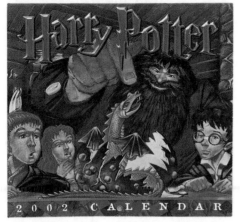

2002 – Harry Potter and the Sorcerer's Stone: literary..$5-$10

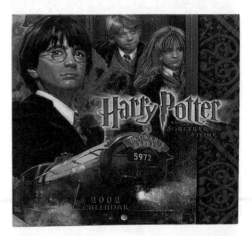

2002 – Harry Potter and the Sorcerer's Stone ....$5-$10

2003 – Harry Potter and the Chamber of Secrets: literary......................................$5-$10

2004 – Harry Potter Inside Hogwarts. $5-$10

2005 – Harry Potter: literary ....$5-$10

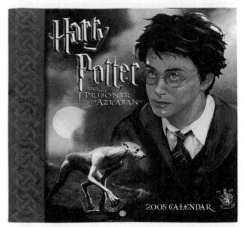

2005 – Harry Potter and the Prisoner of Azkaban..$5-$10

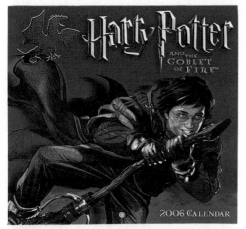

2006 – Harry Potter and the Goblet of Fire
....$5-$10

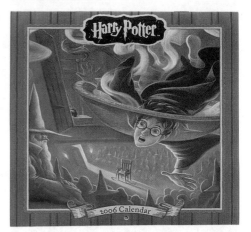

2006 – Harry Potter: literary ....$5-$10

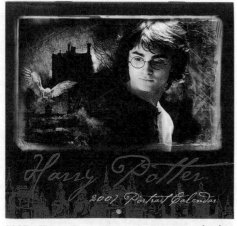

2007 – Harry Potter Portrait Calendar .$5-$10

2008 – Harry Potter and the Order of the Phoenix ....$5-$10

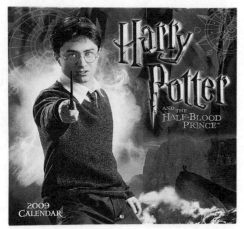

2009 – Harry Potter and the Half-Blood Prince ....$5-$10

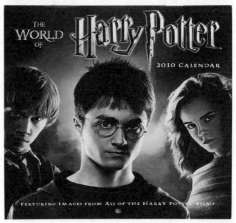

2010 – The World of Harry Potter (Scenes from all the films)..................................$5-$10

Large Wall Calendars

2001 – Harry Potter (with 16 free stickers): literary ....$15-$20

2002 – Harry Potter and the Sorcerer's Stone
....$15-$20

2002 – Harry Potter (with 17 free stickers): literary ....$15-$20

2003 – Harry Potter and the Chamber of Secrets: literary.....................................$15-$20

2003 – Harry Potter and the Chamber of Secrets...$15-$20

2004 – Harry Potter Heroic Moments ....$15-$20

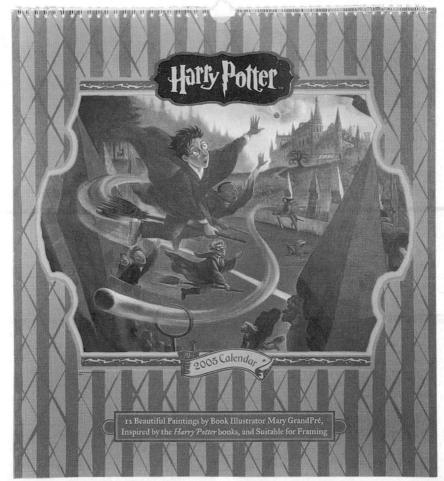

2005 – Harry Potter (with paintings by Mary GrandPre) coil bound at top...................$15-$20

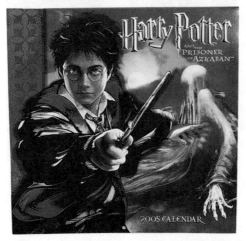

2005 – Harry Potter and the Prisoner of Azkaban...$15-$20

2006 – Harry Potter and the Goblet of Fire. ....$15-$20

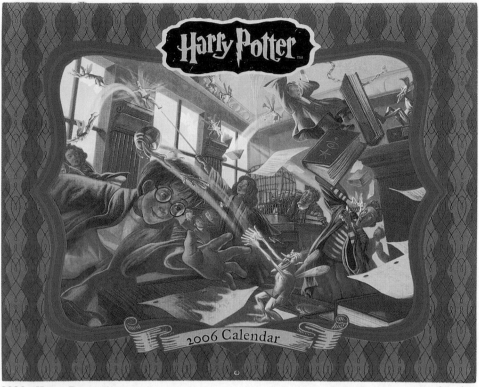

2006 – **Harry Potter:** literary ....$15-$20

2007 – Harry Potter (promotional poster art from all movies)...................................$15-$20

2008 – Harry Potter and the Order of the Phoenix...$15-$20

2008 – Harry Potter (scenes from all films) ....$15-$20

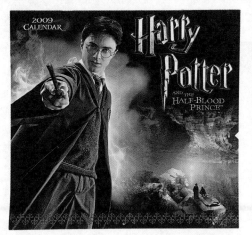

2009 – Harry Potter and the Half-Blood Prince .... $15-$20

2010 – The World of Harry Potter (scenes from first six films) .... $15-$20

Block Calendars
("Open it up to reveal 12 sides! 12 Magical Scenes! 12 Months")

2009 – Harry Potter and the Half-Blood Prince .... $15-$20

2010 – The World of Harry Potter (scenes from first six films) .... $15-$20

Hallmark

2001 – Hogwarts calendar and photo frame, 12" x 16", stands on easel or hangs .... $5-$10

Trends International

2005 – Harry Potter and the Prisoner of Azkaban .... $10-$12

2006 – Harry Potter and the Goblet of Fire .... $10-$12

2008 – Harry Potter and the Order of the Phoenix .... $10-$12

2009 – Harry Potter and the Half-Blood Prince .... $10-$12

People collect for many different reasons but most will tell you they do it for fun. This is not as true for card collectors as it once was due to the fact that a number of the cards command a high price. If a collector is satisfied with the basic sets and perhaps one or two of the special cards, then they are more likely to be "fun" collectors. Those striving for completion are looking at a considerable investment both in money and time spent searching for the elusive cards.

Card collectors today view their collections differently from those who collected in the early days of the hobby. Back in the day there were a certain number of cards issued and that was that, you got them or you didn't. Online auctions have made collecting much easier, and a wider variety of cards has become available to all collectors. Card manufacturers also look at the hobby differently, thus the issuing of cards that only dealers are likely to get and, therefore, sell at a large profit in the secondary marketplace. Inserts, autograph cards, costume cards, and other short run items increase in value rapidly as they are in very limited supply, and once they arrive in a collector's hands are unlikely to appear again on the market any time soon.

The number of insert cards varies from set to set, but on average a collector will find two per box. These could include an autograph card, costume card, or a film cell card. In addition, a single box topper and a lenticular case topper appear in every 10-box case. Using the *Half Blood Prince* sets as an example, the 12 autograph cards appear five to a case; costume cards are one to a box and 10 to a case; prop cards and film cell cards are three to a case. The idea is to provide dealers with more incentive to buy a case lot rather than single boxes.

The best way to maintain the value of your cards is to keep them in the best condition possible. Protective cases, sleeves, or sheets allow easy viewing of the cards and yet keep them free from sticky fingers.

Two of the popular costume cards containing "authentic costume material" from the *Order of the Phoenix* and *Half-Blood Prince* sets from Artbox.

Artbox

Artbox started with the *Prisoner of Azkaban* set, and after the success of the PoA cards, produced cards for the first two films. Since then they have kept up to date with the film releases. The prices of these cards vary, and it is beyond the scope of this guide to price them individually. Condition, popularity of character, and rarity of cards determine the value. The following list can be used as a guide when purchasing cards:

Base cards, set	$5-$10
Chase cards, set	$2-$6
Box toppers	$5-$10
Case toppers	$5-$10
Autograph cards	$10-$30
Costume cards	$5-$15
Prop cards	$10-$20
Film cell cards	$15-$20
Case incentive and show cards	$5-$10
Promo cards	$5-$15
Album binder	$15-$25
Tin	$10-$15

Harry Potter and the Chamber of Secrets, 2006
- 90 base cards
- 9 hobby chase cards
- 4 box toppers
- 2 case toppers
- 10 autograph cards
- 17 costume cards
- 10 prop cards
- 9 film cell cards
- 4 promo cards
- 4 case incentive and show cards box

Harry Potter and the Sorcerer's Stone, 2005
- 90 base cards
- 9 hobby chase cards
- 4 box toppers
- 3 case toppers
- 14 autograph cards
- 12 costume cards
- 13 prop cards
- 9 film cell cards
- 6 case incentive and show cards
- 4 promo cards

Harry Potter and the Prisoner of Azkaban, 2004
- 90 base cards
- 9 hobby chase cards
- 9 mass chase cards
- 4 box toppers
- 3 case toppers
- 10 autograph cards
- 7 costume cards
- 9 prop cards
- 2 case incentive and show cards
- 6 promo cards

Harry Potter and the Prisoner of Azkaban (Update), 2004
- 90 base cards
- 9 hobby chase cards
- 9 mass chase cards
- 4 box toppers
- 3 case toppers
- 18 autograph cards
- 21 costume cards
- 10 prop cards
- 9 film cell cards
- 4 case incentive and show cards
- 4 promo cards

Harry Potter and the Goblet of Fire (Update), 2006
- 90 base cards
- 9 hobby chase cards
- 4 box toppers
- 3 case toppers
- 13 autograph cards
- 15 costume cards
- 11 prop cards
- 9 film cell cards
- 8 case incentive and show cards
- 4 promo cards

Harry Potter and the Goblet of Fire, 2005
- 90 base cards
- 9 hobby chase cards
- 4 box toppers
- 3 case toppers
- 14 autograph cards
- 14 costume cards
- 12 prop cards
- 9 film cell cards
- 7 case incentive and show cards
- 4 promo cards

Harry Potter and the Order of the Phoenix, 2007
- 90 base cards
- 9 hobby chase cards
- 9 film cell cards
- 4 box toppers
- 2 case toppers
- 13 autograph cards
- 18 costume cards
- 12 prop cards
- 5 promo cards
- 6 case incentive and show cards

Harry Potter and the Order of the Phoenix (Update), 2007
  90 base cards
  9 hobby chase cards
  9 film cell cards
  4 box toppers
  2 case toppers
  13 autograph cards
  18 costume cards
  12 prop cards
  5 promo cards

Harry Potter and the Half-Blood Prince (2009)
  90 base cards
  14 costume cards
  12 autograph cards
  12 prop cards
  9 film cell cards
  4 crystal cards – Comic Con exclusive
  4 costume cards – Comic Con exclusive
  1 oversize luna auto card

Six-case incentive and show cards.

Pack of cards.

Harry Potter Memorable Moments (2006)
    72 base cards
    9 hobby chase cards
    4 box toppers
    3 case toppers
    9 autograph cards
    12 costume cards
    8 prop cards
    4 prop and costume card
    4 promo cards
    7 case incentive and show cards

*Harry Potter Memorable Moments – Series 2
(2008)*
72 base cards
27 foils

The World of Harry Potter in 3D (2008)
72 base cards
9 puzzle cards
6 rare chase cards
3 ultra rare chase cards
4 box toppers
2 case toppers
12 autograph cards
13 costume cards
10 prop cards
9 promo cards
4 case incentive and show cards

Harry Potter Poster Set
(Oversized cards, 3-1/2" x 5", first four films.)
32 base cards
4 gold foil border cards
4 gold standard coin cards

Harry Potter Literary Set
(First five films with art by Mary GrandPre.)
45 base cards

Artbox Card Albums
Harry Potter and the Sorcerer's Stone
Harry Potter and the Chamber of Secrets
Harry Potter and the Prisoner of Azkaban
*Harry Potter and the Prisoner of Azkaban
    Update*
Harry Potter and the Goblet of Fire
Harry Potter and the Goblet of Fire Update

Photo from the collection of Megan Barrow

Back

Photo from the collection of Megan Barrow

Front

Harry Potter and the Order of the Phoenix
*Harry Potter and the Order of the Phoenix
    Update*
Harry Potter and the Half-Blood Prince

Photo from the collection of Megan Barrow

World of Harry Potter in 3D
Harry Potter Memorable Moments
Harry Potter Memorable Moments – Series 2
Harry Potter Poster Set
Harry Potter Literary Set

Chocolate Frog Cards

See "Miscellaneous" chapter, "Food" section, for Chocolate Frog Cards.

Artbox Card Tins

Photos from the collection of Megan Barrow

Harry Potter and the Prisoner of Azkaban
Harry Potter and the Goblet of Fire

Photo from the collection of Megan Barrow

Harry Potter and the Order of the Phoenix
Harry Potter Memorable Moments

Wizards of the Coast

**Harry Potter and the Sorcerer's Stone
Movie Trading Cards**

Released in 2001, this set was not a trading card game but was issued with uncommon (#1-40), common (#41-80), and rare cards (#1-40 as foil cards). The cards were 2-1/2" x 4-1/2" and issued in a box of 36 packs of seven cards with a movie poster (19" x 27") in each two-box carton.

Cards #1-5.

Common.. $0.20-$0.50
Uncommon ....$0.50-$1
Rare ....$1-$2

Harry Potter and the Half-Blood Prince

Trading Card Games
Wizards of the Coast

Wizards of the Coast, Inc., of Renton, Washington, was founded in 1990 and successfully produced various trading card games (TCG). In 1999 the company was bought by Hasbro.

The first Harry Potter TCG was previewed in early 2001 at the American International Toy Fair in New York City and officially launched at Gen Con in Milwaukee, Wisconsin in August 2001. The first expansion to the game, Quidditch Cup, was released in November 2001.

Harry Potter Trading Card Games

A trading card game (TCG) is exactly what it implies, a blend of playing a game and trading the cards. There are set rules but no limit to the number of cards a player can have. A satisfactory game can be played with a starter set of two 41-card decks, a play mat, and instructions. Booster packs can be purchased to enable players to expand their collections. As the boosters are random, a player gets a selection of cards: six common, two uncommon, two lesson, and one rare.

The prices of these cards vary, and it is beyond the scope of this guide to value individual cards. Condition, the effect of a card on the game, and popularity of a character are factors in determining value. The type of card is determined by a symbol on the lower right corner. Lesson cards have no mark; common cards have a circle; uncommon cards have a diamond; rare cards have a star; and premium cards are easy to spot as they have a foil pattern (stars and lightning bolts) or a holographic character as well as a star. The following list can be used as a guide when purchasing cards:

Lessons	$.01-$0.20
Common	$0.20-$0.50
Uncommon	$0.50-$1
Rare	$1-$5
Premium	$5-$10+
Starter sets	$10-$15
Booster packs	$3-$4
Theme packs	$7-$8

Photo from the collection of Megan Barrow

Two Player Starter Set

42818-14032 – With two 41-card decks, the set contains duplicate cards and a premium wizard or witch card, a play mat, rulebook, and 12 damage counters.

Cards #3, 4, 23, 20, 60, and 113.

Harry Potter Base Game

Released in August 2001, this set contains 116 cards available in starter sets and booster packs: #1-20 are holographic and foil cards, #21-38 are rare cards, #39-72 are uncommon cards, #73-112 are common, and #113-116 are lesson cards. The *Unicorn* foil card #20 is the rarest.

Cards #2, 19, 42, 61, 71, and rules.

Quidditch Cup Card Game

Released in November 2001, this set contains 111 cards: #1-30 are rare with an additional #1-30 as premium foil and hologram cards, #31-50 are uncommon, #51-75 are common, #76-80 are lesson cards. (Includes one unnumbered rules card.) The rarest is #4, Premium Foil Fluffy.

Adventures at Hogwarts Cards

Released in June 2002, this set contains 110 cards: #1-30 are rare with an additional #1-30 as premium foil and hologram cards, #31-50 are uncommon, #51-75 are common, #76-80 are lesson cards. The rarest is #1, Albus Dumbledore hologram card.

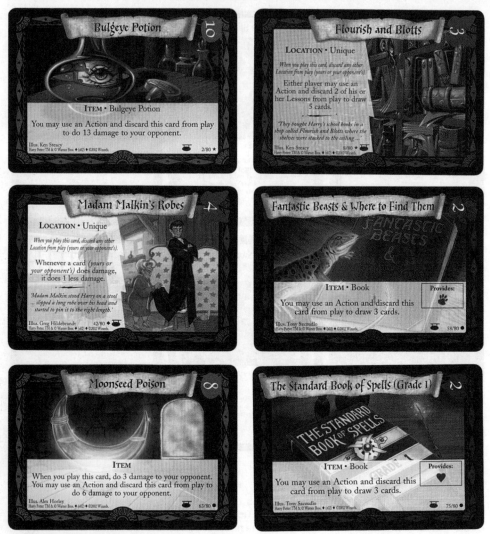

Cards #2, 8, 42, 58, 63, and 75.

Diagon Alley Cards

Released in March 2002, this set contains 110 cards and includes new location cards inserted among the other cards: #1-30 are rare with an additional #1-30 as premium foil and hologram cards, #31-50 are uncommon, #51-75 are common, #76-80 are lesson cards. The rarest is #12, Griphook foil.

Chamber of Secrets Cards

Released in October 2002, this set contains 195 cards: #1-55 are rare with an additional #1-55 as premium foil and hologram cards, #56-90 are uncommon, #91-135 are common, #136-140 are lessons. The rarest is #45, Professor Pomona Sprout hologram card.

Hannah Abbott's Spellcaster Theme Deck: 61 cards, damage counters, one Premium Wizard card, and playmate. ....**$15-$20**

Percy Wesley Potions Theme Deck: 61 cards, damage counters, one Premium Wizard card, and play mat. ....**$15-$20**

Twin Trouble Theme Deck: 61 cards, damage counters, one Premium Wizard card, and play mat. ....**$15-$20**

Costumes

ostumes are another area where unlicensed articles abound. Halloween 2001 was the first to see a plethora of witch and wizard costumes on the market, along with assorted Harry-style glasses, with and without tape. Only two companies were actually licensed, Rubie's Costume Co., Inc. of New Hyde Park, New York, and Elope, Inc., of Colorado Springs, Colorado.

Most people buy costumes to wear them, either for Harry Potter-related events such as movie premieres, book store galas, Halloween parties, or trick-or-treating. Collecting Harry Potter costumes, therefore, becomes a very personal thing. Whether one chooses to wear the costumes or keep them in pristine condition as part of their collection is a completely personal choice. Value is based on condition, and used costumes will have a lower value than unused ones.

Regardless, certain steps need to be taken to maintain your costume if you want it to survive from one year to the next. For example, should it need cleaning, make certain the manufacturer's advice is closely followed. If no instructions are available, proceed with care and test any detergent on an unnoticeable piece of the cloth to check for bleeding dye, fading, or other damage to the fabric.

If the costume has been worn, check for body odor, matting, moisture, and other stains. Carefully brush out wigs to remove tangles and matting. Masks made of plastic or latex should be cleaned with anti-bacterial solutions. Air out any accessories.

It is recommended that stains be spot cleaned, and when washing, use a mild detergent. If in doubt, hand wash, wring out the water, and lay flat to dry. Once it is dry, press out any wrinkles (if the fabric can be ironed) and store carefully. Costumes can either be folded and stored in an appropriate bin or box or hung in a sealed garment bag.

Molded over-the-head masks should be stored on a Styrofoam head and placed in a protective bag. Hats can be stuffed with tissue to retain their shape. Wands, swords, glasses, snitches, brooms, and other Potter accessories should be bubble-wrapped and stored in a box or bin.

*Deluxe Gryffindor Robe
from Rubies Costumes Co. Inc.*

Elope

Elope, Inc. (Everybody's Laughing On Planet Earth) is a high quality manufacturer of authentic character hats and glasses, as well as a leader in new designs of headwear, eyewear, and accessories. Hats are fully lined with a size adjuster and hidden pocket. Elope is certified by Worldwide Responsible Apparel Production (WRAP), and is a socially responsible business dedicated to exceptional customer care, fair trade, and community service. Photos in this section are courtesy of Elope, Inc.

Hogwarts

Hogwarts scarf (LU2360): Acrylic knit 56" scarf with school crest. .... **$15-$20**

Hogwarts knit hat (LU2355): Acrylic with school crest and 56" scarf. .... **$20-$24**

Hogwarts scarf (LU2359): Acrylic black 85" scarf with school crest. .... **$15-$20**

Hogwarts student hat (LS7227): Black velvet, large. .... **$15-$19**

Hogwarts student hat (LU2335): Black velvet, small. .... **$12-$15**

Hogwarts student hat (LU2335): Black velvet, small. ....**$12-$15**

Gryffindor House

Gryffindor House beanie (LU2365): Lamb's wool with house colors and crest. ....$7-$10

Gryffindor House scarf (LU2361): lamb's wool 75" scarf with house colors and crest........................... $15-$20

Gryffindor silk necktie (LU2380): With house colors and crest. .... $16-$19

Hufflepuff House

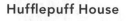

Hufflepuff House beanie (LU2367): Lamb's wool with house colors and crest. ....$7-$10

Hufflepuff House scarf (LU2363): Lamb's wool 75" scarf with house colors and crest........................... $15-$20

Hufflepuff silk necktie (LU2382): With house colors and crest. .... $16-$19

Ravenclaw House

Ravenclaw House beanie (LU2368): Lamb's wool with house colors and crest. ....$7-$10

Ravenclaw House scarf (LU2364): Lamb's wool 75" scarf with house colors and crest. ....$15-$20

Ravenclaw silk necktie (LU2383): With house colors and crest. .... $16-$19

Slytherin House

Slytherin House beanie (LU2366): Lamb's wool with house colors and crest. ....$7-$10

Slytherin House scarf (LU2362): Lamb's wool 75" scarf with house colors and crest. ....$15-$20

Slytherin silk necktie (LU2381): With house colors and crest. .... $16-$19

Hats

Dumbledore tassel hat (LU2370): Embroidered, distressed ultra suede with gold tassel .... **$24-$32**

Sorting Hat (LU2330): Soft, thick fabric puppet hat with features of the face sewn in, cotton and polyester, 18" tall. .... **$20-$24**

Mini Sorting Hat (M2330): Deluxe faux suede with "invisible" string .... **$5-$7**

Dumbledore wizard hat (LU2371): Crinkled chiffon with faux suede brim. .... **$20-$24**

Professor McGonagall faux suede witch hat (LU2341): .... **$20-$24**

Professor McGonagall velvet hat (LU2340): Checkered band and pheasant feather. .... **$20-$24**

Professor McGonagall wool tartan hat (LU2342): Side flaps with tie. .... **$20-$24**

Accessories

Harry's glasses (LS7222): Matte black plastic frame with taped nosepiece and gold logo on frame .... **$5-$7**

Harry's glasses (LS7224): Round wire, brushed metal with gold logo .... **$5-$7**

Mad-Eye Moody patch (LS7227): Faux leather strap, plastic eyepiece with moving eyeball. .... **$6-$8**

Quidditch goggles (LS7225): Padded vinyl with golden Snitch icons .... **$12-$14**

Rubies Costumes

Costumes are available from Rubie's Costumes Co. Inc. in both adult and child sizes for the major characters in the Harry Potter films. Costume designs are based on the actors and the wardrobes they wore in the movies. Many of the costumes are still available from Rubie's and their retailers and are indicated below with a product number. Photos in this section are courtesy of Rubies Costumes Co. Inc.

Some of the original and discontinued costumes include:

Albus Dumbledore: Deluxe costume with a paisley robe like the one worn by Richard Harris. Child ....$25-$30 Adult.........................$30-$40 Wig and beard available separately.................. $10-$15 Dumbledore glasses.....$3-$5

Rubeus Hagrid: Costume consists of jacket, pants, belt, and mask with bushy hair and beard. Child.......$25-$30 Adult.........................$30-$40 Keys and ring...............$6-$7 Pink umbrella ....$5-$6

Professor McGonagall: Costume comes in two layers with white and gray-blue-black pattern.............$40-$50 Wig available separately ....$10-$15 Glasses ....$3-$5

Severus Snape: Black high-collared cloak (wig sold separately) Child ......$20-$25 Adult..........................$25-$30

Harry Potter Costume Kit (5251): Black and burgundy robe with Gryffindor crest, wand, and glasses; large ....$23-$26

Harry Potter Costume Kit (5274): Contains hooded robe, clasp, wand, and glasses; small, medium, and large ....$28-$39

Deluxe Harry Potter Costume (10792): Black and burgundy polyester robe with clasp; small, medium, and large ....$33-$50

Harry Potter Costume Kit (17117): Contains glasses, hooded robe with clasp, wand, and tattoos; standard size............................$25-$30

Harry Potter Pet Costume (50573): Comes with glasses, wizard hat, and Gryffindor crested robes; small, medium, large, and extra large ....$14-$17

Fiber Optic Harry Potter Robe (882763): Black polyester robe with clasp and fiber optic Hogwarts emblem; small, medium, and large..........................$32-$37

Dementor (888346): Long black robe, chest piece, and mask; STD; retail .....$35-$40

Hermoine Granger (883406): Gray cardigan with Gryffindor burgundy and gold stripe tie, small, medium, and large ....$30-$40

Quidditch Kit (3542): Contains goggles, gloves, arm and leg guards..$25-$30

Quidditch Kit (544): Black goggles, gloves, shin guards, and wrist guards......$20-$25

Harry Potter and the Half-Blood Prince Trick or Treat Bag: Eight in package ....$2-$3

Harry Potter Costume Kit (17117): Contains glasses, hooded robe with clasp, wand, and tattoos; standard size..............................$25-$30

Quidditch Costume Kit (17128): Contains goggles, hooded robe, and Golden Snitch.........................$25-$30

Dobby Prop Replica (909883): 2' 4" statue on display base; retail ....$575-$650

Back *Front*

Quidditch Robe (882169): Quidditch robe, Potter and Quidditch number printed on back; small, medium, and large .... **$25-$30**

Harry Potter Task 3 (882182): Black and burgundy shirt, black pants; small, medium, and large .... **$23-$27**

Deluxe Quidditch Robe (882173): Long hooded robe with Hogwarts crest; small, medium, and large ....**$25-$30**

Harry Potter Task 1 Robe (882180): Black robe with red star and "Potter" on back; small, medium, and large ....**$25-$30**

Slytherin Robe (882764): black and green hooded robe with clasp and Slytherin crest; small, medium, and large...........................**$25-$30**

Harry Potter Robe (882765): Black and burgundy robe with clasp and printed Gryffindor crest; small, medium, and large..........................**$23-$26**

Deluxe Gryffindor Robe (882767): Black and burgundy polyester hooded robe with clasp and embroidered Gryffindor crest; small, medium, and large; retail ....**$30-$40**

Deluxe Harry Potter Robe (882769): Black and burgundy polyester hooded robe with clasp and embroidered Gryffindor crest; small, medium, and large ...**$30-$40**

Gryffindor Robe (882766): Black and burgundy hooded robe with clasp and embroidered Gryffindor crest; small, medium, and large..........................**$25-$30**

Deluxe Slytherin Robe (882768): Black and green polyester hooded robe with clasp and Slytherin crest; small, medium, and large ....**$30-$40**

Death Eater (882770): Black hooded robe and mask; small, medium, and large; retail ....**$25-$30**

Deluxe Death Eater (882771): Silver character mask, black hooded robe and shirt front; small, medium, and large; retail ....$30-$40

Dementor (882775): Mask, black robe, and chest piece; small, medium, and large ....$30-$35

Deluxe Hedwig Costume (885506): Plush headpiece with attached jumpsuit; TSM............................$37-$50

Voldemort (882774): Partial face mask and black robe; small, medium, and large; retail ....$27-$33

Bellatrix (882966): Mask, dress with hood and cummerbund; small, medium, and large.....................$27-$33

Harry Potter (888337): Black and burgundy robe with clasp, iron on Gryffindor crest; STD ....$30-$35

Dementor (888338): Black mask and robe with chest piece; STD ....**$35-$40**

Bellatrix (888341): Black dress with hood, silver mask, and cummerbund; STD ....**$45-$40**

Death Eater (88839): Silver mask with black hooded robe and shirt front...........**$32-$37**

Deluxe Death Eater (888340): Silver mask with hooded robe and shirt front, STD, retail ....**$37-$50**

Voldemort (888345): Black robe with bell sleeves, character mask; STD ....**$35-$40**

DELUXE ADULT LATEX MASKS

Deluxe Voldemort Latex Mask (68130): One size over-the-head mask with molded facial features. .... **$25-$35**

Dementor Deluxe Mask (50696): Over-the-head latex design with molded facial features (mesh covering for the eyes). .... **$35-$45**

Dobby (4450): 3/4 vinyl child mask; one size. .... **$13-$17**

Rubeus Hagrid (4019): Adult overhead latex mask with hair. .... **$30-$60**

Professor Flitwick: Adult overhead latex mask with hair. .... **$50-$60**

Albus Dumbledore Latex Mask (68129): One size with molded latex facial features has wire-rimmed glasses, hair, and beard attached, and a fabric hat. .... **$45-$55**

Deluxe Mad-Eye Moody Latex Mask (68148): Over-the-head mask with molded facial features, hair, and "Mad-Eye." .... **$50-$60**

Sorting Hat (49047): 18" tall with features sewn on soft, thick fabric, secret pocket in lining ....$25-$35

Professor McGonagall's Hat (49048): With feather $20-$26

McGonagall's Witch Hat (49050): Black, one size ....$14-$17

Hogwarts School Hat (49049):......................$17-$20

Economy Sorting Hat: Light foam and black fabric with character details screen printed in purple and gray ....$7-$13

Harry Potter and the Half-Blood Prince Trick or Treat Bag: Eight in package.. **$2-$3**

Cauldron Candy Cups (7255): Six-piece pack............... **$6-$8**

Harry Potter Tie (520): Gryffindor colors, burgundy and gold..................... **$10-$17**

Harry Potter Trick-or-Treat Cauldron (3558): Comes in small, medium, and large...... **$5-$6, $10-$12, and $16-$17, respectively**

Harry Potter Safety Lantern (7256): Battery - operated plastic lantern with Hogwarts crest, 5-1/2" tall with a round base ....**$7-$10**

Harry Potter Scarf (7257) (8655): Gryffindor colors without crest............... **$9-$13**

Dobby Adult Hands (7208): .... **$13-$16**

Voldemort Hands (7280): one size, adult.................. **$15-$20**

Golden Snitch (8652):..**$5-$8**

Accessory Kit (8651) (17124):
Contains glasses and wand
.... **$9-$11**

Hedwig (7253): Made with real feathers, 12".......**$10-$14**

Harry Potter Scar and Makeup Kit (19866): Includes a four-color makeup tray, sponge/brush applicator, packet of face adhesive, 3-D latex scar, scar wax, and instructions.............. **$5-$7.50**

Broom: Nimbus 2000 (8644): 36" long.....................**$14-$20**

Eye glasses (8649): .....**$7-$10**

Warner Bros.

Harry Potter Costume (HM161): Kid's size..	$20-$24
Harry's Glasses (HM186):	$3-$4
Temporary Tattoos (HM195):	$2-$3

People from all walks of life, women and men, collect dolls as historical objects, antiques, costume models, film characters, or nostalgic old friends. Harry Potter dolls are of recent vintage and only a small portion of the doll collector's world.

Having said that, it should be remembered that age is not always a determining factor for price. Most dolls do not increase in price within a few years of purchase, though brands like Robert Tonner are an exception as they are sold in limited editions and designed as collectibles. With that in mind, you should still collect what you enjoy, not what you think will increase in value.

Leading doll collectors agree that dolls should not be purchased as an investment unless you are buying very expensive antique dolls. This does not apply to Harry Potter dolls, so buy the dolls you like, take them out of the box (many boxes are generic and do not increase the value by much), display them, play with them, and enjoy your collection.

However, it should be stressed that while changing the clothing on your dolls is all a part of playing with them or displaying them, it is not recommended that alterations be made to the doll. The hair, body, clothes, and accessories should be maintained in an unaltered state. Changing clothes is fine, but changing heads or other body parts is not recommended primarily due to the fact that damage is likely to occur.

In order to keep your doll in as good a condition as possible and still display or play with it, it is important to be careful when handling the doll. Most dolls have synthetic hair and fine fabrics that should not be subjected to rough treatment or, if cleaned, harsh detergents. For information on cleaning and caring for your dolls, I recommend the Robert Tonner website Doll Hospital at http://www.tonnerdoll.com/dollcare.htm.

Price guides are an essential part of collecting but should not be regarded as bibles. They are guides to assist you in making an educated purchase. Prices are dependent on condition and availability. For example, if you see a mint condition doll but it is priced above book value, don't decide not to buy it for that reason. By the same token, don't grab up every doll on sale below book price, either. Keep in mind that the doll market, like any other collectibles market, can be volatile. That is why it is important to buy what you like so even if the price does go down, it is not that important because you love the item you have.

Mattel

Big Feast, The (89100): Released 2002, 12" accessory set, comes with table, dishes, and candelabra (twist and dishes fill with food and pitcher fills with juice). ....**$25-$35**

Hogwarts Heroes: Harry: Released 2002, 8" Harry wearing black robe and Gryffindor colors, includes wand and Sorcerer's Stone, "Rub stone on robe to reveal crest." ..**$50-$80**

Hogwarts Heroes: Hermione: Released 2002, 8" Hermione wearing black robe and Gryffindor colors, includes wand and Sorcerer's Stone, "Rub stone on robe to reveal crest." ..**$50-$80**

Hogwarts Heroes: Ron (50687): Released 2002, 8" Ron wearing black robe and Gryffindor colors, includes wand and Sorcerer's Stone, "Rub stone on robe to reveal crest." .**$50-$80**

Magical Powers: Harry Potter (C3172): Released 2002, 12" Harry wearing Quidditch uniform, comes with Mirror of Erised, sorting hat, and broom; can "levitate" a ball, turn the pages of a book, make bubbles in a cauldron, etc.; window box..................................**$30-$35**

Magical Powers: Hermione: Released 2002, Hermione wearing white blouse with Gryffindor scarf and gray skirt, comes with a cauldron, trunk, stool, magic wand, and Crookshanks; can make the cat disappear, the cauldron's green flames pop up, and bottles illuminate..............................**$25-$30**

Magical Talking: Hermione: Released 2002, Hermione wearing black sweater, colorful blouse, red skirt, white leotards, comes with a witch's hat and a trunk full of mix-and-match beads that can be attached to Hermione— "Connect magic charms and Hermione talks!"................................**$30-$35**

Magic Lessons Playset: Released 2002, 12" accessory set, comes with chair, table, books, and other accessories for the dolls..**$25-$35**

Snitch Chasing Harry: Released 2002, 11" electronic figure with Harry in Quidditch uniform riding a broom. "Fly" Harry to activate magical Quidditch sound. ....**$26-$30**

Wizard Sweets: Harry (54868): Released 2002, Harry wearing red shirt and white pants, comes with special bracelet and chocolate frogs. ....**$15-$18**

Wizard Sweets: Hermione: Released 2002, Hermione wearing red and gray sweater over blue blouse and brown skirt, comes with bracelet and Bertie Bott's beans. ....**$15-$18**

NECA, Inc.

Harry in black and red Maze Task outfit: 12" with vinyl head and plush body...............**$10-$25**

Harry in casual clothes: 12" with vinyl head and plush body. ....**$10-$25**

Harry in Quidditch robes: 12" with vinyl head and plush body.......................................**$10-$25**

Harry in Yule Ball dress robes: 12" with vinyl head and plush body. ....**$10-$25**

Tonner Character Figures*

Tonner refers to its products as character figures with high quality craftsmanship, hand-painted facial detail, and articulation. Many of the Harry Potter characters are represented from *Goblet of Fire* onwards and are designed to resemble the actors who portray the characters. The figures are approximately 17" tall and have 14 points of articulation to permit unlimited movement so that owners can pose them in a variety of positions for play or display. Clothes are not interchangeable between Ron and Harry as Ron is about a half-inch taller than Harry. The first Harry Potter character figures appeared in 2005.

Prices vary widely due to condition, the existence of various clothing pieces, and the original box.

Bellatrix Lestrange (T9-HPDD-02): Limited edition of 1,000, released 2009; 17" tall with rooted hair and hand-painted face wearing black dress, faux leather corset, necklace, and hosiery; comes with wand and stand. ....**$180-$190**

Dobby (T7-HPDD-08): Open edition, released 2007; the 9-1/2" house elf is made of resin with neck, shoulders, and hips joints; comes in pillowcase and includes stand. (Sock not included.) ....**$75-$85**

Cho Chang at Hogwarts (T8-HPDD-01): Limited edition of 2,500, released 2008; rooted hair figure with hand-painted face wearing white cotton shirt, pleated wool skirt, cardigan, Ravenclaw tie, gray tights, and faux leather shoes under school robe; comes with wand and stand.....................**$140-$150**

Draco Malfoy at Hogwarts (T7-HPDD-04): Limited edition of 5,000, released 2007; wigged figure with hand-painted face wearing white shirt and tie under sweater with flannel pants under school robe with Slytherin crest decal; comes with wand, socks, shoes, and stand.................... **$140-$150**

Ginny Weasley at Hogwarts (T9-HPDD-04): Limited edition of 1,000, released 2009; rooted hair figure with hand-painted face wearing cotton Oxford shirt, pleated skirt, knit tights, faux leather slip-ons, custom knit sweater, Gryffindor tie, and robe with Hogwarts crest; comes with wand and stand. .. **$150-$160**

Harry Potter at the Yule Ball (T5-HPDD-01): Limited edition of 2,500, released 2005; wigged figure with hand-painted face wearing white formal shirt, white bow tie, and vest with matching pants under dress robe; comes with glasses, wand, socks, shoes, and stand. Owl not included. .... **$150-$175**

Harry Potter at Hogwarts (T5-HPDD-02): Limited edition of 5,000, released 2005; wigged figure with hand-painted face wearing white shirt and tie under knit sweater with flannel pants under school robe with Hogwarts crest decal; comes with glasses, wand, socks, shoes, and stand. ....**$140-$150**

Hermione Granger at Hogwarts (T6-HPDD-02): Limited edition of 5,000, released 2006; rooted hair figure with hand-painted face wearing white shirt and tie under knit sweater with flannel pleated skirt under school robe with Hogwarts crest decal; comes with wand, tights, shoes, and stand. ....**$140-$150**

Ron Weasley at Hogwarts (T6-HPDD-01): Limited edition of 5,000, released 2006; wigged figure with hand-painted face wearing white shirt and tie under custom knit sweater with flannel pants under school robe with Hogwarts crest decal; comes with wand, socks, shoes, and stand. ....**$140-$150**

Harry Potter, Gryffindor Seeker (T6-HPDD-06): Limited edition of 2,500, released 2006; wearing custom knit sweater over trousers under his Gryffindor house robes; comes with gloves, shin guards, shoes, socks, and stand. (Firebolt broomstick sold separately.) .... $150-$160

Kreacher (T8-HPDD-03): Open edition, released 2008; Sirius Black's house elf is 10" tall, wearing a sack and has hand-painted face, rooted hair, and acrylic eyes. .... $90-$100

Luna Lovegood at Hogwarts (T8-HPDD-04): Limited edition of 2,000, released 2008; rooted hair figure with hand-painted face wearing white cotton shirt, pleated wool skirt, cardigan, Ravenclaw striped tie, gray tights, and faux leather shoes under Ravenclaw robe with crest; comes with wand, earrings, necklace (to ward off Nargels), and stand. .... $150-$160

Hermione Granger at the Yule Ball (T6-HPDD-04): Limited edition of 2,500, released 2006; rooted hair figure with hand-painted face wearing gown with satin bodice and continuous layers of chiffon ruffles; comes with earrings, corsage, hose, shoes, and stand. ....$150-00-$175

Lucius Malfoy Death Eater (T9-HPDD-03): Limited edition of 1,000, released 2009; Death Eater costume of faux leather shirt, tailored trousers, socks, faux leather belt and boots, and embroidered robe; comes with resin mask and stand. .... $240-$250

Professor Dumbledore (T9-HPDD-01): Limited edition of 500, released 2009; 19" figure with rooted hair and applied beard over hand-painted face in the likeness of Richard Harris, wearing brocade under robe and outer robe in jacquard trimmed in metallic brocade with velvet hat and boots; comes with stand. ....**$240-$250**

Ron Weasley at the Yule Ball (T6-HPDD-03): Limited edition of 2,500, released 2006; wigged figure with hand-painted face wearing white formal shirt and bow tie under vest with black pants under "vintage" lace-trimmed tapestry robe; comes with wand, socks, shoes, and stand. Note: Ron is approximately a half-inch taller than Harry... **$150-$175**

Voldemort (T8-HPDD-05): Limited edition of 1,500, released 2008; He-Who-Must-Not-Be-Named stands 19" with hand painted face wearing black three-layer costume and no shoes; comes with wand and stand ....**$150-$160**

Accessories

Crookshanks (T6-HPAC-05): Open edition; Hermione's 4" pet is sculpted in resin and hand painted. ....**$20-$30**

Firebolt (T6-HPAC-02): Open edition; 16" broomstick is sculpted in resin and hand-painted with runic symbols, gold tone bands to secure the straw, and leg hooks. ....**$50-$60**

Quidditch Set (T6-HPAC-06): Open edition; incredibly detailed 8" trunk contains a quaffle, two bludgers, beater bat, and golden Snitch, sculpted in resin and hand painted. ....**$90-$100**

Sorting Hat, The (T7-HPAC-06): Open edition; 4-1/2" hat is made from molded fabric and does not include a stool. ....**$30-$40**

Fawkes (T7-HPAC-07): Open edition; Dumbledore's phoenix is sculpted in resin and detailed with feathers; comes with a 9" stand. ....**$70-$80**

Hedwig (T6-HPAC-01): Open edition; sculpted in resin with feathers, this owl is fitted with a rod to allow her to be held by the characters; comes with 8" tree stand and base. ....**$50-$60**

Triwizard Cup (T6-HPAC-04): Open edition; sculpted in resin and hand painted, this 4.5" cup is an authentic reproduction. ....**$40-$50**

Outfits Only

Casual Set, Ron Weasley (T6-HPOF-03): Limited edition of 1,000; outfit includes hooded jacket, long-sleeve sweater, pants, socks, and shoes. .... **$70-$75**

Weekend Togs, Hermione Granger (T6-HPOF-04): Limited edition of 1,000; outfit includes turtleneck sweater, belted jacket, jeans, socks, and shoes. ...... **$70-$80**

Out of the Classroom – Harry Potter (T6-HPOF-01): Limited edition of 1,000; outfit includes denim jacket, T-shirt, hooded sweater, jeans, socks, and shoes. .... **$70-$80**

Tonner dolls in original box.

2008 San Diego Comic-Con Exclusive

Draco Malfoy, Slytherin Seeker (T7-HPSO-01): Limited edition of 100, released 2008; dressed in a custom knit sweater over trousers under his Slytherin house robes; comes with wand, gloves, shin guards, shoes, socks, and stand. San Diego Comic-con exclusive (Booth #5540)........**$200-$220**

F.A.O. Schwarz Exclusive

Harry Potter at Hogwarts (T5-HPDD-03): FAO Schwarz special edition of 400, same as the line doll but includes Hedwig (later sold separately). ....**$190-$200**

Hermione Granger at Hogwarts (T6-HPSD-01): FAO Schwarz special edition of 200, same as the line doll but includes Crookshanks (later sold separately). ....**$200-$220**

Voldemort (T7-HPSD-03): FAO Schwarz Exclusive limited edition of 150; You-Know-Who is hand-painted with black suit and shoes; comes with stand. **$200-$220**

Cho Chang at the Yule Ball (T8-HPSD-01): FAO Schwarz Exclusive limited edition of 100; tooted hair figure with hand-painted face wearing floor-length white gown embroidered with flowers. ....**$200-$220**

Draco Malfoy at the Yule Ball (T7-HPSD-01): FAO Schwarz Exclusive limited edition of 200; wigged figure with hand-painted face wearing white bow tie and vest with matching pants under dress robe; comes with socks, shoes, and stand. .**$200-$220**

Prototype of Voldemort.

Harry Potter and The Goblet of Fire Triwizard Trunk Set (T6-HPSD-02): FAO Schwarz Exclusive limited edition of 300; wardrobe trunk contains a figure of Harry, five different outfits, the Triwizard cup, Firebolt, and a golden dragon's egg that is exclusive to this set. (The Triwizard cup and Firebolt are available separately.) .... **$120-$130**

Ornaments
& Decorative Collectibles

Harry Potter ornaments come in a wide variety of types. The earliest ones were based on the artwork of Fred Bode and started to appear in late summer of 2000. These items consisted of secret boxes, waterglobes, bookends, figurines, Christmas tree ornaments, and more.

The main producers of the first lines were Department 56, Enesco, Kurt S. Adler, and Hallmark. At that time the ornaments were only available in Warner Bros. Studio Stores. Fortunately there were well over 100 of these stores in most states, and they could be ordered online as well. As the Harry Potter phenomenon grew, so did the amount and quality of ornaments available. In time the WB Stores closed, and Potterphiles bought their collectibles in different locations.

Ornaments are designed to be displayed. Unfortunately, as they serve their purpose they are most vulnerable to damage. This is true of Harry Potter ornaments as well. It is recommended that if you wish to display your collection, the ornaments should be kept out of direct sunlight, preferably in an enclosed case to also keep them dust free. Should this not be possible, an occasional cleaning might be necessary. Compressed air, available in most computer shops, works well to remove any dust that might accumulate.

When purchasing an ornament, inspect it carefully for nicks or cracks. Be wary of price stickers as they might be covering a flaw or may damage the paint when removed. This is true of any ornament, whether wooden, plastic, or ceramic. Some ornaments may fade with age, and this should be taken into consideration for pricing.

Christmas tree ornaments should be carefully placed on the tree, preferably not on the ends of branches where they could be subject to being knocked off and damaged. When removing the decorations, place them in their original boxes for storage.

*Harry Playing Quidditch,
Kurt S. Adler.*

Department 56, Inc.

DEPARTMENT

Department 56's unusual name comes from its origins at a floral products company that numbered each of its departments: The wholesale imported gift division was #56. It was founded in 1976 and is now based in Eden Prairie, Minnesota. Photos of Department 56 items are courtesy of Department 56, Inc.

Animated and Lighted Scenes

Harry Potter Animated Scene (59006): Released in 2000, this 17" scene winds up, making Harry, Ron, and Hermione chase the flying keys; retired 2002..**$150-$180**

Hogwarts School Lighted Scene (59036): Light-up Hogwarts School three-dimensional diorama, retired 2002..........**$80-$115**

Journey to Hogwarts Lighted Scene (59027): First years in boats, retired 2001..**$80-$115**

Secret Boxes

Department 56's first major Harry Potter offering was the first series of limited edition plastic "secret boxes" issued in 2000. Series 1 boxes come apart in two pieces. A hollow area in the base conceals a bronze-looking charm. Retired in 2000, unless otherwise indicated.

Golden Snitch (59007): Broomstick charm. ... **$15-$20**

Hagrid and Harry at Gringotts (59012): With Griphook, charm resembles a small package..........**$25-$30**

Hermione the Bookworm (59011): Stack of books charm.........................**$20-$25**

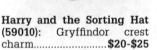

Harry and the Sorting Hat (59010): Gryffindor crest charm.........................**$20-$25**

Hedwig the Owl (59009): Birdcage charm. ....**$20-$25**

Quidditch Harry (59008): Golden Snitch charm. ....**$20-$25**

Series 2 secret boxes came out in fall 2001, just before *Harry Potter and the Sorcerer's Stone* was released. The boxes in Series 2 are all-in-one hinged containers in highly detailed plastic. Retired in 2002, unless otherwise indicated.

Golden Snitch, The (59020): Quidditch charm...**$15-$20**

Hermione Granger (59017): Hourglass charm $25 $35

Invisibility Cloak, The (59015): Stack of books charm. .... $25-$35

Mirror of Erised (59018): Mirror charm... $25-$35

The Potter Family Fortune (59019): Coin charm.. $25-$35

Professor Snape (59016): Potions Class, potion bottle charm. ....$27-$42

Enesco

Enesco, based in Itasca, Illinois, has created a number of different collectibles.

Bookends

Each set is composed of sculpted polyresin plastic. Issued in 2000 with literary figures.

Bookend Buddies (836265): Harry with Quidditch book (843113), Hermione with Magic book, sold as two of the same or set of one Harry and one Hermione................................... **$15-$20 ea.**

Sorting Hat, The (823260): Sorting Hat with Quidditch and Hogwarts books on one bookend and Spells, Wizards, and Potions books on the other. .... **$20-$30 pair**

Christmas Ornaments

These figures come with gold strings to hang on the tree. These average 2" to 3" and are similar in design to other Enesco items. I recently found a set of four of these on eBay in which the characters were in the wrong boxes (i.e., Harry was in a box marked "Albus Dumbledore"). I don't know if this was because they had been switched around by the original owner by accident or design, or if they had been accidentally packaged that way by Enesco. The seller stated that the boxes had not been opened. This fact did not seem to affect the price......**$5-$7**

Albus Dumbledore with wand.
Harry on a broom catching the Snitch.
Hermione with a book.
Ron with Scabbers.
Rubeus Hagrid with hatching Norbert.
Severus Snape with folded hands.

Collectible Figurines

The Heroes Series features plastic characters on stone-like floor bases that interlock to form one tableau. Issued in 2000, each figure comes with a colored story scope. ....**$10-$15 ea.**

Hagrid holding Norbert (811874).
Harry catches the Golden Snitch (811831).
Hedwig atop books (811904).
Hermione plays the magic flute (811858).
Professor Dumbledore (811866).
Ron with Scabbers (811947).

From the collection of Harry Silvester

Harry catches the Golden Snitch (811831).

Cookie Jars

Crafted in literary style, these ceramic jars can be used for cookies or trinkets. .... **$45-$50**

Harry Potter standing over bubbling cauldron.
Rubeus Hagrid standing with Ron, Harry, and Hermione.
Seeker Harry flying over Hogwarts School.

Cookie jar of Rubeus Hagrid standing with Ron, Harry, and Hermione.

Magic Trinket Boxes

"Among the three layers of each trinket box lies an enchanting surprise," promises Enesco...**$5-$10 ea.**

Fat Lady in Portrait: Harry and the staircase to Gryffindor dormitory.
Gringotts: Hagrid and Harry at the Potter vault in Gringotts.
Hermione Granger: Trunk opens to reveal her school supplies.
Mirror of Erised: Harry sees his long-dead parents.
Norbert: The baby Norwegian Ridgeback hatches from his egg.
Scabbers: Hides inside *Magical Theory* textbook.

Masterpiece Collection
Limited edition literary resin figurines showing a scene from *Harry Potter and the Sorcerer's Stone*, hand numbered.

Through the Trapdoor (823597): Issued in 2000, Ron and Hermione peer into the trapdoor as Harry plays the flute and lulls Fluffy to sleep; door opening lights up. .... **$40-$50**

Troll Battle, The: Harry and Ron battle the Mountain Troll to rescue Hermione, 7-1/2" tall. .... **$40-$50**

Story Scopes
Similar to the story scopes included with the six Heroes Series figurines. Attached tags are gold metallic-looking with a lightning bolt Harry Potter title and clip. Designs each sold separately. Issued in 2000 (847852). .... **$2-$4 ea.**

1) Harry Potter Scope, purple pyramid
2) Hermione Granger Scope, maroon flame
3) Rubeus Hagrid Scope, blue jewel
4) Fluffy Scope, amber rectangular (2)
5) Ron Weasley Scope, green diamond
6) Hogwarts Scope, yellow oval
7) Slytherin Scope, purple diamond
8) Gryffindor Scope, maroon jewel
9) Hufflepuff Scope, blue flame
10) Ravenclaw Scope, amber oval
11) Severus Snape Scope, green pyramid
12) Hedwig Scope, yellow rectangular
13) Potions Scope, amber diamond
14) Sorting Hat Scope, amber rectangle
15) Sorcerer's Stone Scope, maroon square
16) Bertie Bott's Beans Scope, amber lightning
17) Harry's Glasses Scope, yellow diamond
18) Spells Scope, yellow diamond
19) Scabbers Scope, yellow flame
20) You-Know-Who Scope, maroon diamond
21) Flying Keys Scope, maroon diamond
22) Norbert Scope, purple lightning
23) Mrs. Norris Scope, purple diamond
24) Golden Snitch Scope, gold on white lightning

Storyteller Series

Made of polyresin, the Storytellers have a book-shaped base and an eyepiece to view the rotating story frames on a plastic wheel; issued in 2000...$10-$15 ea.

Fluffy (823635): Looking ferocious.

Harry Potter (8236009): Harry with Hedwig.

Hermione Granger (823619): Levitates a feather.

Ron Weasley (823627): Holding a bag of Bertie Bott's Every Flavor Beans.

Waterglobes

Musical waterglobes featured literary scenes from *Harry Potter and the Sorcerer's Stone*, released in 2000, average 4"-5" tall. ....**$5-$10 ea.**

Harry and Hedwig: Plays *Eine Kleine Nachtmusik*.
Harry and Norbert: Harry observes the hatching of baby dragon Norbert.
Hermione Granger: Hermione holds a scroll and looks at potion bottles.

Photo from the collection of Megan Barrow

Journey to Hogwarts: Four students in boats, castle is in waterglobe, plays *Eine Kleine Nachtmusik*.
Quidditch Harry: Harry catching the Golden Snitch.
Ron Weasley: Ron in Snape's potions class, plays *Hungarian Dance No. 5*.

Gentle Giant Ltd.

Bust-Ups

These are 2" to 3" tall busts and statuettes similar in form and detail to the mini-busts above. They were released in two series, Classic Moments and Order of the Phoenix.
.... **$5-$7 ea.**

Photos of Gentle Giant Ltd. items are courtesy of Gentle Giant Ltd.

Harry Potter (9790-1)   Ron Weasley (9790-2)

Classic Moments

Triwizard Tournament Harry Potter (9790-4), Riddle Grave (9790-5), Hermione Granger (9790-3), Harry Potter (9790-1), Ron Weasley (9790-2), Harry Potter (9790-1)

Order of the Phoenix

Neville Longbottom (9791-4), Ginny Weasley (9791-3), Dumbledore (9791-5), Draco Malfoy (9791-2), Harry Potter (9791-1)

Bust-Ups Box Sets

Harry Potter Death Eater Bust-Up Box Set (10735): Released in 2008, 2" tall, includes Bellatrix Lestrange, Malfoy, Dolohov, Rookwood, and a Death Eater. Chase figure, Death Eater "Masked Bellatrix." .... **$25-$30**

Harry Potter Order of the Phoenix Bust-Up Set: Includes Harry Potter, Draco Malfoy, Professor Dumbledore, Neville Longbottom, Ginny Weasley, and a Thestral. .... **$15-$20**

Harry Potter: Quidditch Bust-Ups Box Set 1 (10641): Released in 2009, includes 3" tall figures on clear bases: Harry Potter, Madam Hooch, and Cho Chang figures. Also includes Quidditch Equipment Accessory Pack: Quidditch trunk, the Snitch, quaffle, two bludgers, and two bats. .... **$25-$30**

Harry Potter: Quidditch Bust-Ups Box Set 2 (11542): Released in 2009, includes 3" tall figures on clear bases: Draco Malfoy, Fred and George Weasley. Also includes Quidditch Equipment Accessory Pack parts: Quidditch trunk bottom, two bludgers, and a bat. .... **$25-$30**

Classics Busts

A new line started in 2009 with detailed busts being an average of 5" tall, based on the Triwizard Tournament Champions.

Cedric Diggory (11630): Limited edition..**$30-$40**

Fleur Delacour (11628): Limited edition. ....**$30-$40**

Harry Potter (11931): Limited edition...**$30-$40**

Viktor Krum Classics Bust (11626): Limited edition...**$30-$40**

Gallery Collection

Gallery Collection Harry Potter Statue (10271): Preparing to fight Voldemort, released in 2008, limited edition, in 1:4 scale, 16" inches tall, wearing a tailored fabric costume. ......**$290-$300**

Gallery Collection Voldemort Statue (10272): Preparing to fight Harry Potter, released in 2008, limited edition, in 1:4 scale, 17-1/2" tall, wearing a tailored fabric costume. **$315-$325**

Mini-Busts

The Gentle Giant mini-bust line of figures started in 2005. The figures are designed in 1:6 scale and average about 6-1/2" to 7" tall.

Albus Dumbledore (7590): Modeled after Michael Gambon, released in 2005, limited edition of 1,500. ....$50-$60

Promotional piece, promo/ artist proof piece limited to 30 pieces. ....$200-$215

Cho Chang (8778): Wearing Ravenclaw colors with wand in hand, released in 2007, limited edition of 2,500. ....$50-$60

Death Eater (8690): Torch carrying Death Eater, released in 2006, limited edition of 1,500.........$50-$60

Dobby (7645): Wearing pillowcase and with sock in hand, released in 2006, limited edition of 2,000. ....$50-$60

Draco Malfoy (9779): Dressed as a Slytherin prefect, released in 2007, limited edition of 3,000.........$50-$60

Fenrir Greyback (11390): Poised to attack, released in 2009, limited edition, 6-3/4" tall..............................$60-$70

Fred & George Weasley two-pack (10624): Weasley twins dressed in brown sweaters, released in 2008, limited edition of 2,000, 2008 Comic Con Exclusive.................................. **$90-$100**

Ginny Weasley (11605): Wearing patterned sweater, released in 2009, limited edition. ....**$55-$65**

Harry Potter (7396): Wearing robes and wand in hand, released in 2005, limited edition of 2,000.........**$45-$50**

Harry Potter in Quidditch Gear (11387): Harry caught the Snitch, released in 2009, limited edition, 9" tall. ....**$55-$65**

Harry Potter, Year 5 (8792): With wand ready and holding prophecy orb, released in 2007, limited edition of 5,000. ....**$50-$60**

Hermione Granger (7633): Carrying the *Monster Book of Monsters*, released in 2006, limited edition of 2,500. ....**$50-$60**

Kreacher (10605): Malicious old elf, released in 2009, limited edition. ....**$50-$60**

Light-Up Harry Potter, Year 5: Same as 8792, but the prophecy orb lights up, released in 2007, limited edition of 1,000, F.Y.E. and Suncoast Exclusive. .**$55-$65**

Mad-Eye Moody (9486): Hands resting on his staff, released in 2007, limited edition of 1,750. ....**$50-$60**

Nearly Headless Nick (7631): Gryffindor house ghost shows how he got his nickname, released in 2006, limited edition of 1,500. ....**$50-$60**

Nymphadora Tonks (10546): Purple hair and matching jacket, released in 2008, limited edition of 2,500, 7-1/2" tall. ....**$55-$65**

Professor McGonagall (10603): Dressed in black with tall pointed hat, released in 2008, limited edition of 1,400, 9-1/2" tall. ....**$55-$65**

Remus Lupin (10600): Wearing brown jacket and staring up at a full moon, released in 2008, limited edition of 1,250. ....**$55-$65**

Ron Weasley (7632): In dress robes for the Yule Ball, released in 2006, limited edition of 2,000.........**$50-$60**

Ron Weasley in Quidditch Gear (11604A): Wearing keeper uniform, released in 2009, limited edition of 700, 7.25" tall.....................**$55-$65**

Rubeus Hagrid (7652): Carrying crossbow and lantern, released in 2007, limited edition of 2,000, 7-1/2" tall. .... **$50-$60**

Severus Snape (7565): Wearing black robes and with raised hand, released in 2005, limited edition of 1,500. .... **$50-$60**

Voldemort (9241): Black robe and wand at the ready, released in 2007, limited edition of 2,500. .... **$50-$60**

Wanted: Sirius Black (8157): As he appeared on Azkaban wanted poster, released in 2005, limited edition, holding gray board. .... **$45-$55**

Wanted: Sirius Black: As he appeared on Azkaban wanted poster, released in 2005, limited edition of 500, San Diego Comic-Con 2005 Exclusive, holding sepia brown board. .... **$175-$200**

Werewolf Lupin (11079): Similar to 10600 but with more hair and fangs as Lupin transforms, limited edition of 500, Premier Guild Exclusive; purchases were limited to one per person. .... **$55-$65**

Statues

Harry Potter on Thestral (10645): Released in 2008, limited edition of 700, Harry can be removed from Thestral, 12" tall and 14" wide. .... **$90-$150**

Hungarian Horntail Dragon (8069): Dragon hovers above the golden egg, released in 2006, limited edition of 1,500, stands over 16" tall with a wing span of 21". ....**$200-$220**

Riddle Grave, The (9144): Winged death in front of the Riddle tombstone, released in 2007, limited edition of 1,500, 7" tall. ....**$60-$70**

Hallmark
Figurines

Photo from the collection of Jordan

Photo from the collection of Jordan

Hermione Granger holding book (1895SFF3111): Released in 2001. ...... **$15-$20**

Ron Weasley with Scabbers in trunk (1895SSF3104): Released in 2001. ...... **$15-$20**

Photo from the collection of Padfoot

Photo from the collection of Padfoot

Hermione Granger sits on the computer monitor, reading a book called *Spells*. .... **$10-$15**

Norbert the Dragon (149SSF3114): Released in 2001. .... **$10-$15**

Professor Dumbledore with House Cup (1895SFF3124): Released in 2001. ..... **$15-$20**

Quidditch Harry Potter (1895SSF3101): Released in 2001, retail. .... **$15-$20**

Rubeus Hagrid with Norbert (2495SFF3131): Released in 2001. .... **$20-$25**

Keepsake Ornaments

Hallmark's Keepsake Ornaments are a highly sought-after collectible in all subjects. Some come in a storybook-type box with a silver strap with Velcro to hold the "book" closed. Unless noted otherwise, photos of Keepsake Ornaments are from the collection of Jordan.

Cauldron Trouble (QXI4359): Released in 2007. .... $24-$26

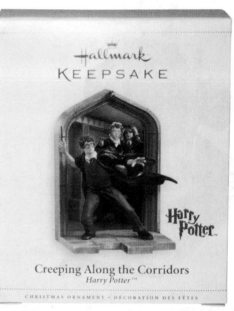

Creeping Along the Corridors (QXI6156): Released in 2006. .... $15-$18

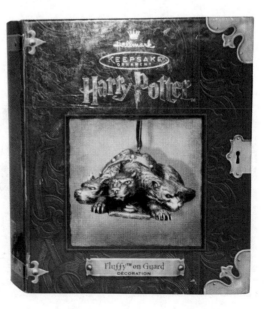

Fluffy: Released in 2000. .... $13-$18

Fluffy on Guard (QXE4415): Released in 2001. .... $13-$18

Gargoyle Guard, The: Released in 2008. .... $40-$45

Hagrid and Norbert (QXE4412): Released in 2001 .... $16-$20

Harry Potter (QXE4402): Released in 2001. .... $13-$17

Harry Potter and Hedwig (QXI4044): Released in 2004. .... $15-$1

Harry Potter Catching Snitch (QXE4381): Released in 2000 .... $13-$18

Hedwig (QXE4394): Released in 2000. .... $13-$18

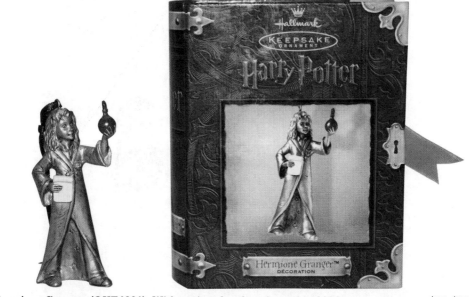

Hermione Granger (QXE4391): With potions bottle, released in 2000. ....$13-$21

Hermione Granger's Trunk, Set of 6 (QXE4422): Released in 2001................................$15-$19

Hogwarts Charms (QXE4404): Released in 2000 (set of six: sorting hat, flying key, potions bottle, Snitch, Norbert, book)..$13-$17

Photo from the collection of Harry Silvester

Hogwarts School Crests (QXE4452): Released in 2001 (set of five: Hogwarts, Gryffindor, Slytherin, Hufflepuff, and Ravenclaw). ....$13-$18

Invisibility Cloak, The (QXI8663): Released in 2002. ....$13-$28

Mirror of Erised (QXI8645): Released in 2001. ..... **$16-$19**

Platform 9-3/4 (QXI4279): Released in 2003. ..... **$13-$19**

Potions Master (QXI8652): Released in 2001. ..... **$15-$19**

Professor Dumbledore (QXE4384): Holding parchment rolls, released in 2000.............**$13-$18**

Photo from the collection of Megan Barrow

Quidditch Match (QXI8915): Released in 2005. ....**$15-$18**

Quidditch Season (QXI8656): Released in 2002...**$24-$28**

Ron Weasley and Scabbers (QXE4405): Released in 2001................................**$13-$28**

Room Decor

Fat Lady Bookends: Harry entering portal on one side and Ron sitting in chair on other. ....$40-$45

Fluffy and Trapdoor: A motion-activated door stop. ....$35-$40

Golden Snitch Lamp...........................$40-$45

Hagrid: Door decoration, 6" x 8". ....$10-$15

Trinket Box

Fluffy on Trapdoor (1495SSF3134): Released in 2000...$15-$20

Waterglobes

Issued in 2000, each shows a scene from *Sorcerer's Stone*; average size is 2-1/2" high.

Chess Game with Ron standing beside a knight...$10-$15

Devil's Snare holding Harry and Ron...$10-$15

Fluffy guarding trapdoor. ....$10-$15

Mirror of Erised with Dumbledore and Harry. ....$10-$15

Potions Riddle with Hermione. ....$10-$15

Winged Keys pursued by Harry on broom. ....$10-$15

Kurt S. Adler, Inc.

One of the world's largest importers and distributors of holiday decorations, Kurt S. Adler Inc. of New York has produced enough decorations to fill most Christmas trees.

Appliqué Stocking

Harry Potter lighting tree with his wand, issued in 2000. ....$25-$30

Bas Relief Resin Ornaments

Each bas relief ornament has the character's name on the base; released in 2000. ....$8-$10 ea.

Harry Potter with wand and Hedwig.
Hermione Granger with wand and potion bottles.
Ron Weasley with wand and Scabbers.
Rubeus Hagrid with baby Norbert.

Blow Mold Ornaments

Harry Potter catching the Golden Snitch. $5-$6

Harry Potter with Christmas gifts. ......$5-$6

Collector's Ornaments

Harry Potter plastic figure on a wooden Nimbus 2000. ....$15-$20

Hedwig carrying a letter to Harry's house on Privet Drive. ....$15-$20

Fabric Maché Table Pieces

These elaborate Christmas at Hogwarts pieces have fabric clothing over the plastic bodies.

Harry Potter flying his Nimbus 2000, 7". $25-$30

Harry Potter with a sweater from Mrs. Weasley....$45-$50

Ron Weasley with a sweater from Mrs. Weasley, 7-1/2". ....$40-$45

Rubeus Hagrid brings a Christmas tree into the school. The tree lights up, 10"......$48-$52

Full Round Resin Ornaments

Flying Key ....$10-$15

Harry Potter mixing potions. ....$45-$50

Hedwig with letter..............................$18-$20

Hermione Granger with wand and potions bottle...$18-$20

Mirror of Erised ....$10-$15

Nimbus 2000 Broomstick ....$10-$15

Norbert hatching from egg. ....$18-$20

Ron Weasley under the Sorting Hat. $18-$20

Sorting Hat ....$10-$15

Injection Plastic Ornament

Lightning Bolt Ornaments: Set of three, 6", plastic. ....$6-$10

Light Set

Harry Potter trying his wand; string of 10 lights. ....$20-$25

Movie Scenes Ornaments

Harry Potter chasing the Golden Snitch; decoupage ball with painted scene. .. $8-$10

Harry, Ron, and Hermione chasing flying keys; printed glass ball ornament, issued in 2000. ....$8-$10

Harry, Ron, and Hermione in the Room of Keys; decoupage ball with painted scene. ....$8-$10

Polonaise Collection

Issued in 2000, these limited edition, hand-blown and hand-decorated ornaments were created by Polish artisans. These ornaments were available individually or in a set of four. If purchased in a set, the ornaments came in a wooden presentation box with the Fred Bode scene titled "Journey to Hogwarts" on the cover and a bonus "HP" lightning bolt/Golden Snitch logo ornament inside. Photos are courtesy of Kurt S. Adler.

Boxed set $200

Hermione With Book of Scales (AP1265) ....$55-$60

Harry and Hedwig (AP1266) ....$55-$60

Ron With Scabbers (AP1264) ....$55-$60

Harry Playing Quidditch (AP1263): Sold by itself. ....$50-$70

Resin Stocking Hanger

Harry, Ron, and Hermione: Red base with gold HP logo and stars with the trio and Hedwig as well as a red Harry Potter stocking, with stars, Harry with his wand, and a fabric Golden Snitch. ....**$20-$25**

Three-Dimensional Ornaments

These ornaments were issued in 2001, are about 4" to 4-1/2" in size, and are made of plastic.

Hagrid on Sirius' motorbike............... **$15-$18**

Harry Potter on his Nimbus 2000. .... **$15-$18**

Harry Potter with a box of chocolate frogs. ....**$15-$18**

Harry Potter with gifts, 4".................**$15-$18**

Hogwarts Express/Platform 9-3/4.....**$18-$20**

Ron Weasley with one of his mother's hand-knitted sweaters. ....**$15-$18**

Rubeus Hagrid carrying a Christmas tree. ....**$15-$18**

Tin Ornaments

These ornaments are made of tin and feature props from the books and movies, issued in 2000. ....**$10-$12 ea.**

Bag of Bertie Bott's Every Flavor Beans
Nimbus 2000 broomstick
Silver key from the Room of Keys

Photo from the collection of Megan Barrow

Photo from the collection of Megan Barrow

Potions Lessons with Ron, Harry, and Hermione, 4-1/2"...**$18-$20**

Mattel

Classic Scenes Collection

These ornaments are meticulously sculpted and feature hand-painted scenes from *The Sorcerer's Stone,* based on Fred Bode's artwork.

Chamber of Keys: Chasing the flying keys. ....**$10-$20**

Hagrid's Gift: Harry receives Hedwig in Diagon Alley. ....**$25-$30**

Mirror of Erised: Harry sees his family. ....**$20-$30**

Collector's Figurines

Four Horsemen of New Jersey designed and sculpted these four figures for Mattel in 2001 in a limited edition of 5,000 each. Four Horsemen also designed the Deluxe Creature Collection figures of Hagrid, Fluffy, and the mountain troll. (See Action Figures section.)

Battling the Mountain Troll (29443): Harry is about to stuff his wand up the troll's nose while Ron and Hermione watch, 12".......... **$100-$135**

Gryffindor Victory (29442): Harry flies over Hogwarts holding a Golden Snitch..**$90-$100**

Hogwarts Homework (29444): Harry, Ron, and Hermione gather around a bubbling cauldron. ....**$90-$100**

NECA, Inc.

Bookends

Harry & Hedwig Bookends: 8", both ends the same, Hedwig on Harry's arm. ....**$30-$35**

Hogwarts Express Bookends: 7", locomotive on one end, coach on the other. ....**$35-$40**

Diorama

Hand-painted resin scenes with 7" tall figure on detailed background and stand.

Harry Potter Diorama (NC60562): Fireplace and chandelier background. ....**$25-$30**

Hermione Granger Diorama (NC60564): Fireplace and chandelier background. ....**$25-$30**

Ron Weasley Diorama (NC60565): Death Eater practice dummy background. ....**$25-$30**

Severus Snape Diorama (NC60563): Potions class background. ....**$40-$45**

Lamps

Hogwarts Tiffany Style (NC60293): 13" lamp in blue and yellow with Hogwarts school on one side and crest on the other. ....**$40-$55**

Triwizard Cup (NC60435): 12-1/2" silver-colored lamp modeled after cup in *Goblet of Fire*........................**$45-$60**

Snowglobe

Harry Potter Quidditch: Released in 2007, 4-1/2", Harry chasing Snitch inside globe. ....**$25-$50**

Tins

Harry Potter Honey Dukes Tin Assortment: Set of six, three round (5-1/4") and two rectangular (7-1/2" x 5" x 2-3/4") tins, labeled Fresh Pumpkin Pasties, Cauldron Cakes, Acid Pops, Fizzing Whizzbees, Pumpkin Juice, and Honey Dukes.......................................**$35-$40**

Votive Holder

Cauldron Votive Candle Holder (NC59576): Black cauldron on stand, released in 2009. ....**$15-$17**

Goblet of Fire Votive Holder (NC60202): Shaped like goblet of fire, 9" tall, released in 2007. ....**$15-$20**

Noble Collection

Bookends

Basilisk Bookends (NN7139): Pair of basilisks from *Harry Potter and the Chamber of Secrets*, 7". ....**$80-$85/pair**

Dumbledore and Voldemort Bookend Set (NN7923): Limited edition of 1,500, 10", hand-painted. ....**$195-$225/pair**

Hungarian Horntail Bookend (NN7659): 9" ....**$65-$75**

Individual Basilisk Bookend (NN7148): 7" ....**$45-$55 ea.**

Broomsticks

Firebolt (NN7387): 13", die-cast miniature on base. ....**$60-$65**

Nimbus 2001 (NN7388): 13", die-cast miniature on base. ....**$60-$65**

Christmas Ornament

Hogwarts Tree Ornament (NN7333): Set of five Hogwarts and house crests in collector box, 4", die-cast and plated................**$55-$65**

Crystal Balls

Dementors Crystal Ball (NN7062): Dementors circling ball on Hogwarts Castle base, 5", pewter and wood with a clear glass ball. ....**$65-$75**

Divination Crystal Ball (NN7364): As seen in *Harry Potter and the Prisoner of Azkaban*, 5", with a solid glass ball.........................**$50-$60**

Prophecy, The (NN7467): 5" globe on bronze-plated stand with metal snakes and label as in *Harry Potter and the Order of the Phoenix*. ....**$35-$45**

Doorstopper

Dobby Doorstopper (NN7259): 6" hand-painted house elf................................**$30-$35**

Figurines

Chinese Fireball Dragon (NN7066): 3-1/2" hand-painted fine pewter on a cut glass.........**$45-$55**

Hungarian Horntail Dragon (NN7065): 3-1/2" hand-painted fine pewter on a cut glass. ....**$45-$55**

Swedish Short Snout Dragon (NN7063): 3-1/2" hand-painted fine pewter on a cut glass. ....**$45-$55**

Welsh Green Dragon (NN7064): 3-1/2" hand-painted fine pewter on a cut glass.....**$45-$55**

All Four dragons listed above (NN7667): ....**$145-$155**

Buckbeak Takes Flight (NN7918): Limited edition of 5,000, 10" pewter on wood base. ....$195-$215

Centaur, The (NN7381): 9" pewter figure on wooden base.....................................$145-$155

Dobby is Free (NN7439): Limited edition of 5,000, 10" pewter figure on wood base. ....$195-$200

Dragons of the First Task Sculpture (NN7764): 12" with hand-painted details and patina in solid bronze on wood base. ....$495-$510

Fawkes the Phoenix (NN7200): 14" Dumbledore's Phoenix on his stand. ....$125-$135

Fluffy (NN7954): 12" on base..........$195-$210

Goblet of Fire (NN7885): Limited edition of 5,000, 8" pewter..............................$125-$135

Golden Snitch (NN7144): 7" die cast metal with silver and gold plating on wood base. ....$55-$65

Hedwig (NN7098): 10" Hedwig in her cage on arched pedestal display.......................$75-$85

Hogwarts Castle (NN7074): 13" hand-painted, detailed sculpture of Hogwarts set atop a cliff on hardwood base...........................$300-$350

Hogwarts Express (NN7800): 21" 1:50 scale die-cast model on base....................$145-$155

Mechanical Death Eater (NN7789): 8" on base. ....$60-$65

Mirror of Erised, The (NN7856): 16-1/2" x 8-1/2" mirror can be wall mounted or placed on tabletop. ....$70-$80

Sorcerer's Stone (NN7386): Cut glass red stone in 6" glass dome......................$95-$100

Thestral is Free (NN7672): 12" on wooden base. ....$195-$200

Triwizard Cup (NN7156): 8" die cast metal and pewter on wooden base from *Harry Potter and the Goblet of Fire*. ....$125-$135

Masks

Bellatrix Lestrange's Mask (NN7325): 9" Death Eater mask on black wood board. ....$75-$85

Death Eater Mask Collection (NN7396): Twelve 3" masks mounted on black wood board. ....$95-$100

Lucius Malfoy's Mask (NN7118): 11" Death Eater mask on black wood board. ......$75-$85

Letter Openers

First Task Dragons Letter Opener Set (NN7908): Four 8" dragon-topped letter openers on Triwizard Tournament display.........$75-$85

Gryffindor Sword (NN7855): 9" letter opener on die-cast Gryffindor lion base holder......$35-$45

San Francisco Music Box Company

Figurines

These highly detailed scenes from various films were released in 2008 and average 5-1/2" x 8" x 7-1/2" in size and are hand-painted on cold cast resin. All SFMBC items play *Prologue, Harry Potter and the Sorcerer's Stone* by John Williams, unless noted otherwise.

Dumbledore's Army (200900011397): Six members of the Dumbledore's Army in front of the door to the Room of Requirement. ....$65-$100

Harry Potter (200900011412): 13" figure of Harry from *Harry Potter and the Half-Blood Prince*. ....$70-$100

Ollivanders Wand Shop (200900000080): Harry and Hagrid outside Ollivanders, detailed interior from the back on lighted base. ....$45-$85

Order of the Phoenix (200900011394): Harry, Hermione, and Ron confer with Sirius Black in a fireplace...$50-$100

Hourglasses

Dementor Hourglass (200900011405): Released in 2008, Harry, Hermione, and Ron are at the bottom with a dementor at the top. ....$70-$140

Harry Potter and the Sorcerer's Stone Hourglass (200900000082): Released in 2008, Harry stands at the bottom of the hourglass with Hedwig. ....$70-$140

Music Boxes

Harry Potter Hinged Box (200900000083): A revolving miniature of Harry in front of a Hogwarts Castle painting on the inside of the lid, 4-1/2" x 4-1/2", released in 2008. ... $25-$55

Harry Potter Poster Lacquer Box (200900000127): Poster from *Sorcerer's Stone*, lid opens to play music, 9" x 7" x 3".....$33-$65

Harry Potter and the Half-Blood Prince Jewelry Box (200900010828): Artwork from Half-Blood Prince, lid opens to play music, 7.2" x 5.4" x 3".......................................$25-$50

Ollivanders Wand Shop (200900000080): Harry and Hagrid outside Ollivanders, detailed interior from the back on lighted base. ....$45-$85

Order of the Phoenix (200900011394): Harry, Hermione, and R on confer with Sirius Black in a fireplace. ....$50-$100

Hourglasses

Dementor Hourglass (200900011405): Released in 2008, Harry, Hermione, and Ron are at the bottom with a dementor at the top. ....$70-$140

Harry Potter and the Sorcerer's Stone Hourglass (200900000082): Released in 2008, Harry stands at the bottom of the hourglass with Hedwig. ....$70-$140

Music Boxes

Harry Potter Hinged Box (200900000083): A revolving miniature of Harry in front of a Hogwarts Castle painting on the inside of the lid, 4-1/2" x 4-1/2", released in 2008 ...$25-$55

Harry Potter Poster Lacquer Box (200900000127): Poster from *Sorcerer's Stone*, lid opens to play music, 9" x 7" x 3". ....$33-$65

Harry Potter and the Half-Blood Prince Jewelry Box (200900010828): Artwork from *Half-Blood Prince*, lid opens to play music, 7.2" x 5.4" x 3". ....$25-$50

Waterglobes

These detailed waterglobes are hand-painted on cold cast resin, were released in 2007, and feature the tune *Prologue, Harry Potter and the Sorcerer's Stone* by John Williams, unless noted otherwise.

Final Battle from Harry Potter and the Sorcerer's Stone Waterglobe, The (200900000081): Released in 2008, Harry, Quirrell, and the Mirror of Erised with battle against Voldemort on base..................$45-$85

Gryffindor Robes Waterglobe (200900000079): Released in 2008, Harry, Hermione, and Ron in robes................$30-$60

Harry Potter at the Yule Ball Waterglobe (200900000031): Released in 2008, Harry in his dress robes with scenes from the ball on base, plays *Entry into the Great Hall and the Banquet.* ....$22-$45

Harry Potter, Fawkes in the Chamber of Secrets Waterglobe (200900000074): Fawkes heals Harry with his tears. ....$22-$45

Harry Potter, Harry Potter and the Sorcerer's Stone Waterglobe (200800012423): Harry catches the Golden Snitch..................$17-$35

Harry Potter, The First Task Waterglobe (200900000073): Released in 2008, Harry reaches for the dragon's egg to complete the first task of the Triwizard Tournament. ....$22-$45

Hedwig Wateregg (200800010438): Hedwig perches on a pile of books, plays *Hedwig's Theme* by John Williams.....................$25-$50

Hermione Granger at the Yule Ball Waterglobe (200900000033): Released in 2008, Hermione in her ball gown with scenes from the ball on base, plays *Entry into the Great Hall and the Banquet*.................$22-$45

Hermione Granger, Polyjuice Potion Waterglobe (200900000076): Hermione brews polyjuice potion. ....$22-$45

Hermione Granger, Wingardium Leviosa Waterglobe (200800012424): Hermione learns the levitation spell....................$17-$35

Hogwarts Express Waterglobe (200800010437): Harry pushes his trolley at Platform 9-3/4 while the train rotates around the base...$35-$70

Hufflepuff Crest Waterglobe (200800010441): Plays *Entry into the Great Hall and the Banquet* by John Williams, reads, "Just and loyal... true.... Yes, clearly...Hufflepuff!" ....$22-$45

Prisoner of Azkaban Waterglobe, The (200900011400): Released in 2008, Ron, Hermione, and Harry behind pumpkins. ....$25-$50

Professor Dumbledore with Fawkes the Phoenix Waterglobe (200900000077): Released in 2008, features Professor Dumbledore and Fawkes, plays *Entry into the Great Hall and the Banquet*.................$25-$50

Quidditch Waterglobe (200800010436): Harry chases the Snitch, plays *The Quidditch Match* by John Williams......................$25-$50

Ravenclaw Crest Waterglobe (200800010440): Plays *Entry into the Great Hall and the Banquet* by John Williams, reads, "Ahh, yes. A ready mind.... You belong in...Ravenclaw!". ....$22-$45

Ron Weasley at the Yule Ball Waterglobe (200900000032): Released in 2008, Ron in his ancient dress robes with scenes from the ball on base, plays *Entry into the Great Hall and the Banquet.* ....$22-$45

Ron Weasley, Harry Potter and the Sorcerer's Stone Waterglobe (200800012422): Ron plays Wizard's Chess. ....$17-$35

Ron Weasley, Howler Waterglobe (200900000075): Ron berated by a Howler from his mother. ....$22-$45

Slytherin Crest Waterglobe (200800010439): Plays *Entry into the Great Hall and the Banquet* by John Williams, reads, "Cunning... shrewd...hmmmm.... Let's see...Slytherin!" ....$22-$45

Yule Ball Waterglobe (200900011401): Released in 2008, Harry, Hermione, and Ron in their Yule finest, plays *Entry into the Great Hall and the Banquet* ....$25-$50

Schylling

The Schylling Toy Co. of Rowley, Massachusetts specializes in metal tins, lunchboxes, and signs. The company released Harry Potter items in 2000.

Boxes

Harry Potter Box: Flat tin box with handle; Harry flobs the flying key as Ron and Hermione watch...**$5-$8**

Seasonal Specialties

Christmas tree ornaments (015130500): Set of five: Hermione, Harry, Hedwig, Scabbers, and Ron........**$5-$6**

Warner Bros.

Harry Potter: Released in 2000, Harry on Nimbus 2000 reaching for Snitch.......**$10-$15**

Hedwig Messenger Owl: Released in 2000, owl with wings spread wide and holding envelope addressed to Harry.................**$8-$12**

Warner Bros. Platform 9-3/4 Bookends (GM568): Released in 2000, platform 8 and 9 on one side, Harry and Hogwarts Express on the other. ....**$20-$35**

Snowglobes

Dumbledore and Students: Headmaster Dumbledore with Harry, Ron, and Hermione over cauldron; base is books...............**$20-$25**

Hagrid's New Arrival (29445): Inside his hut, Hagrid holds newborn Norbert by the tail; limited edition of 5,000......................**$90-$100**

Promotional Bobblehead

Dobby the House Elf: Promotional item, never sold, for the release of the *Harry Potter and the Chamber of Secrets* DVD in 2002. Approximately 6" tall. ....**$25-$30**

Miscellaneous

I often find the miscellaneous section of a book the most interesting for here we find almost anything one can imagine that has some relationship to the Harry Potter world. This is the muggle equivalent to Diagon Alley.

To use this section effectively, it should be noted that the items are arranged alphabetically by collectible type, ranging from audio books to wands. Not everything Harry Potter is listed, but there are enough items here to provide a cross-section and allow buyers and sellers to determine the price of the item they have or want to add to their collection. Finding the closest description to the item in question is often sufficient to establish a reasonable price. The prices in this section are relative to one another and therefore useful regardless of the age of this book. The data collected is the result of hundreds of hours of searching and the assistance of many businesses and individuals. Some manufacturers went out of their way to be helpful. Secondary sources also had to be relied upon to complete listings.

Items are listed in alphabetical order with subsections by manufacturer's name, again in alphabetical order. Where a picture of the item is not available, a detailed description is provided to aid in identification. If known, manufacturer's numbers, dates of issue, and details of interest are also included. Some of the items listed, such as chocolate frogs and edible cake decorations, are not true collectibles as they tend to deteriorate over a short period of time, but they are included nonetheless as they are part of Harry Potter merchandising.

As with the earlier parts of this book, the items listed are from the North American market, though many items from other countries such as Great Britain are readily available due to Internet purchasing. Many of these can be priced by comparing them with similar North American items. The vast amount of Harry Potter material produced in a relatively short period of time makes it necessary to restrict what is included, due to space requirements.

Harry Potter items are still being produced and will no doubt continue to appear on a regular basis for some time to come. As older items become rare, collectors will focus more on newer items, making it possible for anyone to be a Harry Potter collector. The depth of our pockets usually decides where our focus will be. Character appeal, perceived value, and the need to own will set the prices. When purchasing collectibles, always remember the golden rule of collecting: Collect what you like, not what you think will be worth the most.

Audio Books

All of the audio books released in the United States are unabridged. Jim Dale performs the voices of all the characters and the narrative. His work has been recognized internationally, winning him a Grammy award, three Grammy nominations, a Tony award, three Audie awards, four Drama Desk awards, and an Academy award nomination. Dale is also a member of the Order of the British Empire.

As cassettes are becoming less popular, the prices are likely to decrease, and in time the same will be true of CDs. Most copies will be in the hands of collectors and not casual listeners.

Listening Library is an imprint of Random House.

Harry Potter and the Sorcerer's Stone
Six cassettes, 8 hours, 17 minutes
Listening Library (October 1999) .... **$10-$15**
Seven compact discs, 8 hours, 17 minutes
Listening Library (December 1999) ...**$25-$30**

Harry Potter and the Chamber of Secrets
Six cassettes, 9 hours
Listening Library (December 1999) ... **$10-$15**
Eight compact discs, 9 hours
Listening Library (December 1999) ...**$25-$30**

Harry Potter and the Prisoner of Azkaban
Seven cassettes, 11.8 hours
Listening Library (February 2000)..... **$10-$15**
10 compact discs, 11.8 hours
Listening Library (February 2000).....**$25-$30**

Harry Potter and the Goblet of Fire
12 cassettes, 20 hours, 52 minutes
Listening Library (July 2000) ....**$15-$20**
17 compact discs, 20 hours, 52 minutes
Listening Library (July 2000) ....**$30-$35**

Harry Potter and the Order of the Phoenix
17 cassettes, 27 hours
Random House Audiobooks (June 2003)
....**$15-$20**
23 compact discs, 27 hours
Random House Audiobooks (June 2003)
....**$30-$35**

Harry Potter and the Half-Blood Prince
12 cassettes, 19 hours
Random House Audiobooks (July 2005)
....**$15-$20**
17 compact discs, 19 hours
Random House Audiobooks (July 2005)
....**$30-$35**

Harry Potter and the Deathly Hallows
12 cassettes, 21 hours
Random House Audiobooks (July 2007)
....**$15-$20**
17 compact discs, 21 hours – Children's Version
Random House Audiobooks (July 2007)
....**$30-$35**

Harry Potter Special Edition
42 compact discs, each book in a clamshell
case..**$100-$125**

Listening Library
Harry Potter and the Sorcerer's Stone
  (CB004)

Harry Potter and the Chamber of Secrets
  (CB005)

Harry Potter and the Prisoner of Azkaban
  (CB006)

Harry Potter and the Goblet of Fire
  (CB007)

Autographed Pictures

Great care must be taken when investing in autographed photographs. Highly prized, these items are easily faked by anyone with calligraphic skills. Buy only from a reputable firm, preferably one with a membership in an organization such as Universal Autograph Collectors Club or International Autograph Collectors Club and Dealers Association, which have a policy of naming dealers who deal in forgeries. It is also wise to shop around and compare prices, for these can vary widely. A certificate of authenticity is preferable but does not guarantee authenticity as anyone with a printer can make one. Belonging to an autograph club will help you to recognize real signatures.

The cheapest way to obtain autographs is by writing to the stars themselves. This way you can build a collection just for the cost of postage. Tips to remember when writing: Keep your letters brief and legible; be polite; ask questions a fan would ask; show some knowledge of the actor's character; be specific about your reason for writing; send a self-addressed, stamped (or international reply coupon) envelope large enough to accommodate a typical size photograph; and be patient. Remember, not all photos you receive are actually signed by the actor; some are pre-printed. The Harry Potter actors can be reached by writing to them at:

Actor's name
c/o Harry Potter Production
Leavesden Studios
PO Box 3000, Leavesden
Hertfordshire WD2 7LT
United Kingdom

Autographed photos generally range in price from about $10 to $50, depending on the popularity of the character or actor. Photos in this section are from the collection of Megan Barrow.

Black and white photo signed by Bonnie Wright (Ginny Weasley).

Black and white photo signed by Devon Murray (Seamus Finnegan).

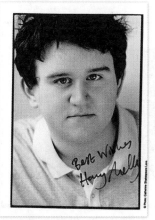

Black and white photo signed by Harry Melling (Dudley Dursley).

Black and white photo signed by Katie Leung (Cho Chang).

Black and white photo signed by Mark Williams as Arthur Weasley.

Black and white photo signed by Matthew Lewis (Neville Longbottom).

Color photo of Rob Pattinson (Cedric Diggory).

Black and white photo signed by Shirley Henderson as Moaning Myrtle.

Photos with printed autographs usually sell for between $2 and $5. Following are a few examples:

Harry Potter and the Goblet of Fire color photo of Ron and Padma Patil, signed by Afshan Azad.

Harry Potter and the Prisoner of Azkaban black and white photo of Hermione, Ron, and Harry exiting Hagrid's Hut, signed by Emma Watson, Daniel Radcliffe, and Rupert Grint.

Harry Potter and the Order of the Phoenix black and white photo signed by Evanna Lynch as Luna Lovegood.

Best Wishes

Daniel Radcliffe

Black and white photo signed by Daniel Radcliffe (Harry Potter).

Black and white photo signed by Emma Watson (Hermione Granger).

Black and white photo signed by Robbie Coltrane as Rubeus Hagrid.

Black and white photo signed by Ralph Fiennes (Lord Voldemort).

Black and white photo signed by Miranda Richardson (Rita Skeeter).

Black and white photo signed by Rupert Grint (Ron Weasley).

Banks

Accessory Network

Harry Potter Bank: Released in 2000, this 7" x 3-1/4" bank has Harry, Ron, and Hermione pictured on the front............................ **$5-$10**

Enesco

Gringotts Action Bank: Features Hagrid, Harry, and Griphook in a Gringotts cart. Inserting a coin and pulling a string releases the cart, which rolls down a track on a 7" high bank; batteries required. .... **$5-$10**

Gryffindor Entrance: Released in 2001, this 6" bank features a slot at the top and Harry and Ron with a laminated Fat Lady Portrait at the entrance to the Gryffindor Common Room.. **$5-$10**

Hasbro

Fluffy Security System and Bank: Manufactured in 2001 by Tiger Electronics, which was later taken over by Hasbro, the 7" x 9" bank features Fluffy with three activation modes. He moves and barks when a button is pushed, money is deposited, or the movement sensor is activated; after a short time a flute plays and Fluffy goes back to sleep. ... **$15-$20**

Schylling

Gringotts Wizarding Bank: Shaped like the bank.. **$5-$10**

Hedwig Mechanical Bank: Harry's pet owl winks at you when a coin is inserted and a message like "Sickles are silver" appears at the bottom.. **$5-$10**

Unknown

Vaults of Gringotts, The: This 2001 plastic bank is inscribed "The Vaults of Gringotts" on the front. Harry is standing on a gold-colored bank with the entrance to a vault behind him and stacks of galleons on either side. It is about 6-1/2" tall, and the coins go in the top. .... **$5-$10**

Photo from the collection of Jordan

Hallmark

Gringotts Bank: Released in 2001, this bank features a red-coated goblin at the door to Gringotts. A see-through window at the bottom has a scene of Harry, Hagrid, and Griphook and the place where the money falls. The ceramic bank is 14" tall....... **$10-$15**

Bookmarks
Antioch Publishing

(Antioch Publishing was bought out by Trends International in 2008.) Antioch Publishing bookmarks photos are from the collection of Megan Barrow.

Standard Bookmarks: Four-color printing on sturdy stock, foil accents, collectible metal charm, silky tassel.
.... $3-$4

Large bookmarks:
2-1/2" x 7-1/2"

Expecto Patronum Bookmark
(0-7824-9549-4)

Priori Incantatem Bookmark
(0-7824-9550-8)

Mirror of Erised Bookmark
(0-7824-9547-8)

Sirius Black Escapes on Buckbeak Bookmark
(0-7824-4375-3)

Small bookmarks: 1-1/2" x 6"

Ford Anglia Over Hogwarts Bookmark (1-4017-0033-0)

Harry Fighting Dragon Bookmark (1-4017-0035-7)

Quidditch Bookmark (1-4017-0032-2)

Film Cells Ltd.

The Film Cell Ltd. bookmarks contain an image and a frame of 35mm movie film. The piece comes laminated with a classic-style tassel. Cells vary from piece to piece because they are hand selected from reels of film. Photos of Film Cells Ltd. bookmarks are courtesy of Film Cells Ltd.

Harry Potter and the Chamber of Secrets (USBM529): 2009, Harry Potter. .... **$8-$12**

Harry Potter and the Goblet of Fire (USBM531): 2009, three scenes: Hermione and Viktor at Yule Ball; Ron and Harry in dress robes; Dumbledore unveiling Triwizard Cup... **$8-$12**

Harry Potter and the Half-Blood Prince (USBM527): 2008, Bellatrix Lestrange....**$8-$12**

Harry Potter and the Order of the Phoenix (USBM532): 2009, Harry Potter. .... **$8-$12**

Harry Potter and the Order of the Phoenix (USBM533): 2009, Voldemort................**$8-$12**

Harry Potter and the Prisoner of Azkaban (USBM535): 2009, Hermione and Harry helping Ron. .... **$8-$12**

Harry Potter and the Sorcerer's Stone (USBM528): 2009, Harry pushing his cart at Kings Cross... **$8-$12**

Harry Potter and the Half - Blood Prince (USBM525): 2008, Harry Potter. .... **$8-$10**

Harry Potter and the Half - Blood Prince (USBM526): 2008, Hermione Granger. .... **$8-$12**

Noble Collection

Broomstick Bookmark Collection, The (NN7498): Set of three die-cast miniature Nimbus 2000, Nimbus 2001, and Firebolt brooms that can be used as bookmarks. Each measure approximately 6-1/2". ....**$30-$35**

Hogwarts Bookmarks (NN7039): Set of four, plated in 24-karat gold and silver on plaque. ....**$20-$25**

Order of the Phoenix Bookmark Collection (NN7392): Seven finely detailed metal bookmarks with collector box. ....**$40-$45**

Scholastic

Set of six bookmarks (1-1/2" x 5-3/4") in plastic protective sleeves with 5" cord and plastic star attached. Released in 2000 with Fred Bode literary art. ....**$2-$3**

Photo courtesy Scholastic Inc.

Harry and Hermione going to Hogwarts in boat (0-439-25429-9)

Harry and Ron under invisibility cloak (0-439-25428-0)

Harry and the Mirror of Erised (0-439-25427-2)

Harry, Hagrid, and goblin in Gringotts cart (0-439-25425-6)

Harry, Ron, and Hermione confronting Fluffy (0-439-25430-2)

Snape looking over Harry's shoulder (0-439-25426-4)

Trends International

Standard Bookmarks: Four-color on sturdy card stock (1-1/2" x 5-3/4") with foil accents, collectible metal charm, silky tassel. Released in 2009. ....**$4-$5**

Dumbledore Hogwarts (F04520)
Half-Blood Prince (01064)
Harry Potter Patronus (F04506)

Photo from the collection of Austin Hall-Silvester

House Crests (F04544)
Order of the Phoenix (F04551)
Voldemort (F04537)

Die-Cut Bookmarks: (8-3/4" x 2-3/4"), four-color on sturdy oversized card stock and embellished. ....**$4-$5**

Albus Dumbledore (F21374)
Harry Potter (F21381)
Harry Potter and Friends (F21398)
House Banners (F21367)

Fold-Out Bookmarks: (8-3/4" x 2-3/4") with fold-out poster. ....**$6-$7**

Dumbledore Army (F21350)
Harry Potter and the Half-Blood Prince (Bm60002)

Beaded Bookmarks: Four-color on sturdy card stock with beads, charms, or coins and silky tassel. ....**$7-$8**

Harry Potter and the Half-Blood Prince, Bad Group Collectors (Bm50008)
Harry Potter and the Half-Blood Prince, Dumbledore Collectors (Bm50006)
Harry Potter and the Half-Blood Prince, Good Group Collectors (Bm50007)
Harry Potter and the Half-Blood Prince, Harry Collectors (Bm50005)

Card Games

Klutz

Building Cards Hogwarts School of Witchcraft and Wizardry: Extra set of cards for building a bigger Hogwarts. .... **$13-$15**

Harry Potter Hogwarts Building Cards (55 KLU 400X): Includes 275 cards with slot to slot construction, illustrations, directions, and a custom Harry Potter figure. ...... **$17-$20**

Mattel

Gnome Toss Card Game (43179): Released in 2001, contains 112 cards and instructions for this "frenetic game of fast, flinging fun!" .... **$4-$6**

Harry Potter and the Sorcerer's Stone Quidditch Card Game (42753): Released in 2001, one of two Quidditch card games (see below) featuring Gryffindor vs. Slytherin. .... **$7-$9**

Harry Potter MagiCreatures Card Game (C3170): Released in 2004, contains 52 creature and point cards. .... **$15-$20**

The United States Playing Card Company

Magical Cards Deck, The: Released in 2001, illustrated by Warner Bros. artist Fred Bode with the Hogwarts crest on the back. The storage box could be used for a disappearing card trick. .... **$5-$8**

Standard Card Deck: Released in 2001, illustrated with movie scenes with Harry Potter title on the back. Comes in a metal book-shaped tin with Harry, Ron, and Hermione on the cover. .... **$6-$9**

UNO – Harry Potter Edition: Released in 2001, the classic International Games, Inc. game got a Harry Potter makeover with Fred Bode illustrations and some rule variations. .... **$15-$20**

Photo from the collection of Megan Barrow

UNO – Harry Potter Edition (42797): Released in 2002, the classic International Games, Inc. game was reissued with Sorcerer's Stone illustrations. .... **$10-$15**

UNO – Harry Potter Special Edition (42751): Released in 2001, the classic International Games, Inc. game got a Harry Potter makeover with Fred Bode illustrations and some rule variations. Comes in trunk-shaped box with faux wood finish, gold detailing, and a felt-covered plastic insert to hold the cards. .... **$45-$50**

Clothing and Accessories

Backpacks
Warner Bros.

Prices are for never used, original packaging and based on the original price as these are not a popular collectible; the used price is dependent on condition. Applicable to most items listed below.

Gadgets Backpack (GM367): Black with school crest and lightning bolt on front pocket. ....**$15-$20**

Gryffindor Backpack (HM169): Gray with house crest and seeker logo. ....**$15-$20**

Harry Potter Denim Backpack...........**$15-$18**

Hedwig Plush Backpack....................**$15-$18**

Hogwarts Backpack...........................**$10-$15**

Hogwarts Denim Padded Backpack ... **$20-$25**

Hogwarts Pink Canvas Fabric Backpack
....**$10-$15**

Hogwarts Toddler Denim Red Backpack
.... **$10-$15**

Quidditch Sports Bag (HM223): Black with red and yellow Quidditch logo on side. ...... **$20-$24**

Quilted Backpack: Pink with Harry Potter logo and icons.....................................**$10-$12**

Slytherin Backpack: Large size. ....**$20-$25**

Ball Caps
Warner Bros.

Gryffindor Cap: HP logo on front. ...... **$10-$15**

Hogwarts Crest Cap (GM437): Navy, adult size...**$14-$16**

Lightning Bolt Cap (GM438): Black, adult size...**$14-$16**

Quidditch Cap (HM202): Navy, adult size. ....**$14-$16**

Quidditch Cap (KA004): Black, child size. .... **$10-$14**

Coin Purses and Wallets
Accessory Network Group, Inc.

Coin purses..**$5-$10**
  Bertie Bott's Beans
  Eyeglasses case
  Hedwig
  Sorting Hat

Harry Potter and the Sorcerer's Stone with icons and Sorcerer's Stone logo. ....**$5-$7**

WBShop.com

Half-Blood Prince Wallet: Built-in coin purse, white with silver snap on top, school crest in gold, embroidered houses crests........ **$12-$14**

Hogwarts Folding Wallet: Attached coin purse, black with silver Hogwarts crest .... **$12-$14**

Footwear
Shoes.com

These three styles of sneakers or running shoes bear logos as designed for the Warner Bros. film. ....**$15-$20**

Gryffindor: Hogwarts shield on the tongue and the HP Snitch logo on the soles.

Hogwarts: HP Snitch logo on the tongue and lightning bolt logo on the soles.

Quidditch: Crossed-broom logo on the sides and the HP Snitch logo on the soles.

Hoodies, Jerseys, and Sweatshirts
Hot Topic

Photo from the collection of Megan Barrow

Gryffindor Crest: Black zippered hoodie with red and yellow striped lining..............**$48-$50**

Photo from the collection of Megan Barrow

Hogwarts Crest: Silver on black zippered hoodie.. **$48-$50**

Warner Bros.

Gryffindor House: Black Gryffindor and lion with yellow and burgundy stripes on sleeve and hem..**$38-$40**

Harry Potter: Star background, black fleece pullover, adult size. ....**$38-$40**

Hogwarts: School name and "H" crest, charcoal fleece, boys' size..................**$26-$28**

WBShop.com

Dumbledore's Army: Hoodie, adult size.
....**$30-$35**

Hogwarts: Denim jacket, kids' size. ...**$45-$50**

I Solemnly Swear...: Hoodie, junior size.
....**$35-$40**

S.P.E.W.: Zippered hoodie, adult size.
....**$40-$45**

Messenger Bags
WBShop.com

Bludgers Messenger Bag: Crossed beater's bats on black and gray stripes, zippered pocket inside, adjustable straps.........**$35-$40**

Dumbledore's Army Elite Messenger Bag: Felt Dumbledore's Army logo, zippered pocket inside, adjustable straps. ....**$25-$27**

Gryffindor Messenger Bag: Nylon with red and gold stripes with Hogwarts crest on flap, elasticized inner pocket with yellow drawstrings and red shoulder strap. ....**$35-$40**

Harry Potter and the Half-Blood Prince Messenger Bag: Black canvas with large Gryffindor crest and smaller embroidered house crests..**$30-$35**

Scarves and Ties
Noble Collection

Gryffindor House Scarf (NN7632): 100% lamb's wool, scarf measures 12" x 85", comes with collector's box..............................**$65-$70**

Gryffindor House Tie (NN7634): 100% silk, comes with collector's box..................**$35-$40**

Socks
High Point Knitting, Inc.

Gryffindor: Small lion crest and house color stripes..**$3-$4**

Harry Potter: Women's size, with Fred Bode art of Harry waving his wand. ....**$5-$6**

Harry Potter: Harry waving his wand, single picture. ....**$5-$6**

Harry Potter: Boy's size, glow-in-the-dark with HP logo and Harry's lightning bolt name..**$6-$7**

Hedwig: Women's size, purple and pink. ....**$5-$6**

Hedwig: Children's size, blue and purple. ....**$5-$6**

Nimbus 2000: Boys' size, dark gray, tan, or white, with Harry's face and broom logo. ....**$6-$7**

Owl Post: Girls' anklet socks, owl on shield with letter. ....**$4-$5**

Quidditch: Children's and women's size, lenticular socks with logo that appears to move when tilted. ....**$4-$5**

Sunglasses
Pan Oceanic Eyewear, Inc.

These sunglasses were offered in 2001 and designed for children. The lenses had holographic designs and coating for protection from ultraviolet rays. Most came with Harry Potter stickers.....................................**$10-$13**

Golden Snitch: Snitch on lenses and Harry chasing Snitch on temples.

Gryffindor: Lion head on lenses and house crest on temples.

Lightning Bolt: Harry on broom on temples.

Round Style 1: Lightning bolt on lenses and title on temples.

Round Style 2: Title on temples and faux tape on nose bridge.

Stars Style 1: Yellow stars on lenses and lenticular hourglass on temples.

Stars Style 2: Purple stars on lenses and Harry on broom and logo on temples.

Suitcases
Accessory Network Group, Inc.

The suitcases were about 10" x 18" and had extending handles and wheels.........**$10-$15**

Harry carrying Hedwig and suitcase
Hogwarts Crest
Room of Keys, Style 1
Room of Keys, Style 2

Totes
WBShop.com

Gryffindor Tote: Burgundy and black with house crest...**$18-$20**

Hogwarts Tote: Tan canvas with school crest...**$18-$20**

Slytherin Tote: Black and green with house crest...**$18-$20**

T-Shirts

T-shirts are one of the easier items to produce unauthorized; check for the copyrights and HP logos. There are a wide variety of styles and sizes available, and this is only a small sampling. Prices are for new clothing; used clothing should reflect thrift store prices. Prices often vary according to size.

Photo from the collection of Megan Barrow

Hot Topic

Draco Malfoy: In the Room of Requirement on black, logo on back..............................**$20-$22**

Dumbledore: Headmaster from Half-Blood Prince, name in gold on right side......**$20-$22**

Photo from the collection of Megan Barrow

Photo from the collection of Megan Barrow

Dumbledore's Army: Red images on black of Army members.....................................**$18-$20**

Harry Potter and the Half-Blood Prince: Cast of film on black. ....**$18-$20**

Harry Potter and the Half-Blood Prince: Cast of film on black, size 2XL. ....**$19-$21**

Harry Potter and the Half-Blood Prince: Close-up of Harry with Dumbledore's reflection in his glasses......................**$18-$20**

Photo from the collection of Megan Barrow

Photo from the collection of Megan Barrow

Gryffindor: House crest on front, name on back, red with gold trim......................**$18-$20**

Gryffindor Crest: Gold outline around crest on black. ....**$20-$22**

Gryffindor Sword: Gryffindor crest with sword and yellow rays emitting from center. ....**$19-$20**

Harry and Ron: Watching their backs, Half-Blood Prince logo.................................**$20-$22**

Harry Potter and the Goblet of Fire: Harry, Ron, and Hermione on black shirt.......**$18-$20**

Hermione: Black shirt with picture of Hermione Granger................................**$18-$20**

Hogwarts: School crest on black with V-neck. ....**$20-$22**

Luna Lovegood: Black shirt with Luna wearing 3D spectacles. ....**$20-$22**

Photo from the collection of Megan Barrow

My Hero: Black shirt with picture of Neville Longbottom. ....**$18-$20**

Muggle: Word Muggle, white on red. **$20-$22**

Ron Weasley: Photo of Ron and name written on right. ....**$20-$22**

Photo from the collection of Megan Barrow

Slytherin: House crest in front, name on back, green with silver trim. ....**$18-$20**

Photo from the collection of Megan Barrow

Slytherin: House crest on green. ....**$18-$20**

Warner Bros.

Various companies manufactured numerous t-shirts for Warner Bros. stores and other retail outlets. Most do not have the manufacturer's name on them, simply Harry Potter markings. These shirts came in a variety of colors and were designed for both genders and sizes. Most listed below were available through the Warner Bros. stores from 2000.

Fluffy: Black shirt with snarling Fluffy. .... **$12-$14**

Gryffindor House: Black or gray shirt with house crest in color. ....**$16-$18**

Harry Potter: Black shirt with gold name logo. ....**$12-$15**

Harry Potter: Black shirt with white name logo. ....**$12-$15**

Harry Potter: Blue, pink, or plum long sleeve shirt with "Harry Potter" name surrounded by numerous glittering stars. ....**$14-$16**

Harry Potter: Pink shirt with Harry behind cauldron on pocket................................**$12-$14**

Harry Potter: White long sleeve shirt with name logo, crescent moon, lightning bolt, and wizard hat...**$14-$16**

Hogwarts Crest: Gray long sleeve shirt with school crest in black and gold.............**$24-$26**

Hogwarts Crest: Gray shirt with school crest in color. ....**$12-$15**

Hogwarts Crest: Navy shirt with school crest in color. .... **$16-$18**

Hufflepuff House: White shirt with house crest in color. .... **$12-$14**

Ravenclaw House: Gray shirt with house crest in color. .... **$12-$14**

Quidditch: Navy with "Quidditch" in red, and Snitch and crossed broomsticks in gold outline. .... **$16-$18**

Quidditch: White long sleeve shirt with "Quidditch" and lightning bolts in gold. .... **$16-$18**

Slytherin House: Gray or black shirt with house crest in color. .... **$12-$14**

Sorting Hat: Turquoise shirt with sorting hat and swirls. .... **$12-$14**

Voldemort: Black shirt with "Voldemort" and eyes... **$16-$18**

Wizard: Pink shirt with wizard's accessories: owl, hat, hourglass, book, etc. .... **$12-$14**

Photo from the collection of Megan Barrow

Hogwarts School Crest: Jeweled short sleeve jersey by Bejeweled, limited edition, hand embellished with Swarovski crystals and studs. ....**$80-$90**

WBShop.com

Chudley Cannons: Adult size............. **$16-$18**

Dumbledore's Army: Charcoal, junior size. ....**$17-$19**

Dumbledore's Army: Exclusive, women's fitted. .... **$13-$15**

Dumbledore's Army: Sketch art, reversible. .... **$15-$17**

Dumbledore's Army Faces: Kid's size. .... **$14-$16**

Forbidden Forest: Adult size.............**$17-$19**

Harry Potter Retro Crest: Adult size. **$16-$19**

I Solemnly Swear that I am up to no good; Mischief Managed on back; women's fitted size... **$16-$19**

I Solemnly Swear that I am up to no good:; Mischief Managed on back; adult size. ....**$17-$19**

Proclamation Educational Decree No. 30: Adult size. .... **$16-$19**

Voldemort: Adult size. ....**$17-$19**

Umbrellas
Totes Isotoner Co.

Totes Isotoner Co., of Cincinnati, marketed a few Harry Potter umbrellas in 2001 and 2002. They folded up to an easily portable size.

Hagrid: 2002, with literary artwork of Hagrid on Sirius Black's motorcycle and Hagrid handle..**$8-$10**

Harry Potter: 2002, with literary artwork of Harry in Potions class with Harry handle. .... **$8-$10**

Hedwig: Literary artwork of Harry's owl and Hedwig handle. .... **$8-$10**

Journey to Hogwarts: 2001, in adult and youth sizes with Fred Bode artwork.. **$10-$12**

Quidditch: 2001, with Golden Snitch and the HP lightning bolt logo..........................**$10-$12**

Backpack umbrellas with different style carrying cases were small enough to be attached to a backpack or zipper........ **$12-$14**
Norbert
Hogwarts Crest
Lightning Bolt

Coins

Noble Collection

Gringotts Coin Collection (NN7234): This set of Gringotts bank coins are beautifully re-created and set in a collector's coin sleeve. Each galleon, sickle, and knut is individually struck in rich detail and plated in 24 karat gold, silver, or copper. .... **$20-$30**

Royal Canadian Mint

The first issue of Harry Potter ReelCoinz was released in 2001 by the Royal Canadian Mint. The blister pack contained five collectible silver-colored medallions in a 5-1/2" x 5" heavy cardboard folder with a sticker booklet and a sheet of reusable stickers. The artwork was based on the book, *Harry Potter and the Philosopher's Stone,* not the movie. The second issue was released in 2002 and was based on the book *Harry Potter and the Chamber of Secrets.*

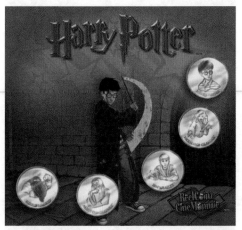

ReelCoinz: Harry Potter, five character medallions, *Philosopher's Stone*, 2001. The designs on the coins were Harry Potter, Hermione Granger, Ron Weasley, Albus Dumbledore, and Rubeus Hagrid. .... **$5-$15**

ReelCoinz: Harry Potter, five crest medallions, 2001. The designs on the coins were Slytherin crest, Ravenclaw crest, Hufflepuff crest, Gryffindor crest, and Hogwarts crest. .... **$5-$15**

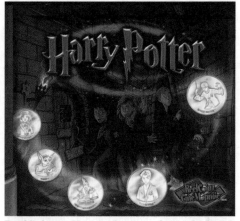

ReelCoinz: Harry Potter, five character medallions, *Chamber of Secrets*, 2002. The designs on the coins were Harry Potter, Ginny Weasley, Dobby, Professor Lockhart, and Tom Riddle. .... **$5-$15**

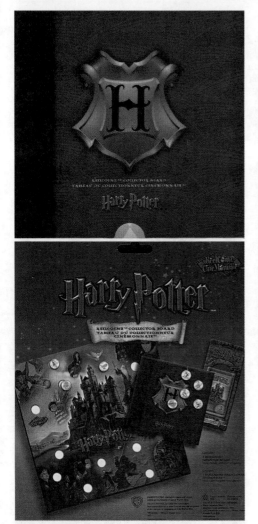

Warner Bros.

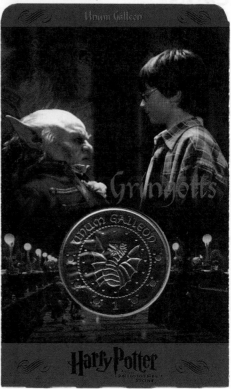

Gringotts Galleon: Released in 2002 as a promotion for the release of *Harry Potter and the Philosopher's Stone* on VHS and DVD. These are apparently exact replicas of the galleon coins issued by Gringotts Bank and used in the film. The coins are approximately 1-1/2" in diameter and come sealed in a cardboard frame with scenes from the movie on the front and the Gringotts Bank seal on the back...**$6-$10**

Harry Potter Official ReelCoinz Collector Board was also issued in 2001. This 7-1/2" x 8" heavy cardboard folded out to a 15" x 16" display board with slots for 12 Harry Potter ReelCoinz Mystery Medallions. These coins were sold separately in packages of three, different from the coins available in the regular ReelCoinz series. The Collector Board sold for $12.95, and the three medallion packs sold for $7.95 each. The 12 coins included: Potions, Bertie Bott's Beans, Diagon Alley Sign, Unicorn, Severus Snape, Professor Quirrell, Centaur, Hedwig, Seeker Harry, Draco Malfoy, Harry Potter, and Chess Knight.

Board	**$5-$10**
Coins, 3-pack	**$5-$7.50**
Board with 12 coins	**$10-$15**
Individual coins	**$1-$3**

Harry Potter Elongated Coin: Pressed from a 1¢ coin at Six Flags Magic Mountain theme park in Valencia, California, inscribed with *Harry Potter's Magic Coin* and Harry's head. ....**$0.50-$1**

Compact Discs

Compact discs were recorded at Air Lyndhurst and Abbey Road Studios, London, England, with music composed by John Williams. *Harry Potter and the Sorcerer's Stone* was nominated for a 2003 Grammy Award for "best score soundtrack album for a motion picture, television, or other visual media." "Hedwig's Theme" was nominated for a 2003 Grammy Award for "best instrumental composition." *Harry Potter and the Chamber of Secrets* was also nominated for "best score soundtrack" at the 2006 Grammy Awards. *Sorcerer's Stone* and *Prisoner of Azkaban* received Academy Award nominations in 2001 and 2004, respectively, for "original score." Following is a representative list. Prices range from used to mint wrapped. Photos of compact discs are from the collection of Megan Barrow.

Label: Atlantic/Wea

Harry Potter and the Chamber of Secrets: By John Williams and William Ross (2002), soundtrack. ....**$2.50-$7.50**

Harry Potter and the Chamber of Secrets: Original Soundtrack (2008), soundtrack. ....**$2.50-$7.50**

Harry Potter and the Philosopher's Stone: Original Motion Picture Soundtrack plus Bonus CD by John Williams (2006), enhanced. ....**$8-$10**

Harry Potter and the Chamber of Secrets: Original Soundtrack (2008), soundtrack. ....**$2.50-$7.50**

Harry Potter and the Philosopher's Stone: Original Motion Picture Soundtrack plus Bonus CD by John Williams (2006), enhanced. ....**$8-$10**

Harry Potter Soundtrack Bundle: Amazon Exclusive (2009), box set of soundtracks from the first five films. ....**$40-$50**

Hedwig's Theme from Harry Potter and the Philosopher's Stone: By John Williams (2002), soundtrack. ....**$2.50-$7.50**

Hedwig's Theme from the Harry Potter Movie: (2003), single. ....**$1.50-$3**

Music from Harry Potter and the Chamber of Secrets: By Hollywood Star Orchestra and John Williams (2006). ....**$5-$10**

Music from Harry Potter and the Sorcerer's Stone: By John Williams (2002), soundtrack. ....**$2.50-$7.50**

Label: Warner Bros. Pictures

Harry Potter and the Sorcerer's Stone: Original Motion Picture Soundtrack by John Williams (2002)..............................**$2.50-$7.50**

Harry Potter and the Goblet of Fire: By Patrick Doyle (2005), soundtrack........**$5-$7.50**

Harry Potter and the Goblet of Fire: By Patrick Doyle (2005), extra tracks......**$5-$7.50**

Harry Potter and the Half-Blood Prince: By Nicholas Hooper (2009), soundtrack. ....**$14-$16**

Harry Potter and the Order of the Phoenix: By Nicholas Hooper (2007), soundtrack. ....**$5-$7.50**

Harry Potter and the Prisoner of Azkaban: By John Williams (2004), enhanced... **$2.50-$7.50**

Music from Harry Potter: The Goblet of Fire: By Patrick Doyle (2005), soundtrack. ....**$5-$7.50**

Music from the Harry Potter Films: By Patrick Doyle, John Williams, James Fitzpatrick, Nic Raine, and City of Prague Philharmonic Orchestra (2006), soundtrack.............**$5-$7.50**

Crafts
Activity Kits
Delta Education

Honored by the Oppenheim Toy Portfolio and Parenting for High Potential Magazine, these Spells and Potions Activity Kits were first released in 2001 in conjunction with Harry Potter and the Sorcerer's Stone. Originally available only through the Troll Book Club, a second series was released with Chamber of Secrets, making a total of 16 kits. The kits come with just about everything required to perform the experiments, including a binder for keeping notes, collectible cards, and instructions. (Some require additional common household ingredients.) Great as teaching aids and just plain fun, the kits were reissued in 2004.

Spells and Potions Series I.....................**$2-$4**
- 501: Chemistry 1
- 502: Chemistry 2
- 503: Flight
- 504: Alchemy
- 506: Tracking
- 507: Optics
- 508: Astronomy
- 509: Physics

Photo from the collection of Megan Barrow

Spells and Potions Series II....................**$3-$5**
- 701: Unpredictable Potions
- 702: Fascinating Fossils
- 703: Spiders and Snakes
- 704: Sounds of Hogwarts
- 705: Mystery Motions
- 706: Secret Sightings
- 708: Herbology and Other Plant Sciences
- 709: Invisible Inks and Secret Codes

Spells and Potions 2004 Series

Cast a Golden Snitch Ball (WH-110-6386)... **$11-$13**
Cast Lightning Bolt and Shield Amulets (WH-110-6560)...**$11-$13**
Cast Sorcerer's Stone Amulets (WH-110-6375)...**$11-$13**
Eeylops Owl Emporium (WH-110-6364)...**$8-$10**
Hogwarts Nature Study.........................**$8-$10**
Hogwarts Optics..................................**$8-$10**
Hogwarts Secret Sightings....................**$6-$8**
Invisibility Crystals Potion (WH-181-0135)...**$3-$5**
Physics Demonstration Science Activities Kit (WH-110-6342)....................................**$12-$15**
Potion of Drought (WH-181-0124)..........**$3-$5**
Secret Sounds of Hogwarts..................**$8-$10**
Slithering Slime Potion (WH-181-0102)..**$3-$5**
Spiders and Snakes.............................**$8-$10**
Teleidoscope Construction (WH-110-6353)**$12-$15**
Troll Boogers Potion (WH-181-0113)......**$3-$5**
Unpredictable Potions...........................**$8-$10**

Elmer's Products, Inc.

Disappearing Glue Sticks: In package of three clear glue sticks illustrated with Harry, Hermione, and Professor Snape..............**$2-$3**

Every Scent Markers: Comes in eight colors and scents "ranging from the delightful to the despicable."..**$3-$4**

House of Hogwarts Glitter Quills: Four plastic tubes of glitter illustrated with the four Hogwarts house crests....................**$3-$4**

Magical Art Glaze: This clear coat liquid comes in a miniature cauldron and makes your craft project "shimmer and shine." ....**$3-$4**

Photo from the collection of Megan Barrow

Troll Booger Glue: 4 oz. "picked fresh from the troll's nose"; comes from a troll's head dispenser...**$2-$3**

Trends International

Harry Potter Doodle (10278): Contains 12" x 12" line art and eight felt-tipped markers. ....**$4-$5**
Harry Potter Flitter Velvet Doodle (13673): Contains 11" x 15" velvet line art, 11" x 15" line art, and eight felt-tipped markers. ....**$4-$5**

Cutouts

Harry Potter
Life-size Cardboard Standup Cutout: Harry standing sideways, pointing wand, 26" x 66". ....**$30-$35**
Hermione Granger
Life-size Cardboard Standup Cutout: Hermione standing sideways, pointing wand, 15" x 66"...**$30-$35**
Professor Dumbledore
Life-size Cardboard Standup Cutout: Dumbledore standing sideways with hands at sides, 25" x 73"................................**$30-$35**
Professor Snape
Life-size Cardboard Standup Cutout: Snape standing facing front with hands on hips, 37"x 74"...**$30-$35**
Ron Weasley
Life-size Cardboard Standup Cutout: Ron facing front with arms crossed, 23" x 69". ....**$30-$35**

Film Cells
Film Cells Ltd.

Film Cells is located in Illinois and started business in 2003. The company's products contain actual pieces of hand-selected 35mm film mounted in custom black frames and issued in limited editions. They are released in a variety of formats. Photos of film cells are courtesy of Film Cells Ltd.

3 Cell Standard
11" x 13" framed, limited edition 2,500 ....**$75-$80**
Harry Potter and the Sorcerer's Stone (S1), USFC5063
Harry Potter and the Chamber of Secrets (S1), USFC5066
Harry Potter and the Prisoner of Azkaban (S1), USFC5069
Harry Potter and the Goblet of Fire (S1), USFC5073
Harry Potter and the Goblet of Fire (S2), USFC5074
Harry Potter and the Order of the Phoenix (S1), USFC5077
Harry Potter and the Order of the Phoenix (S2), USFC5145
Harry Potter and the Order of the Phoenix (S3), USFC5172

Double

11" x 13" framed, limited edition 2,500
....**$70-$75**
Harry Potter and the Sorcerer's Stone (S3), USFC5131

Harry Potter and the Chamber of Secrets (S4), USFC5134

Harry Potter and the Prisoner of Azkaban (S4), USFC5136

Harry Potter and the Prisoner of Azkaban (S3), USFC5070

Harry Potter and the Goblet of Fire (S5), USFC5139

Harry Potter and the Order of the Phoenix (S3), USFC5078

Harry Potter and the Order of the Phoenix (S4), USFC5140

Harry Potter and the Order of the Phoenix (S5), USFC5146

Harry Potter and the Half-Blood Prince (S1), USFC5106

Harry Potter and the Half-Blood Prince (S2), USFC5107

Harry Potter and the Half-Blood Prince (S4), USFC5244

Mini Montage

11" x 13" framed, limited edition 2,500
Harry Potter and the Sorcerer's Stone (S3), USFC5132...**$90-$95**
Harry Potter and the Prisoner of Azkaban (S4), USFC5137 ....**$90-$95**
Harry Potter and the Order of the Phoenix (S3), USFC5142 ....**$90-$95**
Harry Potter and the Order of the Phoenix (S2), USFC2870 ....**$55-$60**
Harry Potter and the Order of the Phoenix (S2), USFC2870 ....**$55-$60**
Harry Potter and the Half-Blood Prince (S1), USFC5174...**$90-$95**
Harry Potter and the Half-Blood Prince (S2), USFC5253 ....**$90-$95**

Minicell

5" x 7" framed, special edition.............**$30-$35**
Harry Potter and the Sorcerer's Stone (S2), USFC5064

Harry Potter and the Sorcerer's Stone (S3), USFC5065

Harry Potter and the Chamber of Secrets (S3), USFC5067

Harry Potter and the Chamber of Secrets (S4), USFC5068

Harry Potter and the Prisoner of Azkaban (S3), USFC5071

Harry Potter and the Prisoner of Azkaban (S4), USFC5072

Harry Potter and the Goblet of Fire (S3), USFC5075

Harry Potter and the Goblet of Fire (S4), USFC5076

Harry Potter and the Order of the Phoenix (S3), USFC5079

Harry Potter and the Order of the Phoenix (S4), USFC5080

Harry Potter and the Sorcerer's Stone (S4), USFC5130

Harry Potter and the Chamber of Secrets (S5), USFC5133

Harry Potter and the Prisoner of Azkaban (S5), USFC5135

Harry Potter and the Order of the Phoenix (S5), USFC5141

Harry Potter and the Order of the Phoenix (S6), USFC5147

Harry Potter and the Prisoner of Azkaban (S6), USFC5152

Harry Potter and the Half-Blood Prince (S1), USFC5153

Harry Potter and the Half-Blood Prince (S2), USFC5154

Harry Potter and the Half-Blood Prince (S3), USFC5155

Harry Potter and the Half-Blood Prince (S4), USFC5156

Deluxe
20-1/4" x 11" framed, limited edition 2,500
....**$150-$160**
Harry Potter 1-6 (S1), USFC5108
Harry Potter 1-6 (S2), USFC5168
Harry Potter and the Half-Blood Prince (S1), USFC5188

Mixed Montage
20" x 19" framed, limited edition 2,500
....**$190-$200**
Harry Potter and the Half-Blood Prince (S1), USFC5164

Harry Potter and the Half-Blood Prince (S1), USFC5173

Food and Drink
CAP Candy/Hasbro

The earliest Harry Potter food products appeared in Warner Bros. Studio Stores in December 2001 and featured a Muggle version of Bertie Bott's Every Flavor Beans. The manufacturing of the first beans was a cooperative effort as Warner Bros. licensed the beans to CAP Candy, Inc., a division of Hasbro, Inc.

CAP went to Herman Goelitz, Inc. (creator of Jelly Belly gourmet jelly beans), and Goelitz made the beans in most of the flavors described in the books. It is not advisable to consume food products that have been kept as collectibles for any length of time. Food collectibles should be checked periodically for deterioration.

Photos are from the collection of Megan Barrow, unless otherwise noted.

Basilisk Candy Shaker (11475): Basilisk's eyes light up when candy dispenses; green sour powder included; 12 in display box. .... **$2-$3**

Exploding Bon Bons: Assorted fruit flavors, 4.25 oz. .... **$1-$2**

Gringotts Coins Bubble Gum (11407): Wizard coin bubble gum stamped like the coins in the films, in collectible blue pouch, 24-pack gravity feed display box. .... **$2-$3**

Harry Potter Acid Pop (11810): Package of three sour lollipops with a sweet flavor inside. .... **$1-$2**

Harry Potter Bertie Bott's Every Flavor Beans Candy (11601): 20 "Magical" flavors, including the new flavors, sausage and pickle; 3.5 oz. plastic bag of beans comes in a purple velvet-like drawstring bag with "Bertie Bott's Every Flavor Beans" screen printed in gold. A hangtag describes the different flavors and shows pictures of each bean. .... **$4-$5**

Various flavors chart.

Harry Potter Bertie Bott's Every Flavor Beans: 10 individual flavors in a box, two more flavors, 1.6 oz............................. **$2-$2.50**

Harry Potter Bertie Bott's Every Flavor Beans: 10 individual flavors in a box, four more flavors, 1.75 oz............................ **$2-$2.50**

Harry Potter Blood Pops: Five strawberry-flavored lollipops in a package. .... **$1-$1.50**

Harry Potter Chocolate Frog (11408): Comes with one of 24 Harry Potter lenticular wizard cards, chocolate frog filled with crisped rice, first released in 2002; being faithful to the book, these Chocolate Frogs don't move, .55 oz. ..**$3-$4**

Set of 24 includes:
1. - Adalbert Waffling
2. - Beaumont Marjoribanks
3. - Bertie Bott
4. - Bowman Wright
5. - Cliodne
6. - Cornelius Agrippa
7. - Daisy Dodderidge
8. - Derwent Shimpling
9. - Devlin Whitehorn
10. - Donaghan Tremlett
11. - Gifford Ollerton
12. - Gunhilda of Gorsemoor
13. - Gwenog Jones
14. - Helga Hufflepuff
15. - Hengist of Woodcroft
16. - Ignatia Wildsmith
17. - Lord Stoddard Withers
18. - Merlin
19. - Morgan Le Fay
20. - Newt Scamander
21. - Quong Po
22. - Rowena Ravenclaw
23. - Sacharissa Tugwood
24. - Uric the Oddball

Harry Potter Chocolate Frog, Series 2: A second series of lenticular cards was released in 2004 with only 12 cards, but with more familiar witches and wizards, .55 oz. .....**$3-$4**

Set of 12 includes:
1. - Albus Dumbledore
2. - Madam Rolanda Hooch
3. - Minerva McGonagall
4. - Pomona Sprout
5. - Severus Snape
6. - Rubeus Hagrid
7. - Madam Pince
8. - Mr. Ollivander
9. - Gilderoy Lockhart
10. - Voldemort
11. - Filius Flitwick
12. - Quirinus Quirrell

Chase Card - The Potter Family: Red back instead of purple; was inserted randomly in packs.

Harry Potter Cockroach Clusters Candy (2274): 2" juicy candy underneath with crunchy shell. ....**$2-$3**

Harry Potter Drooble's Best Blowing Gum (11830): .53 oz. gumballs turn your mouth blue; come in a collectible pouch in display box of 16. ....**$0.50-$1 each**

Harry Potter Fudge Flies: Approximately 70 milk chocolate flies with fudge filling in each five oz. box. ....**$3-$4**

Harry Potter Ice Mice (11791): Four ice melted candies, .85 oz. ....**$3-$4**

Harry Potter Jelly Slugs: 2.25 oz., average 12 to 15 slugs per pack. ....**$2-$3**

Harry Potter Spin Pops (11608): A rotating strawberry-flavored sucker coming out of Harry's head, arms can be posed; includes two different Harrys, Professor Snape, Ron, and Hermione; 12 in display box...........**$5-$6**

Harry's Wizard Wand Candy (11412): Light-up wand contains lightning bolt-shaped candies; 12 in display box.......................**$5-$6**

Mandrake Lollipop Dipper (11476): Comes with vanilla pop and grape candy for dipping; 12 in display box. ....**$1-$2**

Coca-Cola Company

In 2001 the Coca-Cola Company paid Warner Bros. $150 million for global rights to put images from *Harry Potter and the Sorcerer's Stone* on bottles, cans, and displays for Coke, Hi-C, and Minute Maid products. The bottler used only icons such as owls and castles. No character images were permitted.

Despite the fact that Coca-Cola donated part of the profits to the charitable organization RIF (Reading is Fundamental), the company managed to draw the ire of activists from the Center for Science in the Public Interest. They contended that the Coke campaign encouraged obesity and health problems in children by promoting the sale of "liquid candy." As a result, J.K. Rowling received over 16,000 letters from the Save Harry Campaign that followed. The campaign officially began on Oct. 15, 2001, with TV commercials using John Williams' *Hedwig's Theme* from the film but no character images. Specially marked packages provided chances to win a trip to a United Kingdom castle ("Hogwarts Castle Adventure").

Harry Potter and the Chamber of Secrets 8 oz. bottle...$5-$7

Harry Potter and the Sorcerer's Stone 8 oz. bottle..$6-$8

Harry Potter and the Sorcerer's Stone: Coke promotional banner, 6' x 34", shows Santa and "Win a School Library" promotion. ....$17-$20

Coca-Cola Contest Cards

Set of six cards, four of which are imprinted "Keep Searching" and one each with "Castle Adventure" and "Harry Potter Video Game" in a center box. The last two are very rare because they would have been turned in to claim the prize (value unknown). Found in Coca-Cola 12 packs. The cards can be linked together "in magical ways" to "build a wall, castle and more!" Contest ended Dec. 31, 2001; there were 10 winners in all.

Gryffindor – Golden Snitch;
Slytherin – Assorted Potions;
Ravenclaw – Flying Key;
Hufflepuff – Quidditch box;
set of four ....$1-$2

Coca-Cola Contest Cards

Mattel

Cast-A-Spell Candy Maker Harry Potter (B0722): Released in 2004, edible spells made by shooting colored spell mix out of the wand and into a spinning vortex container; also includes three creature vials, a measuring spoon, two packets of powdered mix, and spell indicator. ....$25-$30

Harry Potter Iced Pumpkin Drink Maker (57608): Released in 2003, comes with ice shaver machine, mixing cup, measuring spoon, one packet of Pumpkin Spice and one of Wizard Sprinkles Powdered Mix.......$5-$10

Harry Potter Polyjuice Potion Maker Edible Activity Set (55692): Released in 2002, makes drinkable potions. ....$15-$20

Harry Potter Professor Snape's Potions Class Edible Activity Set (29449): Released in 2001, "Motorized Lab! Wand magically stirs potions by itself! Brew 15+ droolicious drinks and 100+ treats in the bubbling cauldron!"; comes with mixing tools and food mixes.......$25-$30

Harry Potter Snake Bites Edible Activity Set (55456): Released in 2002, creates gummy creatures and includes Snake Bites and Spider Web Spinner..$15-$20

Professor Sprout's Fungus Field Trip: Edible activity set like the Potions Class set, it has mushrooms, bugs, and slugs to dig up and eat with chocolate dirt and pond slime to drink; comes with shovel, food mixes, and watering can. ....$25-$30

Wilton Baking Products

Wilton Industries, Inc. is the United States' largest manufacturer and distributor of cake decorating and baking supplies. It released a number of licensed Harry Potter items in the last half of 2001.

Cake Supplies

For instructions on how to bake a Harry Potter Cake, visit:
www.wilton.com/downloads/
paninstructions/2105-5000HarryPotter.pdf.

Harry Potter Baking Cups (415-5000): Standard size, microwave-safe paper in package of 50..**$2-$3**

Harry Potter Cake Pan (2105-5000): One-mix aluminum pan measures 11-1/2" x 9-1/2" x 2", includes a color picture and decorating guide.......................................**$10-$15**

Harry Potter Candle Set (2811-5002): set of four, 2"; hand-painted for Ravenclaw, Hufflepuff, Slytherin, and Gryffindor.....**$4-$5**

Harry Potter Cauldron Candle (2811-5000): 3-1/2" hand-painted, clean-burning. ......**$4-$5**

Harry Potter Edible Cake Decoration Set (711-5000): Magical icing decoration shapes and happy birthday message.................**$3-$4**

Photo courtesy Bonds Corner

Harry Potter Edible Cake Topper, Harry with book and cauldron, 3".

Harry Potter Edible Cake Toppers
Harry in Gryffindor robe and with Snitch..**$8-$10**
Harry Potter Quidditch cake top decoration.**$5-$6**
Harry with book and cauldron, 3"..........**$5-$6**
Hogwarts crest cake topper....................**$5-$6**
Professor Snape's Potions cake toppers. **$8-$10**

Harry Potter Icing Color Kit (601-5000): 4-1/2 oz. jars called Enchanted Sky Purple, Darkening Black, Lightning Bolt Gold, and Cauldron Copper; set of four...................**$5-$6**

Harry Potter Icon Icing Decorations: Package of 12, features four Harry glasses and five lightning bolts in mint flavored shapes.
....**$2-$3**

Harry Potter Petite Icing Decorations (710-5001): Four each assorted colorful sugar shapes includes sorting hats, lightning bolts, moons, and Nimbus 2000 brooms. .... **$6-$8**

Harry Potter Sprinkle Decorations (710-5002): Four-cell container for pouring and storing; contains 7 oz. each lightning bolts, sorting hats, Nimbus 2000, and moons. ....**$6-$7**

Harry Potter Standard Icing Decorations (710-5000): Mint-flavored edible shapes in a package of nine. ....**$3-$4**

Cupcakes, Cookies, and Suckers

Harry Potter Baking Cups: Standard baking cups with icon print as above, sold separately, 50 in package.....................................**$1.50-$2**

Harry Potter Cupcake Kit (2104-9913): Includes 50 standard baking cups with icon print, nine standard and 12 small icing decorations, and 1 oz. sprinkle decorations in sorting hat, lightning bolt, and moon shapes.
....**$8-$10**

Harry Potter Icon Toppers: Can double as bookmarks when the treat is gone. Four each of Nimbus 2000, Bertie Bott's Beans, Harry's glasses, and books in set of 12. ....**$1.50-$2**

Harry Potter Large Plastic Cookie Cutters: Includes 4" cutter shapes of glasses, sorting hat, lightning bolt, and Nimbus 2000.
....**$2-$3 each**

Harry Potter Lollipop Kit (2115-5002): Mold in four designs (chocolate frog, Fluffy, Norbert, and Hedwig), 10 oz. of Candy Melts Light Cocoa, three disposable decorating bags, a brush, 10 bags with ties, and 10 sticks.
....**$8-$10**

Harry Potter Miniature Plastic Cookie Cutters: Set of four 2-1/4" miniature copper cookie cutters of flying key, Snitch, star, and potion bottle. ....**$8-$9**

Plastic Cupcake Toppers: Four Hogwarts house crests in set of 12. ....**$1.50-$2**

Greeting Cards

Hallmark

Hallmark is the largest manufacturer of greeting cards in the United States and has been in business since 1910. The company has produced a number of Harry Potter cards as well as its famous Keepsake Collection ornaments. The prices are for used to mint condition and range from $3-$4. Cards that have been written in are worth less. Following is a sampling of what are available with the wording as description. Photos of greeting cards are from the collection of Megan Barrow, unless otherwise noted.

The time has come to celebrate YOU – which can only mean one thing...
Magical Possibilities! Happy Birthday

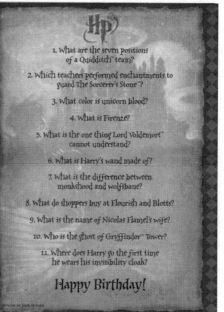

At Hogwarts, you'd surely be one of the best – You're smart, so let's see how you do on this test!

1. What are the seven positions of a Quidditch team?
2. Which teachers performed enchantments to guard the Sorcerer's Stone?
3. What color is unicorn blood?
4. What is Firenze?
5. What is the one thing Lord Voldemort cannot understand?
6. What is Harry's wand made of?
7. What is the difference between monkshood and wolfsbane?
8. What do shoppers buy at Flourish & Blotts?
9. What is the name of Nicholas Flamel's wife?
10. Who is the ghost of Gryffindor Tower?
11. Where does Harry go the first time he wears his invisibility cloak?
Happy Birthday!

The first task of your birthday…
…is to find as much fun and adventure as is wizardly possible!

Until his birthday came along, Harry never knew there was magic there inside him…
Like the magic that's in YOU! Hope Your Birthday's the Best One Ever!

Nephew…
Hope your birthday in filled with never-ending excitement!

You know who is sending you this birthday card...
No, not he-who-must-not-be-named – me!

Every birthday begins a yearlong journey of surprises!
Hope you'll find all kinds of wizardly fun!
(Hallmark [s07] – "Hedwig's Theme" plays when the card is opened)

Birthday Magic Is So Powerful...

...Even the Strongest Spell Couldn't Keep These Wishes From Finding You!

Have a Magical Day and a Year Filled With Adventures!

(Hallmark [s07] – with detachable bookmark)

You may be destined for greatness...

But on your birthday, you're destined for fun

Valentines
Paper Magic Group

Paper Magic Group, Inc., of Scranton, Pennsylvania, made these sets of Harry Potter movie Valentines for the U.S. market.

Harry Potter and the Order of the Phoenix: 34 Valentines with stickers. .... **$3-$4**

Harry Potter Valentines: 30 cards with shiny foil-effect scenes from Sorcerer's Stone (2002). .... **$3-$4**

Harry Potter Valentines: 32 fold-and-seal Valentine cards with seals. .... **$3-$4**

Harry Potter and the Goblet of Fire: 32 Valentines and tattoos, poster inside. ...**$3-$4**

Jewelry
Noble Collection
Bracelets

Harry Potter Icon Charm Bracelet (NN7034): Sterling silver and 24K gold plating, charms (stars, wand, broom, sorting hat, school crest, Quidditch Cup, key, owl, and Harry Potter logo) on bracelet. .... **$140-$150**

Quidditch Golden Snitch Bracelet (NN7254): Sterling silver and selective 24K gold plating. ....**$75-$80**

Brooch

Flying Hedwig Brooch (NN7014): Sterling silver and 24 karat gold-plated details; wingspan measures 1-3/8". ....**$50-$55**

Earrings

Hermione's Yule Ball Earrings (NN7689): Sterling silver set with pink crystals. **$55-$60**

Hogwarts House Earrings – Gryffindor (NN7106): Sterling silver and selective 24K gold plating. ....**$60-$65**

Hogwarts House Earrings – Hufflepuff (NN7108): Sterling silver and selective 24K gold plating. ....**$60-$65**

Hogwarts House Earrings – Ravenclaw (NN7107): Sterling silver. ....**$60-$65**

Hogwarts House Earrings – Slytherin (NN7105): Sterling silver. ....**$60-$65**

Lightning Bolt Earrings (NN7142): Sterling silver, measures three-quarters inch in length. ....**$50-$55**

Lightning Bolt Earrings (NN7622): 14 karat gold, measures three-quarters inch in length. ....**$90-$95**

Necklaces

Luna Lovegood Jewelry Set (NN7819): Includes necklace, ring, and earrings. ....**$45-$50**

Quidditch Golden Snitch Necklace (NN7276): Sterling silver and selective 24K gold plating; comes with an 18" sterling silver chain. ....**$75-$80**

Ron Weasley's Sweetheart Necklace (NN8112): Heart and arrow, crafted in sterling silver, plated in 24K gold, comes with chain. ....**$65-$70**

Pendants

Dark Mark Pendant, The (NN7715): Sterling silver with 18" sterling silver chain....**$55-$60**

Death Eater Mask Pendant – Bellatrix (NN7588): Sterling silver....................**$50-$55**

Death Eater Mask Pendant – Lucius Malfoy (NN7589): Sterling silver....................**$50-$55**

Dumbledore's Army Pendant (NN7592): Solid sterling silver with 18" leather chain. **$40-$45**

Dumbledore's Army Scroll Pendant (NN7749): Sterling silver, plated in 24K gold with chain...**$60-$65**

Golden Egg Pendant (NN7533): Gold-plated pendant with petals that bloom open, comes with chain and wood display box. .....**$45-$50**

Gringotts Bank Pendant (NN7591): Sterling silver with 18" sterling silver chain; copper-plated Gringotts Bank Knut...............**$60-$65**

Hogwarts House Pin/Pendant – Gryffindor (NN7244): Sterling silver and selective 24K gold plating..**$70-$75**

Hogwarts House Pin/Pendant – Hufflepuff (NN7241): Sterling silver and selective 24K gold plating..**$70-$75**

Hogwarts House Pin/Pendant – Ravenclaw (NN7242): Sterling silver.....................**$70-$75**

Hogwarts House Pin/Pendant – Slytherin (NN7243): Sterling silver.....................**$70-$75**

Lightning Bolt Pendant (NN7189): Sterling silver, 1-3/4", comes with 18" sterling silver chain..**$45-$50**

Lightning Bolt Pendant (NN7601): 14 karat gold and set with three diamonds. Measures 1-1/4", comes with 18" sterling silver chain... **$140-$145**

Phoenix Pendant (NN7265): Sterling silver, comes with 18" chain...........................**$70-$75**

Sorcerer's Stone Pendant (NN7570): Cut glass pendant, comes with gold-plated chain. ....**$50-$55**

Time Turner Pendant (NN7763): Sterling silver, gold plated, with a working miniature hourglass and rotating inner rings, 1-3/8" in diameter, comes with display.........**$120-$125**

Photo from the collection of Megan Barrow

Time Turner Pendant (NN7017): Working miniature hourglass with rotating inner rings, plated in 24 karat gold, 1-3/8" with 18" chain; comes with display case...................**$50-$60**

Quill

Hogwarts Writing Quill (NN7595): With collector box. ....$30-$35

Rings

Gryffindor Ring (NN7794): Sterling silver gold plated with Gryffindor house symbols with enamel and crystals. .... $90-$100

Hogwarts House Ring – Gryffindor (NN7101): Sterling silver and selective 24K gold plating. ....$90-$95

Hogwarts House Ring –Hufflepuff (NN7104): Sterling silver and selective 24K gold plating. .... $90-$95

Hogwarts House Ring – Ravenclaw (NN7103): Sterling silver. .... $90-$95

Hogwarts House Ring – Slytherin (NN7102): Sterling silver. .... $90-$95

Quidditch Golden Snitch Ring (NN7266): Sterling silver and selective 24K gold plating. .... $65-$70

Slytherin House Ring (NN7745): Sterling silver with Slytherin house symbols with enamel and crystals. .... $95-$100

Slytherin House Ring (NN7757): 10K white gold ring features the Slytherin house symbols with enamel and diamonds. ....$285-$295

Watches

Watches are another of those gray area collectibles that are easily manufactured without license. Dozens of cheap watches have been produced and sold on auction sites, and, while popular, are unauthorized. The watches listed here are confirmed as licensed. There are no doubt many more, but these should give a respectable cross section of what is available and the prices one might expect to pay. There may be some overlap as Fossil and SII made watches for Warner Bros. stores.

Fossil

Dumbledore's Pocket Watch (HC0302): Replicates the headmaster's watch with planets in place of the numbers and 12 hands instead of two, as described by J.K. Rowling in *Philosopher's Stone*. Comes in a mahogany finish case bearing a brass Hogwarts crest. ....$95-$105

House Crest Watches: One for each house (Gryffindor, Hufflepuff, Ravenclaw, and Slytherin) with the Warner Bros. version of the house crest. Leather strap edged in the house color. Comes in a plastic sorting hat case; limited edition of 1,000 for each house. ....$100-$110

Mirror of Erised Watch, The: Red sun ray dial with Sorcerer's Stone at 12 o'clock, Harry Potter name logo in gold. Watch face appears when the light is turned on.................$80-$90

Mood Watch and Tin Set (WB17630122): 2000, made for WB Store, Fred Bode art, Harry Potter, comes with mood ring in silver box. ....$55-$65

Quidditch Watch (LI-2074): Limited edition of 2,000, Fossil Limited Edition Quidditch inscribed on back with limited edition number and model number. Both a pocket watch and a tabletop watch, includes a pull-out metallic ring stand so the watch can be set up on display. Comes in a tin box designed like a foot locker featuring the house mascots. .... $90-$100

SII Marketing International, Inc.

Based in Austin, Texas, SII is a joint venture between Seiko and Fossil. Seiko's Hong Kong division made the watches and SII sold them worldwide. They are "SII" brand, not Lorus or Fossil, coming in a distinctive metal tin like Fossil products.

Golden Snitch Watch: Clip-on watch shaped like a Golden Snitch. ....$15-$20

Golden Snitch Watch, The: Harry disappears and reappears through a rotating disk. ....$20-$25

Gryffindor and Slytherin Light Show Watch: Gryffindor lion and Slytherin snake in stars and night sky. ....$25-$30

Harry and Crest Watch: Literary art of Harry holding his wand with the Hogwarts crest; brass or silver with black or brown strap. ....$15-$20

Harry Potter and the Goblet of Fire Collectors Pocket Watch (HC0220): Antique bronze case with closing lid featuring Hogwarts crest; comes in red suede drawstring pouch and Harry Potter watch box. ....**$180-$200**

Harry Potter and the Prisoner of Azkaban Timescape Watch (HP0085): Includes "spell meter," "muggle meter," and "flyback meter" with faux black leather strap; comes in collectible watch tin. ....**$65-$75**

Harry Potter Goblet of Fire Flip Top Watch (HC0216 SII): Comes in red metal Goblet of Fire tin and outer box. ....**$120-$125**

Harry Potter Goblet of Fire Jeweled Crystal Watch: Comes in *Goblet of Fire* collectible watch tin. ....**$100-$125**

Harry Potter Golden Snitch Logo Watch: Logo on face in silver or antiqued brass finish..**$15-$20**

Harry Potter Logo Watch: Harry Potter name logo with moon and star in two shades of purple. ....**$20-$25**

Harry Potter Magical Car Watch: Harry and Ron flying Ford Anglia with Velcro strap........**$14-$16**

Harry Potter Watch: Hogwarts crest and drawing of Harry in brass or silver with black or brown strap. ....**$25-$30**

Harry Potter Watch and Pin Set (HP0047): Released in 2000, limited edition of 1,000, literary Harry with H crest at 6 o'clock; box includes a small bronzed Hogwarts crest pin with silvertone backing, considered the rarest of Harry Potter watches. ....**$1,000-$1,500**

Hogwarts Crest Watch: Hardened blue plastic case around colorful school crest with fabric strap..**$20-$25**

Hogwarts Express Watch (HC0301): Limited edition, released 2004 in conjunction with Harry Potter and the Prisoner of Azkaban; rectangular watch tin featuring the scene from the dial. ....**$45-$50**

Hogwarts House Crests Watch: 2001, Hogwarts shield flip top reveals all house crests, with black or brown strap.......**$15-$20**

Magic Potions Watch: Potions and bottles on face. ....**$25-$30**

Metamorphosis Watch: Harry pursues the Snitch and dodges a bludger...............**$25-$30**

Potions Watch: Bottles move around the watch face on the second hand. ....**$25-$30**

Prisoner of Azkaban Gold Icon Watch: Released in 2004, Harry chasing Snitch, gold icon crest on leather strap.................**$80-$100**

Quidditch Crossed Broomsticks Logo Watch: Comes with black or brown strap. .....**$20-$25**

Quidditch Watch (HC000): 2001, made for WB Store, Snitch and word "Quidditch" on black face, 3D effect, comes in literary art collectible box. ....**$20-$25**

Snitch Light Show Watch: Literary drawing of Harry about to grab a Snitch that seems to move; leather strap stamped with Snitches. ....**$20-$25**

Time Turner Pocket Watch: Limited edition of 1,000, time turner case front opens to reveal Harry and Hermione riding Buckbeak; antiqued bronze silver case and chain; comes with red velvet pouch and swivel top wooden case..**$450-$500**

Triwizard Tournament: Silver face and square case watch with three schools' crests and names; comes in Goblet of Fire box. ..**$35-$40**

Violet Potion Bottle Analog Watch (HP0006): Jewel and potion bottle accents, squared watchcase with violet leather and nylon strap...**$30-$40**

Winking Hedwig Watch (HC007): Hedwig with one eye closed on face with white faux fur strap; comes in metal box. ....**$60-$80**

Warner Bros.

Bertie Bott's Beans (HP0017PS): Bag of Bertie Bott's Beans in center of face. .... **$12-$15**

Disappearing Harry Watch (HP0014): Made by Fossil for WB, Snitch circles the face while Harry lights up. ....**$22-$35**

Fawkes (HP0053): Orange phoenix on black face with Velcro strap..........................**$15-$17**

Harry Potter Blue Digital Quidditch Watch (HP0002): Literary art with Harry about to grab Snitch...**$12-$15**

Harry Potter Blue Quidditch Analog Watch (HP0062): Harry on broom on blue face with darker blue case and plastic strap. ....**$15-$17**

Leather Strap Watch and Tin Set: 2000, Fred Bode art, Harry chasing Snitch on blue face, comes in silver box.............................**$10-$15**

Light Up Watch and Tin Set (GM452): 2000, Harry Potter name on black face, comes in silver box..**$10-$15**

Velvet Strap Watch and Tin Set (GM453): 2000, Harry Potter and stars on blue face, comes in silver box.............................**$10-$15**

You-Know-Who Watch (HP0013): Sinister eyes and "You-Know-Who" on dark face with Velcro strap, imprinted Voldemort and Slytherin logo.......................................**$15-$20**

Key Chains

Key chains or key rings can be classified as toys, as functional items, or as collectibles in their own right. Easily manufactured, there are many unauthorized key chains on the market.

Cedco Publishing Co.

Bertie Bott's Beans Photo Album: 2000, 3" x 3-1/2", literary art, mini book key chain has pages for 24 photos. ....**$3-$5**

Famous Witches and Wizards Photo Album: 2000, 3" x 3-1/2", literary art, mini book key chain holds 24 pictures. ....**$3-$5**

Gryffindor Web Sites: 2000, 3" x 3-1/2", literary art, Gryffindor Shield (website directory), mini book key chain has pages for URL, user ID, password clue.....................................**$3-$5**

Norbert's Fantastic Friends: 2000, 3" x 3-1/2", literary art, mini book keychain has pages for information on you and friends, names, nicknames, birthdays, favorite shows, etc. **$3-$5**

Room of Keys Autograph Book: 2000, 3" x 3-1/2", literary art, mini book key chain has pages for autographs, dates, and notes...**$3-$5**

Hallmark

Golden Snitch (2727): Released 2000....**$4-$5**

Silver Harry Potter Logo (2726): Released 2000 ....**$4-$5**

Hasbro

Motion Key Chains: Basically a flashlight on a chain, six different. ....**$4-$5 ea.**
- 1 - Broomstick
- 2 - Fluffy
- 3 - Hagrid on motorcycle
- 4 - Messaging owl
- 5 - Scabbers
- 6 - Wand

LEGO

These key chains are exact copies of the figures that appeared in the LEGO sets except they do not come apart. The arms and legs move but there is a metal spine to prevent them from coming apart.
- 1 – 851030: Harry Potter, 2004 ....**$12-$15**
- 2 – 851031: Hermione, 2004 ....**$12-$15**
- 3 – 851032: Hagrid, 2004 ....**$10-$13**
- 4 – 851033: Dumbledore, 2004............**$10-$13**
- 5 – 851034: Professor Snape, 2004 .....**$10-$13**
- 6 – 851730: Professor Dumbledore, 2006..**$8-$10**
- 7 – 851731: Harry Potter Tournament, 2006 ....**$8-$10**
- 8 – 852000: Hermione, 2007 ....**$5-$8**
- 9 – 852091: Harry Potter without cape, 2007 ....**$5-$8**

NECA, Inc.

Half-Blood Prince Bulbadox Juice Key Chain (NC59521): 2009, potion bottle..............**$7-$8**

Half-Blood Prince Elixir Potion Key Chain (NC59520): 2009, potion bottle..............**$7-$8**

Half-Blood Prince Potion Nr. 113 (NC59522): 2009, potion bottle. ....**$7-$8**

Harry Potter Golden Snitch Plush Key Chain: Gold polyester ball with silver wings, 3" x 5" x 10". ....**$7-$9**

Photo from the collection of Megan Barrow

Harry Potter Gryffindor Crest Metal Key Chain (NC59528): 2009, Harry Potter name logo and Gryffindor house crest in silver with dangling beads...**$7-$8**

Harry Potter Hogwarts Crest Metal Key Chain (NC59528): 2009, Harry Potter name logo and Hogwarts crest in silver with dangling beads.. $7-$8

Harry Potter Quidditch Accessory Key Chain (NC59531): 2009, crossed bats, quaffle and Snitch dangling from a ring. .... $7-$8

Harry Potter Slytherin Crest Metal Key Chain (NC59530): 2009, Harry Potter name logo and Slytherin house crest in silver with dangling beads.. $7-$8

Mad-Eye Moody Key Chain (NC59514): 2009, Mad-Eye's magic eye on faux leather strap. .... $7-$8

Noble Collection

Hogwarts House Crest Key Chain (NN7117): Intricately detailed with the animals of the four Hogwarts houses; plated in 24 karat gold and enameled. .... $20-$25

Warner Bros.

Draco Malfoy: Lucite (clear, hard plastic) with headshot of Draco, images on both sides. .... $5-$6

Fantastic Creatures: From Goblet of Fire, Lucite (clear, hard plastic) with images on both sides.. $4-$6

Golden Snitch: Flexible rubber composite. $5-$6

Golden Snitch Key Ring (GM465):......... $4-$5

Gryffindor Crest: Small 1" x 1" enameled crest of key ring. .... $7-$8

Harry Potter and the Prisoner of Azkaban: Movie logo, Lucite (clear, hard plastic). . $5-$6

Harry Potter Logo (HP60331): Harry Potter name logo; metal logo is 3" x 1". .... $4-$7

Harry Potter Logo with Snitch (HP60205): Silver and black metal key chain, 1-1/2". .... $4-$7

Hermione (HPK0005): Miss Granger on one side and Gryffindor crest on the other. Crystal-clear Lucite key chains with chrome ring, 2" x 1-3/8"..................................... $1.50-$2

Hufflepuff Crest: Lucite (clear, hard plastic) with Hufflepuff crest. .... $5-$6

Quidditch: Lucite (clear, hard plastic) with Harry chasing Snitch on one side and Prisoner of Azkaban logo on the other. .... $5-$6

Quidditch 07: Lucite (clear, hard plastic) with silver and green Harry on broomstick on one side and Prisoner of Azkaban logo on the other... $5-$6

Ravenclaw Crest: Lucite (clear, hard plastic) with Ravenclaw crest. .... $5-$6

Sorting Hat Key Chain: Flip it over and the hat will sort you using a small block inside fluid. .... $10-$12

Unknown

Dark Mark: Lucite (clear, hard plastic) with Dark Mark image on both sides.............. $5-$6

Golden Snitch Key Chain Bagclip: 2-1/2" in diameter (wingspan 4-1/2" wide), metallic gold material with iridescent wings.... $8-$10

Gryffindor: House crest, metal enamel, 2" x 2-1/2" with key ring................................. $5-$7

Hogwarts: School crest with motto "Draco Dormiens Nunquam Titillandus," metal enamel, 2-1/2" x 3" with key ring............ $5-$7

Slytherin: House crest, metal enamel, 1" x 1" with key ring.. $5-$7

LEGO

Warner Bros. Consumer Products announced an alliance with LEGO on July 11, 2000, for worldwide marketing of construction toys based on Harry Potter. It was a four-year agreement, and the first figures were to be released at the same time as *Harry Potter and the Philosopher's/Sorcerer's Stone* in theaters.

The lists below indicate the set number, name, number of pieces, and character figures included. Prices range from "used without box" to "factory sealed."

Harry Potter and the Philosopher's/Sorcerer's Stone

Fourteen sets were released for the first film; of these, 11 were produced in 2001 and the last three in 2002.

4701 Sorting Hat: 48 pieces, Harry Potter. ....**$5-$15**

4704 The Chamber of Winged Keys: 175 pieces, Harry Potter, Ron Weasley, White Queen chess piece. ....**$20-$50**

4705 Snape's Classroom: 163 pieces, Professor Snape, Ron Weasley, Peeves. ....**$14-$40**

4706 Forbidden Corridor: 238 pieces, Harry Potter, Ron Weasley, Hermione Granger. ....**$20-$60**

4707 Hagrid's Hut: 299 pieces, Rubeus Hagrid, Headmaster Albus Dumbledore. ....**$40-$130**

4708 Hogwarts Express: 410 pieces, Harry Potter, Ron Weasley, Hermione Granger. ....**$70-$200**

4702 The Final Challenge: 60 pieces, Professor Quirrell, Harry Potter............**$5-$15**

4709 Hogwarts Castle: 682 pieces, Harry Potter, Ron Weasley, Hermione Granger, Professor Snape, Rubeus Hagrid, Professor Dumbledore, Draco Malfoy, Peeves, Gryffindor Knight...**$100-$300**

4711 Flying Lesson: 23 pieces, Harry Potter, Draco Malfoy...**$5-$10**

4712 Troll on the Loose: 71 pieces, mountain troll, Harry Potter.....................................**$5-$20**

4714 Gringotts Bank: 250 pieces, Griphook, goblin, Rubeus Hagrid, Harry Potter. **$15-$50**

4721 Hogwarts Classrooms: 73 pieces, Harry Potter...**$5-$15**

4722 Gryffindor House: 68 pieces, Ron Weasley...**$5-$15**

4723 Diagon Alley Shops: 80 pieces, Hermione Granger. ....**$5-$15**

Harry Potter and the Chamber of Secrets
Ten sets were released for the movie in 2003.

4719 Quality Quidditch Supplies: 120 pieces, Draco Malfoy...**$8-$24**

4720 Knockturn Alley: 209 pieces, Harry Potter, Lucius Malfoy. ....**$10-$20**

4726 Quidditch Practice: 128 pieces, Harry Potter, Draco Malfoy, Madam Hooch. **$10 -$30**

4727 Aragog in the Dark Forest: 178 pieces, Ron Weasley, Harry Potter. ....**$8-$24**

4728 Escape from Privet Drive: 278 pieces, Ron Weasley, Harry Potter, Vernon Dursley. ....**$25-$80**

4729 Dumbledore's Office: 446 pieces, Headmaster Dumbledore, Professor McGonagall, Harry Potter. ....**$20-$60**

4730 The Chamber of Secrets: 591 pieces, Harry Potter, Tom Riddle, Ginny Weasley, Professor Lockhart, Ron Weasley. ....**$50-$150**

4731 Dobby's Release: 70 pieces, Lucius Malfoy, Dobby...**$5-$15**

4733 The Dueling Club: 129 pieces, Harry Potter, Draco Malfoy, Professor Snape, Professor Lockhart.................................**$8-$24**

4735 Slytherin: 90 pieces, Draco Malfoy, Vincent Crabbe, Gregory Goyle............**$8-$24**

Harry Potter and the Prisoner of Azkaban
Twelve sets were released for the third film, including the first and only Harry Potter Mini Set. The figures now had flesh tones instead of yellow, a change LEGO instituted at this time for all figures based on characters or real people.

4695 Mini Knight Bus: 54 pieces (promo, in bag not box). ....**$4-$6**

4750 Draco's Encounter with Buckbeak: 36 pieces, Draco Malfoy.............................**$5-$10**

4751 Harry and the Marauder's Map: 106 pieces, Harry Potter, Professor Snape. ....**$5-$15**

4752 Professor Lupin's Classroom: 155 pieces, Professor Snape (Boggart), Professor Lupin, Neville Longbottom. ....**$10-$35**

4753 Sirius Black's Escape: 189 pieces, Harry Potter, Dementor, Sirius Black. .... **$10-$30**

4754 Hagrid's Hut: 302 pieces, Hermione Granger, Rubeus Hagrid. .... **$35-$100**

4755 Knight Bus: 242 pieces, Harry Potter, Stan Shunpike .... **$15-$45**

4756 Shrieking Shack: 444 pieces, Peter Pettigrew, Harry Potter, Sirius Black, Professor Lupin .... **$25-$80**

4757 Hogwarts Castle: 928 pieces, Dementors (two), Harry Potter, Hermione Granger, Ron Weasley, Headmaster Dumbledore, Professor Trelawney, Draco Malfoy .... **$80-$250**

4758 Encounter on the Train: 386 pieces, Harry Potter, Ron Weasley, Professor Lupin, Dementor .... **$20-$80**

10132 Motorized Hogwarts Express: 706 pieces, Harry Potter, Ron Weasley, Professor Lupin, Dementor .... **$60-$200**

Harry Potter and the Goblet of Fire

Only four sets were released for the next film, missing many key scenes and characters.

4762 Rescue from the Merpeople: 175 pieces, Harry Potter, Ron Weasley, Hermione Granger, merperson, Viktor Krum with shark head. .... **$15-$40**

4766 Graveyard Duel: 548 pieces, Harry Potter, Lord Voldemort, Lucius Malfoy, Peter Pettigrew, three skeletons. .... **$25-$80**

4767 Harry and the Hungarian Horntail: 265 pieces, Harry Potter, Headmaster Dumbledore, Alastor "Mad-Eye" Moody. .... **$20-$50**

4768 The Durmstrang Ship: 550 pieces, Igor Karkaroff, Viktor Krum. .... **$25-$80**

Harry Potter and the Order of the Phoenix

Only one set was released for the fifth film.

5378 Hogwarts Castle: 943 pieces (including the greenhouse, a room filled with awards and ribbons, and Professor Umbridge's office), Harry Potter, Ron Weasley, Hermione Granger, Headmaster Dumbledore, Professor Snape, Rubeus Hagrid, Draco Malfoy, Death Eater, Dolores Umbridge, and two Thestrals. .... **$90-$260**

With the impending release of a Harry Potter LEGO video game, rumor has it that LEGO will revive the Harry Potter line in the near future as they expect an upsurge in product interest.

Awards Won by Harry Potter LEGO

Harry Potter Hogwarts Castle
2004
Seal of Approval, The National Parenting Center
Gold Award Winner, Oppenheim Toy Portfolio

2004
Parents Choice Approved Award, Parents Choice
Toy of the Year Award Winner, Family Fun

2007
Gold: Best Toy Award, Oppenheims

Harry Potter: Durmstrang Ship
2005
Toy Wishes All Star, Toy Wishes

Harry Potter Motorized Hogwarts Express
2004
Three-star rating, Canadian Toy Testing Council
Best Bet Award, Canadian Toy Testing Council
National Parenting Center's Seal of Approval, The National Parenting Center

Harry Potter Shrieking Shack
2004
Three-star rating, Canadian Toy Testing Council

Harry Potter Chamber of Secrets
2003
Red, Approved, Parent's Choice

Harry Potter Dumbledore's Office
2002
Award Winner, Oppenheim Toy Portfolio

2003
Red, Approved, Parent's Choice

Linens

Despite extensive searching, little information has come to light about prices for early Harry Potter linens. Attempts to contact the manufacturers have largely been ignored.

Most prices given are suggested retail prices (SRP) at the time of release. Present value is dependent upon original packaging and condition. Used linens should sell at thrift store prices.

Goodwin Weavers
Throws and Pillows

Thick, woven cotton throws are blankets with full-color illustrations by Warner Bros. artist Fred Bode. Matching pillows have the same images.

Harry, Hagrid, and Griphook ride the Gringotts cart

Harry chasing the Golden Snitch

Harry mixes a potion under Snape's watching eyes

Hogwarts first years riding in boats to the castle

Quidditch blanket in Gryffindor colors featuring crossed broomsticks, Golden Snitch. SRP.......... **$45-$50** (throws) and **$25** (pillows)

NECA, Inc.
Throw Pillows

Harry Potter Dumbledore's Army A throw pillow ....**$20-$25**

Harry Potter Dumbledore's Army B throw pillow ....**$20-$25**

Harry Potter Hedwig 14" x 14" throw pillow ....**$20-$25**

Blankets

Dumbledore's Army features Harry, Ron, and Hermione with the list of Dumbledore's Army members and Hogwarts Crest: 60" x 80", acrylic and polyester.....................**$25-$30**

Northwest Company
Blankets

Harry Potter: Head and shoulders from *Goblet of Fire*, polyester, 50" x 60". ....**$20-$25**

Comforter

Gryffindor: House crest on red and black background, polyester, twin size. ......**$20-$25**

Springs Industries
Bedroom Ensemble

An entire coordinated sleep ensemble based on *The Sorcerer's Stone* movie. Quilting is done with a special lightning bolt stitch.

Comforter: Harry chasing a Snitch on a maroon and blue diamonds background. .... **SRP $70** (twin) and **$85** (full)

Curtains: Golden stars and streaked twilight sky; draperies and valance. ....**SRP $35-$45**

Dust Ruffle: Same pattern as rest of ensemble. .... **SRP $35** (twin) and **$40** (full)

Pillow Sham: View of Hogwarts........**SRP $25**

Toss Pillows: Winking Hedwig and baby Norbert. .... **SRP $20 each**

Twin Bed Sheets: Harry chasing a Snitch in same pattern as curtains; Harry and Hermione on the pillowcases............. **SRP $40**

Harry Potter Fawkes 14" x 14" throw pillow ....$20-$25

Harry Potter Forbidden Forest throw pillow ....$20-$25

Harry Potter Marauder's Map 17" x 14" throw pillow ....$20-$25

Sheets

Hedwig: Twin sheet set......................**SRP $30**

"In Flight": Twin sheets set. ....**SRP $30**

Sorting Hat: Twin flannel set with Harry getting sorted and Hogwarts house crests; comes in vinyl storage case. ....**SRP $30**

Fabric

Raw cloth for sewing and craft stores. .... **SRP $5-$7 per yard**

Blue Quidditch players and house crests

Harry gets the Snitch

Hedwig and HP logo

Hogwarts house crests with blue diamond pattern

Hogwarts fabric panel to make into a pillow, wall hanging, or quilt, 34" x 45"

HP logo, glittery silver sparkles on navy blue

Terrisol

Beach Towels

Terrisol originally produced seven beach towel designs for sale in the Warner Bros. stores in October 2000, and later in department stores and other retailers. The 30" x 60" towels feature literary art and include the scenes below as well as Hagrid and Professor Snape.

Flying Keys: Harry, Ron, and Hermione pursue flying keys. ....**$12-$15**

Fluffy on Guard: Harry, Ron, and Hermione confront Fluffy. ....**$12-$15**

Quidditch: Harry pursues the Golden Snitch. ....**$12-$15**

Warner Bros.

Twin Bed Set

Harry Potter J'adore Gryffindor: Set includes comforter, pillow case, and flat and fitted sheets with Gryffindor crest on red and black. ....**$80-$90**

Lunch Boxes

Photo from the collection of Jordan

Hallmark

Lunchbox with literary artwork by Fred Bode. Front shows Harry capturing the Snitch and back features "Journey to Hogwarts" artwork. Released in 2000. ....**$10-$15**

NECA, Inc.

Harry Potter and the Sorcerer's Stone Lunchbox: Metal with matching drink bottle, same picture on both sides, 9" x 7" x 4". ....**$15-$20**

Harry Potter and the Chamber of Secrets Lunchbox: Metal with matching drink bottle, same picture on both sides, 9" x 7" x 4". ....**$15-$20**

Harry Potter and the Goblet of Fire Lunchbox: Metal with matching drink bottle, same picture on both sides, 9" x 7" x 4". ....**$15-$20**

Harry Potter and the Prisoner of Azkaban Lunchbox: Metal with matching drink bottle, same picture on both sides, 9" x 7" x 4". ....**$15-$20**

Harry Potter and the Order of the Phoenix (60544): Metal with matching drink bottle, same picture on both sides, 9" x 7" x 4". ....**$15-$20**

Thermos

Lunchbox featuring Harry chasing the Golden Snitch. Soft vinyl sided, 10" x 8" with 10 oz. bottle. Released in 2001. ....**$5-$10**

Magazines With Harry Potter Covers

Since J.K. Rowling's books became international best-sellers and the Warner Bros. films became blockbusters, magazines of every kind have featured a Harry Potter article of some sort. These range from short teasers to full-length, fully illustrated features.

Sometimes the article is mentioned on the cover with the Harry Potter name, other times a small picture appears on the cover, and then there are the covers primarily devoted to the Harry Potter article. It is the latter that is of interest here, and I have only listed magazines with at least 25 percent Harry Potter cover art.

This is only a sampling of what is available and not meant as a comprehensive listing. Condition and subject are the main criteria for prices.

Title and Issue Number	Date	Price
Blast #24	Winter 2002	$3-$5
Channel Guide	January 2008	$4-$6
Cineflex Magazine #88	January 2002	$9-$15
Cineflex Magazine #93	April 2003	$9-$15
Cineflex Magazine #105	April 2006	$9-$15
Details	October 2008	$4-$6
Disney Adventures	September 2005	$2-$3
Entertainment Weekly #614	September 2001	$10-$15
Entertainment Weekly #628	2001	$10-$15
Entertainment Weekly #657	July 6, 2002	$10-$15
Entertainment Weekly #683	Nov. 22, 2002	$10-$15
Entertainment Weekly #769	June 2004	$5-$10
Entertainment Weekly #831	July 2005	$5-$10
Entertainment Weekly #849	November 2005	$5-$10
Entertainment Weekly #928	April 2007	$5-$10
Entertainment Weekly #944	July 2007	$5-$10
Entertainment Weekly #946	August 2007	$5-$10
Entertainment Weekly #966/967	November 2007	$5-$10
Entertainment Weekly #1007/1008	August 2008	$5-$10
Entertainment Weekly #1041	April 2009	$4-$6
Entertainment Weekly #1057	July 2009	$4-$6
Expose Special #29	2005	$8-$10
Expose Special #32	2007	$6-$8
Famous Kids	Fall 2008	$1-$2
Flare	November 2008	$1-$2
Gamepro #160	January 2002	$2-$3
Games Unplugged #13	2001	$3-$5

Title and Issue Number	Date	Price
Girls Life	December 2006	$2-$3
Hit Sensation Kid Series #2	2002	$5-$6
Hit Sensation Kid Series #5	2002	$5-$6
Interview Magazine	May 2009	$5-$8
Kid Planet, Vol. 2, #16	2002	$4-$5
Ladies Home Journal		$4-$5
Lee's Toy Review #172	February 2007	$6-$8
LEGO Magazine	Fall 2001	$3-$5
Life Magazine	November 2005	$5-$7
Life Story Movie Magic #31	2003	$10-$12
Life Story Movie Magic #33	2003	$10-$12
Life Story Movie Magic #42	2004	$10-$12
Life Story Movie Magic #43	2004	$10-$12
Life Story Movie Magic #73	2007	$8-$10
Life Story Movie Magic #74	2007	$8-$10
Life Story Movie Magic #94	2009	$8-$10

Title and Issue Number	Date	Price
Mad Magazine #412	December 2001	$5-$10
Mad Magazine #424	December 2002	$5-$10
Mad Magazine #443	July 2004	$5-$8
Mad Magazine #460	December 2005	$5-$8
Mad Magazine #480	August 2007	$4-$7
Maclean's	July 2007	$5-$8
Newsweek	July 17, 2001	$8-$10
Newsweek	May 31, 2004	$5-$7
Nickelodeon	November 2005	$5-$6
Non-Sport Update, Vol. 18, #3	June/July 2007	$3-$5
Parade (Boston Globe Supplement)	Aug. 7, 2007	$4-$5
People	July 2007	$5-$7
Playthings	October 2000	$15-$20
Premiere	November 2001	$10-$15
Reader's Digest	December 2000	$3-$5
Realms of Fantasy	August 2003	$5-$10
Scott Stamp Monthly, Vol. 25, #6	June 2007	$4-$6
16 Special – Harry Potter	2001	$4-$6
Starlog #340	November 2005	$7-$10
Starlog #357	2007	$4-$6
Time, Vol. 154, #12	September 1999	$5-$7
Time, Vol. 161, #25	June 2003	$5-$7
Toyfare #119	July 2007	$3-$5
TV Week #46	November 2001	$1-$2
Vanity Fair	October 2001	$4-$5

Magnets
NECA, Inc.

Gryffindor Crest (59544):
Resin magnet................$6-$8

Hufflepuff Crest (59546):
Resin magnet................$6-$8

Ravenclaw Crest Magnet (60401): Released 2007 $6-$8

Hogwarts Crest (59545):
Resin magnet................$6-$8

Hufflepuff Crest Magnet (60311): Released 2007 $6-$8

Slytherin Crest (59548):
Resin magnet................$6-$8

Hogwarts Crest Magnet (60284): Released 2007 $6-$8

Ravenclaw Crest (59547):
Resin magnet................$6-$8

Slytherin Crest Magnet (60421): Released 2007 $6-$8

Magnet Sheets

These 7" x 10" sheets, with removable magnets, were released in 2008-2009.

Harry Potter and the Half-Blood Prince (NC59527): Characters magnet sheet, eight pieces. ....$6-$8

Movie Scenes (NC60540): Magnet sheet, eight pieces......$6-$8

Movie Scenes (NC): Magnet sheet, seven pieces. ....$6-$8

Potions (NC59550): Magnet sheet, 10 pieces.....................$6-$8

Snitch Logo Magnet (60332)
....$6-$8

Movies

VHS and DVD

With the increasing popularity of Pay Per View and Video On Demand, the market for home video has declined. The market for VHS has all but disappeared with the arrival of DVD and HD-DVD. In time the DVD market will give way to Blu-Ray.

Though Harry Potter DVDs have historically been best-sellers, each sequel has attracted fewer buyers with a drop in sales estimated at 15 percent between the first and latest releases. Budget-conscious buyers are more selective in the movies they buy, but films like the Harry Potter series are always well ahead of the others. When the release of *Half-Blood Prince* was moved to July 2009 from November 2008, many suspected the move was to help declining DVD sales by pushing the release of the home video version closer to Christmas.

Prices are for used movies in good condition to movies still in original wrapping. Movies with free cards and other bonuses must include the bonuses to command the higher price.

Harry Potter and the Philosopher's Stone

DVD – Special widescreen edition yellow band, two discs, May 2002. ....$5-$7

DVD – Widescreen white band, two discs, December 2007. ....$5-$7

DVD – Full screen edition, no band, two discs, May 2002. ....$5-$7

DVD – Full screen edition, no band, two discs, December 2007. ....$5-$7

Mini-DVD – Full screen edition, white band, one disc, April 2005...$5-$7

HD-DVD – Burgundy band, December 2007. ....$5-$7

Blu-Ray – Blue band, December 2007.............................$15-$17

VHS – 2002...................$2-$3

Harry Potter and the Sorcerer's Stone

VHS – 2002.................... $2-$3

Photo from the collection of Megan Barrow

DVD – Special widescreen edition, yellow band, two discs, May 2002 (includes trading card). .... $8-$10

DVD – Full screen edition, black band (includes trading card)............................ $8-$10

DVD – Widescreen edition, no band (includes trading card)........................... $8-$10

DVD – Full screen edition, no band, two discs, May 2002. .... $5-$7

DVD – Full screen edition, yellow band, two discs, December 2007. .... $5-$7

DVD – Widescreen edition, white band, two discs, December 2007. .... $5-$7

Mini-DVD – Full screen edition, white band, one disc, April 2005............ $5-$7

HD-DVD – Burgundy band, December 2007. .... $8-$10

Blu-Ray – Blue band, December 2007. .... $15-$17

Harry Potter and the Chamber of Secrets

VHS – 2003.................... $2-$3

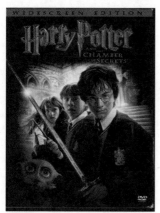

DVD – Widescreen edition, yellow band, two discs, April 2003. .... $5-$7

DVD – Full screen edition, green band, two discs, April 2003. .... $5-$7

DVD – Full frame edition, blue band, two discs. .... $5-$7

DVD – Widescreen edition, black band, December 2007 (includes trading card)....................................... $8-$10

Mini-DVD – White band....................................... $5-$7

HD-DVD – Burgundy band, December 2007. .... $8-$10

Blu-Ray – Blue band, December 2007............................ $15-$17

Harry Potter and the Prisoner of Azkaban

VHS – November 2004...$2-$3

DVD – Full screen edition, blue band, two discs, November 2004...$5-$7

DVD – Full screen edition, yellow band, December 2007. ....$5-$7

DVD – Widescreen edition, white band, December 2007. ....$5-$7

DVD – Widescreen edition, black band, December 2007 (includes trading card).......................................$8-$10

Mini-DVD – White band...$5-$7

HD-DVD – Burgundy band, December 2007. ....$8-$10

Blu-Ray – Blue band, December 2007.............................$15-$17

DVD – Widescreen edition, yellow band, two discs, November 2004............$5-$7

Harry Potter Years 1-3
2004 DVD six-disc set in full screen and widescreen versions for *Harry Potter and the Sorcerer's Stone, Harry Potter and the Chamber of Secrets,* and *Harry Potter and the Prisoner of Azkaban.* Comes gift boxed with three coins: galleon, sickle, and knut. Certificate of authenticity comes with the coins... **$23-$26**

Harry Potter and the Goblet of Fire

VHS – 2005....................$2-$3

DVD – Full screen edition, yellow band, March 2006. ....$5-$7

DVD – Widescreen edition, burgundy band, March 2006.............................$5-$7

DVD – Two-disc edition, Edition Speciale de Deux Disques, widescreen edition, March 2006................. $8-$10

DVD – Two-Disc Deluxe Edition, March 2006 (The deluxe edition was made for Target, and the only difference is the cover art.) ....$8-$10

DVD – Widescreen edition, black band, December 2007 (includes trading card). ....$8-$10

DVD – Full screen edition, black band, December 2007 (includes trading card). ....$8-$10

Mini-DVD......................$5-$7

HD-DVD – Burgundy band, December 2007. ....$8-$10

Blu-Ray – Blue band, December 2007. ....$15-$17

Photo from the collection of Megan Barrow

DVD – Two-disc special edition, silver band, March 2006. ....$8-$10

Harry Potter and the Order of the Phoenix

DVD – Widescreen, no band, December 2007. ....$6-$8

DVD – Widescreen edition, Edition Panoramique, burgundy band, December 2007, different cover art. ....$6-$8

DVD – Two-Disc Special Edition, silver band, December 2007. .... $12-$14

DVD – Full screen, no band, December 2007. ....$5-$7

DVD – Exclusive Limited 2-Disc Edition, silver band, widescreen, December 2007, sold at Best Buy for limited time, included Death Eater mask and collectible art. ....$25-$30

DVD – Wal-Mart 2-Pack Gift Set, widescreen, December 2007, sold at Wal-Mart, included three bookmarks. ....$8-$10

Mini-DVD......................$5-$7

HD-DVD – Burgundy band, December 2007, HD DVD and DVD combo format. ....$6-$8

Blu-Ray – Blue band, December 2007. .... $18-$20

Harry Potter and the Half-Blood Prince

DVD – Widescreen edition, December 2009. .... $8-$10

DVD – Full screen edition, December 2009. ....$5-$8

DVD – Special Edition, 2-Disc Edition, widescreen, December 2009, with Holographic slipcover. ....$10-$15

DVD – Collector's Edition, December 2009, comes with detailed Marauder's Map from Noble Collection. ....$20-$25

Blu-Ray – Single disc, December 2009. ....$10-$15

Blu-Ray – 2-Disc Edition, December 2009. ....$18-$22

Blu-Ray – 3-Disc Edition, December 2009, retailer exclusive limited edition Death Eater storage case, includes DVD and digital. ....$20-$25

Digital† – Future Shop Exclusive, December 2009, limited edition iron pack case...$10-$15

Digital – 2-Disc Edition, December 2009, special limited edition acrylic case...$15-$20

Digital – 2-Disc Edition, December 2009, special edition steel book with DVD...$15-$20

Digital – Download authorization codes. ....$2-$5

†Digital – Comes with disc and instructions that contain an activation code. Once downloaded onto your computer (internet connection required), can be played on iTunes, iPod, Windows Media, PSP, or other digital devices.

Harry Potter Limited Edition Gift Set

DVD seven-disc set comes in a trunk-shaped box with Hogwarts crest on top and includes *Harry Potter and the Sorcerer's Stone, Harry Potter and the Chamber of Secrets, Harry Potter and the Prisoner of Azkaban, Harry Potter and the Goblet of Fire, Harry Potter and the Order of the Phoenix, Harry Potter Interactive DVD Game: Hogwarts Challenge,* and a two-hour disc full of bonus features, plus a five bookmark collection and 16 trading cards. .... **$35-$40**

The Magical World of Harry Potter: The Unauthorized Story of J. K. Rowling: Video Release Productions, released in 2000 on DVD. ....$2-$5

Discovering the Real World of Harry Potter: Discovery Channel, released in 2001 on DVD. .... $10-$15

Biography: Harry Potter Kids: Biography Channel, released in 2009 on DVD. ....$7-$10

It is interesting to note that the six Harry Potter movies released to date, as of December 2009, are all in the top 25 highest grossing films. The following list is for international gross according to The Internet Movie Database.

1. Titanic (1997)
2. The Lord of the Rings: The Return of the King (2003)
3. Pirates of the Caribbean: Dead Man's Chest (2006)
4. The Dark Knight (2008)
5. *Harry Potter and the Sorcerer's Stone* (2001)
6. Pirates of the Caribbean: At World's End (2007)
7. *Harry Potter and the Order of the Phoenix* (2007)
8. *Harry Potter and the Half-Blood Prince* (2009)
9. Star Wars: Episode I – The Phantom Menace (1999)
10. The Lord of the Rings: The Two Towers (2002)
11. Jurassic Park (1993)
12. *Harry Potter and the Goblet of Fire* (2005)
13. Spider-Man 3 (2007)
14. Ice Age: Dawn of the Dinosaurs (2009)
15. Shrek 2 (2004)
16. *Harry Potter and the Chamber of Secrets* (2002)
17. Finding Nemo (2003)
18. The Lord of the Rings: The Fellowship of the Ring (2001)
19. Star Wars: Episode III – Revenge of the Sith (2005)
20. Transformers: Revenge of the Fallen (2009)
21. Independence Day (1996)
22. Spider-Man (2002)
23. Star Wars (1977)
24. Shrek the Third (2007)
25. *Harry Potter and the Prisoner of Azkaban* (2004)

Academy Award Nominations

2001 *Harry Potter and the Sorcerer's Stone*: Best art direction, best costume design, and best original score for John Williams

2004 *Harry Potter and the Prisoner of Azkaban:* Best visual effects and best original music score

2005 *Harry Potter and the Goblet of Fire:* Best art direction

Mugs
Enesco

These Harry Potter mugs are shaped in the faces of the characters with yellow handles and the character name in a circle at the base of the handle. They were released in 2000.

Harry Potter: 4" high. ....$13-$15

Hedwig (2630543BA): One eye winking. .... $12-$14

Hermione Granger: 4" high. ....$13-$15

Mountain Troll .... $12-$14

Ron Weasley (2630473AW): 4" high...................... $13-$15

Decal Mugs

Gryffindor Crest: White with house crest....................$5-$6

Harry Chasing Flying Keys: white with picture. ......$5-$6

Hogwarts Crest: Dark blue with school crest. ....$5-$6

Hufflepuff Crest: White with house crest....................$5-$6

Ravenclaw Crest: White with house crest..........$5-$6

Ron Weasley and Bertie Bott's Beans (851957B): Released in 2001, 12 oz. white with red background and image of Ron and beans, reveals secrets when heated. ....$6-$8

Slytherin Crest: White with house crest....................$5-$6

Hallmark

Hogwarts Emblem Ceramic Mug: Issued in 2000. ....$8-$10

Noble Collection

Gryffindor Mug (NN7668): Fine pewter with raised house crest................$55-$60

Slytherin Mug (NN7669): Fine pewter with raised house crest................$55-$60

NECA, Inc.

Dumbledore's Army stackable mugs: Set of four, 6 oz...........................$18-$20

Gryffindor Decal Mug: White with color house crest. $7-$9

Half-Blood Prince (59551): Released in 2009, black and green with Harry and logo. .... $7-$8

Half-Blood Prince (59552): Released in 2009, black and green with Harry, Ron, and Hermione logo. .... $7-$9

Half-Blood Prince (59553): Released in 2009, thermal, black and green with Harry and logo..................... $15-$16

Half-Blood Prince (59554): Released in 2009, thermal, black and green with Harry, Ron, and Hermione and logo. .... $15-$16

Hogwarts Decal Mug: White with color school crest. .... $7-$9

House Crest stackable mugs: Set of four, 6 oz., black with crest..........................$18-$20

Slytherin Decal Mug: White with color house crest. .... $7-$9

Warner Bros.

Birth of Norbert Mug (NL106): Black with purple dragon. ....$6-$8

Harry Potter Logo Mug (BM254): Black with gold letters. ....$6-$8

Harry Potter With Flying Friends Mug (NL104): White with Harry, Ron, and Hermione on brooms....$6-$8

Hedwig Mug: White with close-up of Hedwig and Harry with wand..........$6-$8

Hogwarts Crest Mug (BM255): Black with school crest..............................$6-$8

I Solemnly Swear That I Am Up To No Good... : Thermal mug. Hot liquid turns it from *I Solemnly Swear That I Am Up To No Good* to *Mischief Managed*, and from black to white..........................$18-$20

Xpres

Xpres, based in North Carolina, featured designs based on the artwork of Warner Bros.' artist Fred Bode. Images are from the *Encore Presents Xpres* catalog, January 2003. Photos of Xpres Mugs are courtesy of Sylvan Lane Shoppe.

Sculpted Black Mugs with Crest: 9 oz.

Slytherin (613345 500 2);
Quidditch (613343 500 2);
Hogwarts (613344 500 2);
Gryffindor (613346 500 2).
....$6-$8

Sculpted Black Soup Bowls with Crest: 16 oz.

Slytherin   (613349 600 2);
Quidditch   (613347 600 2);
Hogwarts   (613348 600 2);
Gryffindor   (613350 600 2).
....$6-$8

Sculpted Window Mugs: Available in black or white with brick-like design, climbing ivy leaves, and an arched window showing a scene from Harry's life, 11 oz.

Harry Gets the Golden Snitch (613352 500 2)

Harry and Hagrid (613351 500 2)

Harry Potter With Wand (613354 500 2)

Harry Gets the Key (613353 500 2)

Added later:
Birth of Norbert
Wild Ride
Potions Class
The Sorting Hat
....$8-$10

Spellbinding Scenes: These black 11 oz. mugs are in full-color with wraparound scenes.............................$6-$8
    1 - Beware Fluffy!
    2 - Invisibility Cloak
    3 - The Sorting Hat
    4 - Your Heart's Desire
       (Mirror of Erised)
    5 - Birth of Norbert
    6 - Vicious Troll
    7 - Wild Ride
    8 - Potions Class

White Mugs: Dobby Drops In (611573 400 2); The Final Chapter (611574 400 2); Quidditch Match (611575 400 2); Watch the Bludger (611576 400 2); Brewing Up Trouble (611578 400 2); Driving to Hogwarts (611579 400 2).
....$6-$8

Wizards of Hogwarts: With a close-up portrait of Harry and a scene from the book and movie......................$5-$7
    1 - Harry and Hedwig
    2 - Harry and Friends
    3 - Harry in Potions
    4 - Harry Gets the Snitch
    5 - Rescued!
    6 - Harry and Hagrid
    7 - The Devil's Snare
    8 - Harry Gets the Key

Wizard's World: This line of 11 oz. black or white mugs features the four Hogwarts houses, each with a crest, the HP Snitch logo, and a carved, castle wall look.............$6-$8
    1 - Owl Post
    2 - Platform 9-3/4
    3 - Quidditch
    4 - Journey to Hogwarts

Party Supplies
Hallmark

Bertie Bott's Goody Bags: Contains one door hanger, four stickers, one backpack clip, one pair novelty glasses, and two suckers. Retail **$2.99**

Goblet of Fire Bubble Blowers: Contains four bubble wands filled with bubble making liquid. .**$5-$6**

Goblet of Fire Dessert Napkins: Sixteen 9-7/8" napkins depicting Harry pointing wand. ....**$3-$4**

Goblet of Fire Dessert Plates: Eight 6-3/4" dessert plates, each depicting Harry and Hogwarts crest. ....**$4-$5**

Goblet of Fire Lunch Napkins: Sixteen 12-7/8" napkins depicting Harry and Hogwarts crest............ **$3-$4**

Half-Blood Prince Rings: Package of nine reusable plastic rings for party favors or decorating cakes or cupcakes, two each of house crests. .... **$3-$4**

Happy Birthday Banner: Reusable plastic banner with "Happy Birthday" in red letters and images of Quidditch Harry............ **$3-$4**

Happy Birthday Banner: Reusable plastic banner with "Happy Birthday" in blue and purple letters and images of Harry, Ron, and Hermione. .... **$3-$4**

Harry Potter Birthday Napkins: Sixteen 12-7/8" napkins depicting Golden Snitch............................ **$5-$6**

Harry Potter Cluster Balloon: One large and four small Mylar star-shaped cluster balloons, 35", Harry on large balloon, Ron, Hermione, logo, and crest on small balloons. .... **$9-$10**

Harry Potter Glasses: Package of four pairs of black soft plastic frames with clear plastic lenses and tape on nose piece. .... **$4-$5**

Harry Potter Rings: Package of nine reusable plastic rings for party favors or decorating cakes or cupcakes, three each of Harry, Ron, and Hermione. .... **$3-$4**

Harry Potter Super Shape Balloon: 21" x 35" seven-point Mylar balloon, depicts Harry on Firebolt on both sides. .... **$7-$8**

Hogwarts Express Cake Topper Set: For use on any rectangular 9" cake, includes a plastic 3" Harry Potter figure, display photo of Hogwarts Express (7" x 4-1/2"), and a luggage cart. .... **$10-$12**

Order of the Phoenix Banner: Red and yellow reusable plastic banner reads, "A Magical Day!" with Harry, Hermione, and Ron between words............................ **$5-$6**

Order of the Phoenix Balloon: 18" round Mylar balloon, depicts Harry and Gryffindor crest.............................. **$3-$4**

Order of the Phoenix Blow-Outs: Package of eight card and paper blow-outs, depicts Harry and Hogwarts crest. .... **$3-$4**

Order of the Phoenix Centerpiece: Cardstock 10-3/4" standup on red wraparound honeycomb, depicts Harry casting spell. .... **$6-$7**

Order of the Phoenix Cups: Eight 9 oz. cups for hot or cold drinks, depicts Harry and Hogwarts crest. ..... **$3-$4**

Order of the Phoenix Dessert Napkins: Sixteen 9-7/8" napkins with Hogwarts crest and list of members of Dumbledore's Army. ..... **$2-$3**

Order of the Phoenix Dinner Plates: Eight 8-3/4" diameter dinner plates, each depicting Harry and five of Dumbledore's Army. ..... **$3-$4**

Order of the Phoenix Invitations: Eight invitations and envelopes, "Your presence is requested..." and Hogwarts crest............. **$3-$4**

Order of the Phoenix Lunch Napkins: Sixteen 12-7/8" napkins with Harry, Ron, and Hermione with wands drawn. .... **$3-$4**

Order of the Phoenix Party Favor Bags: Package of eight plastic party favor bags depicting Harry Potter. **$2-$3**

Order of the Phoenix Party Hats: Eight cone-shaped party hats depicting Harry casting spell. .... **$3-$4**

Photo courtesy Bonds Corner

Order of the Phoenix Dessert Plates: Eight 6-3/4" dessert plates, each depicting Harry and Hogwarts crest. .... **$3-$4**

Order of the Phoenix Table Cover: Reusable plastic table cover, 54" x 102", depicting Harry and Hermione. ... **$5-$6**

Order of the Phoenix Thank You Notes: Eight thank you notes and envelopes, "Thanks," Harry and Gryffindor crest. .... **$3-$4**

Order of the Phoenix Tumbler: 16 oz. reusable plastic tumbler depicting Harry, Ron, and Hermione. .... **$1-$2**

Photo courtesy Bonds Corner

Party Favor T-Shirt Emblems: Contains four Triwizard Tournament Hogwarts Crests, 4-3/4" x 4-1/4". **$8.99**

Patches

Beauxbatons Academy: Gold on blue circle, cut-out, iron-on. .... **$9-$11**

Death Eater: Silver snake symbol on red oval, cut-out, iron-on. .... **$15-$16**

Durmstrang Institute: Gold and red on green circle, cut-out, iron-on........... **$9-$11**

Gryffindor Crest: Red, gold, and silver on black, 4" die-cut. .... **$7-$9**

Gryffindor Crest: Red, gold, and silver on black, cut-out, iron-on. .... **$5-$7**

Harry Potter Logo: HP and snitch logo, gold on black circle, 4" cut-out, iron-on. .... **$8-$9**

Hogwarts Crest: All four house crests combined as one, cut-out, iron-on..... **$5-$7**

Hogwarts Crest: All four house crests combined as one, on black, 4" die-cut..........**$7-$9**

Hogwarts School Crest: Multicolor on black circle, cut-out, iron-on. .... **$7-$8**

Hufflepuff Crest: Gold and silver on black, 4" die-cut. **$7-$9**

Hufflepuff Crest: Gold and silver on black, cut-out, iron-on...**$5-$7**

Owl Post: Orange and silver on black, 4". .... **$9-$10**

Platform 9-3/4: Purple and white with orange train, 6" cut-out, iron-on........... **$8-$10**

Ravenclaw Crest: Gold and blue on black, 4" die-cut. .... **$7-$9**

Ravenclaw Crest: Gold and blue on black, cut-out, iron-on. .... **$5-$7**

Slytherin Crest: Green and silver on black, 4" die-cut.**$7-$9**

Slytherin Crest: Green and silver on black, cut-out, iron-on. .... **$5-$7**

Triwizard Tournament: Green, silver, gold, and red, cut-out, iron-on........... **$8-$10**

Wizard in Training: Gold Hogwarts crest on red circle, cut-out, iron-on........... **$9-$11**

Pens
Hallmark
Light-Up Pens

Set of eight pens, released in 2000. .... **$4-$6 ea.**
- 1 – Bertie Bott's Beans
- 2 – Hedwig
- 3 – Hogwarts House Crests
- 4 – Hogwarts School Crest
- 5 – Lightning Bolts
- 6 – Norbert
- 7 – Potion, Chess, and Key
- 8 – Quidditch Balls

Pen and Paper Gift Sets

Released 2000 .... **$15-$20 ea.**
- 1 – Potion Bottle and Scrolls, includes paper pad and pen.
- 2 – Harry Potter chasing Golden Snitch, includes paper pad and pen.

LEGO

The LEGO Harry Potter Connect & Build writing pen was produced by CDM in 2005. It came with extra connectible beads, a replaceable ink cartridge, and a pen stand with storage container. It was apparently limited to only a few thousand under a special LEGO license and came in two styles.

Harry Potter .... **$5-$10**

Harry Potter & Hermione .... **$6-$12**

Noble Collection

Firebolt Broom Pen (NN7258): 7" broom on stand........................**$20-$25**

Harry Potter's Levitating Wand Pen (NN1590): Harry's 8" wand floating in mid air. ....**$40-$45**

Harry Potter's Wand Pen (NN7121): 8" wand with illuminating tip.........**$18-$20**

Hogwarts House Pen – Gryffindor (NN7280): 7" die-cast, enameled, 24K gold and silver plated. ....**$18-$20**

Hogwarts House Pen – Hufflepuff (NN7282, NN7280): 7" die-cast, enameled, 24K gold and silver plated. ....**$18-$20**

Hogwarts House Pen – Ravenclaw (NN7281, NN7280): 7" die-cast, enameled, 24K gold and silver plated. ....**$18-$20**

Hogwarts House Pen – Slytherin (NN7279): 7" die-cast enameled 24K gold and silver plated. ....**$18-$20**

Sorting Hat Display (NN7284): Porcelain and wood pen holder.......**$30-$35**

Warner Bros.

Pens (GM610): Set of six pens with various patterns and colors with different character names, released 2000. ....**$6-$8**

Personal Care
Johnson & Johnson

Johnson & Johnson, Inc., made these personal care items at the time of the *Sorcerer's Stone* movie in November 2001. They are now hard to find and the contents have probably deteriorated over the years.

Bath

Bedazzled Blue Raspberry Shampoo......................**$2-$3**

Foaming Kiwi Melon Detangler......................**$2-$3**

Hermione Green Apple Body Wash..............................**$3-$4**

Strawberry Vanilla Bubble Bath ....**$3-$4**

Transforming Cherry Liquid Hand Soap ....**$3-$4**

Toothpaste and Brushes

Drooble's Best Blowing Gum Toothpaste ....**$2-$3**

Harry Potter Reach Toothbrush (left)..........**$2-$4**

Hermione Granger Reach Toothbrush (right).......**$2-$4**

Band-Aids

Harry Potter Band-Aids: 25 glow-in-the-dark bandages in each box...................**$2-$4**

Photo from the collection of Megan Barrow

Belae Brands Canada Company
Lip Balm

There are four characters, each on top of a roll of lip balm with a clip. An international product, the characters were made in China, the tube filled in Canada, and the product assembled in United States. The first three were released in 2001, Dobby in 2002. ....**$4-$5 ea.**

1 – Norbert
2 – Hedwig
3 – Scabbers
4 – Dobby

Picture Frames
Fetco International

Fetco, based in Massachusetts, was originally the primary manufacturer of licensed Harry Potter photograph frames. Some of the frames have artwork by Warner Bros. artist Fred Bode.

Harry and Friends: Ron, Hermione, Gryffindor crest, and Harry chasing Snitch. .... **$15-$17**

Harry in Potions Class: From Fred Bode's illustration of Snape watching Harry in potions class. .... **$15-$17**

Harry's Glasses: Pictures can be inserted in lens position.. **$15-$17**

Hogwarts House Crests: Crests of the four Hogwarts houses. .... **$15-$17**

Quidditch Team: In Gryffindor uniforms. ....**$25-$30**

Hallmark
Bertie Bott's Beans: Holds 2-1/2" x 2-1/2" picture. .... **$15-$17**

Lenticular Padded Frame: Changes appearance depending on angle of viewing, issued in 2000, two styles..............**$8-$10 ea.**

1 - Black frame shows lightning bolts and purple frame shows Quidditch balls.

2 - Red frame shows house crests and purple frame shows sorting hats.

Kurt S. Adler, Inc.
Mirror of Erised: Resin picture frame ornament...**$8-$10**

Rubies Costumes

Photo courtesy of Rubies Costumes Co. Inc.

Distressed Black with Gold Lip Picture Frame: 3-1/2" x 5-1/2".............................**$4-$5**

Warner Bros.
Harry Potter: Harry on broom, Hagrid with Norbert and owl. .... **$16-$18**

Pins and Buttons

Many pin sellers on eBay make their own pins using pictures from Harry Potter books and movies. These are infringements of copyright and not listed here. Take care when buying pins; they should have the WB logo or WDEI 2004 or similar copyright on the edge or back. Check with the seller before purchase. Many sellers will have a disclaimer such as "Not mass produced, made for fans only."

McDonalds

Hermione Granger: Very hard to find 2" cloisonné pin released in conjunction with McDonalds to promote *Harry Potter and the Sorcerer's Stone*. Shows Hermione on her broom in green jacket and bright pink pants. Color variations on her clothes exist with pink pants apparently among the most difficult to find. The McDonalds logo appears to the side of the Harry Potter title, and the WB logo is on the back... **$20-$25**

Warner Bros.

These 1-1/2" round back pins all have the WDEI 2004 copyright along the bottom.
Deatheaters: Red text on white Death Mark on black background. ....**$3-$5**
Gryffindor Crest: Gold and burgundy crest on striped background. ....**$3-$5**

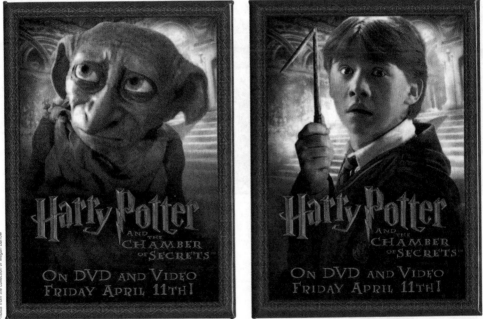

Photos from the collection of Megan Barrow

Harry Potter and the Chamber of Secrets: Rectangular pins from store promotion for the release of the second film on DVD, set of four. ....**$4-$5**

Harry Potter and the Sorcerer's Stone Button Pack: Warner Bros. Store Exclusives from 2000, approximately 1" wide, includes Harry and Mirror of Erised; Owl Post Service; Seeker Harry; Gringotts; Scabbers; Daily Prophet sign, etc...**$10-$15**

Harry Potter Pins: Rectangular pins from Wal-Mart promotions for the release of *Harry Potter and the Sorcerer's Stone* on DVD; feature goblins, Hagrid, Ron, and Hermione..................**$4-$5**

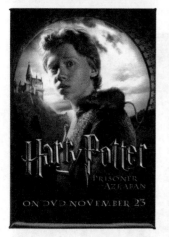 

Harry Potter and the Prisoner of Azkaban: Rectangular pins from store promotion for the release of the third film on DVD in 2004, set of four...$4-$5

Harry Potter Promo Pin: Worn by bookstore employees to promote book IV.......$2-$3

Hermione Granger: Head and shoulders on black and blue background...........$1-$2

I Speak Parsel Tongue: Black print on yellow..............$3-$5

Mudblood: White print on red background. ....$1-$2

Muggle: White print on black and red designed background...................$3-$5

Seeker: Black print on red designed background. ....$3-$5

Sirius Black: Face from wanted poster, black and gray...............................$4-$6

Something Wicked This Way Comes: White print on blue and white background. ....$3-$5

Triwizard Tournament: White text on Harry, Cedric and Viktor. ....$3-$5

Wizard in Training: Yellow print and Hogwarts logo on brown background.......$3-$5

NECA, Inc.

Harry Potter and the Half-Blood Prince Character Pins (NC59512): Release 2009, 1-1/4", set of six.........$7-$8/set

Harry Potter and the Half-Blood Prince Crest Pins (NC59513): Release 2009, 1-1/4", set of six.........$7-$8/set

Noble Collection

Hogwarts House Pins (NN7374): Finely detailed and hand enameled, includes set of four houses and school crests in collector box. ....$20-$25

Slytherin Crest: Green and silver crest with checkered background..$3-$5

Plush
Gund

Gund, Inc., of Edison, New Jersey, a major manufacturer of everyday and collectible stuffed toys, is world renowned for soft quality plush designs. Photos of Gund toys are courtesy of Gund, Inc.

Basilisk: 46" with reptilian print, loosely stuffed with wire running through his body for ease of posing. ....$20-$25

Fluffy: 9" three-headed, brown guard dog wearing a spiked collar. ....$20-$25

Golden Snitch: 36 2-1/2" Quidditch balls displayed in an acetate barrel promotion pack. ....$5-$7 ea.

Display of five Gund animals.

Hagrid: 14" full bearded, soft-bodied figure, wearing green shirt, brown coat, pants, and boots with keys on his belt and Gryffindor scarf around his neck. ....$20-$25

Hedwig: 7" snowy white owl with jeweled collar around her neck and faux leather claws and beak...**$14-$18**

Harry Potter: 11" soft-bodied figure, dressed in jeans and striped shirt under his removable black robe...$25-$30

Hermione Granger: 11" soft-bodied figure, dressed in pink v-neck, jeans, and removable black robe...**$25-$30**

Mrs. Norris: 9" yellow-eyed, softly striped cat wearing a green jeweled collar. ....**$14-$18**

Norbert: 7" reptilian print body with taffeta wings and corduroy chest, this baby dragon sits in a fabric detachable egg. ....**$14-$18**

Ron Weasley: 12-1/2" soft-bodied figure, dressed in purple shirt, jeans, and removable black robe...**$35-$40**

Scabbers: 8" gray rat with black stars on his back, gold collar, and green bracelet. **$14-$18**

Gund Beanies

Gund also released a line of five beanies (5"-5-1/2") similar to the Harry Potter critters above: Fluffy, Hedwig, Scabbers, Norbert, Mrs. Norris. ....**$5-$10 ea.**

Plush Christmas Ornaments

Christmas 2001 saw the release of three plush Gund ornaments for the Christmas tree. These 2-1/2" decorations included Hedwig, the Sorting Hat, and a Golden Snitch. ....**$5-$10 ea.**

Messaging Owls: 4" in assorted colors with fabric message attached to claws. ....**$5-$8 ea.**

Mattel

Messaging Owls: 4" in assorted colors with fabric message attached to claws. ....**$5-$8 ea.**

NECA, Inc.

Buckbeak: 9" stately white hippogriff. ....**$15-$20**

Chinese Fireball Dragon: 11-1/2" reptilian red. ....**$15-$20**

Crookshanks: 8" sitting cat in brown with yellow chest. ....**$15-$20**

Fawkes the Phoenix: 11" mythical bird, red with black features. ....**$15-$20**

Golden Snitch: 10" wing span, golden with silver wings . ...**$8-$10**

Hedwig: 8" white owl with black features. ....**$10-$15**

Hungarian Horntail Dragon: 11-1/2" reptilian brown and black. ....**$15-$20**

Monster Book of Monsters: Brown with protruding yellow eyes and printing vibrates when its pink tongue is pulled, 10-1/2"x8-1/2"x3". ....**$18-$20**

Scabbers: 9" rat, brown with white spots, missing a toe. ....**$10-$15**

Sorting Hat: 18" wearable brown plush. ....**$20-$25**

Swedish Short-Snout Dragon: 11-1/2" reptilian gray with silver. ....**$15-$20**

Talking Sorting Hat: 10", quotes phrases from the movie. ....**$35-$40**

Welsh Green Dragon: 11-1/2" reptilian green. ....**$15-$20**

Warner Bros.

Hedwig: Similar to Gund owl but with wings slightly extended from sides. ....**$16-$20**

Postcards
Artcards
Harry Potter and the Chamber of Secrets
Single postcards issued in 2002...$1-$2 ea.

474 – Harry, Ron, Hermione, and Dobby (ad card)

475 – Harry with Gryffindor sword (ad card)

476 – Hermione pointing wand (ad card)
477 – Ron with broken wand (ad card)

C&D Visionary Inc.
Harry Potter and the Goblet of Fire
Single postcards issued in 2004...$1-$2 ea.

Magical Creatures
– Dark Arts
– Hermione, Ron, and Harry on stairs.

Harry Potter and the Prisoner of Azkaban
Single postcards issued in 2004..$1-$2 ea.

– Dementors (die-cut)
– Dark Arts

GoCard

Harry Potter and the Goblet of Fire
Book IV postcard......................................$2-$3

Harry Potter and the Half-Blood Prince
Book VI postcard......................................$2-$3

– Are You Ready for the New Harry Potter?

– Who is the Half-Blood Prince?

NECA, Inc.

Harry Potter and the Half-Blood Prince
– Crests postcard set of four (59557) issued in 2009. ....$5-$6
Harry Potter and the Half-Blood Prince
– Potions postcard set of four (59558) issued in 2009...$5-$6

Scholastic

Harry Potter and the Chamber of Secrets Postcard Book: 24 postcards, four to a page, perforated for easy removal with scenes from the film, ISBN 0-439-42522-0, cover...........$6-$8

Harry Potter and the Sorcerer's Stone Postcard Book: This postcard-sized book features 32 scenes from the movie, ISBN 0-439-28856-8. ....$6-$8

Sonis
Harry Potter and the Chamber of Secrets | Harry Potter and the Philosopher's Stone

Single postcards...$1-$2 ea.

    – Harry and car flying over Hogwarts (C.1385)
    – Hermione, Ron, Harry and Dobby (C.1390)

First Years approach Hogwarts by water (C.1231) ....$1-$2 ea.

Unknown Publisher
Harry Potter and the Prisoner of Azkaban
Single cards issued in 2004. ....**$1-$2 ea.**
- Dumbledore and Ron
- Dumbledore, Harry, Hermione, and Ron
- Dumbledore, Ron, Hermione, and Harry
- Harry and Gryffindor symbol
- Harry and Hogwarts
- Harry and Hogwarts crest
- Harry and Professor Lupin
- Harry close-up and signature
- Harry reaching for Golden Snitch
- Harry with wand
- Harry, Ron, and Hermione
- Harry, Ron, Hermione, and Hogwarts
- Harry, snitch, and house crest

- Hermione
- Hermione and timeturner
- Hermione, Professor Trelawney, and Hogwarts
- Ron and Dumbledore
- Wormtail and Sirius Black

Harry Potter and the Goblet of Fire
Single cards issued in 2005................**$1-$2 ea.**
- Cedric Diggory (dark background)
- Cedric Diggory (misty background)
- Cedric, Harry, Fleur, Viktor
- Cho and Cedric
- Fleur Delacour
- Fleur, Ron, and flying coach
- Harry pointing wand to left
- Harry Potter
- Harry, Fleur, Cedric
- Harry, Fleur, Cedric, Viktor, Ron, Hermione
- Hermione
- Hermione with lake behind
- Hermione with stairs behind
- Hermione, Harry, Ron
- Mad-Eye Moody with darkness behind
- Mad-Eye Moody with wall behind
- Ron in dress robes
- Ron in sweater
- Ron, Fleur (looking forward), and flying coach
- Ron, Fleur (looking right) and flying coach
- Ron, Harry, Hermione
- Ron, Harry, Hermione closer
- Viktor and Hermione with lake behind
- Viktor Krum (facing left)
- Viktor Krum (facing right)

Harry Potter and the Order of the Phoenix
Single cards issued in 2006................**$1-$2 ea.**
- Harry Potter and Voldemort
- Hermione Granger and Professor Umbridge
- Luna Lovegood and Death Eater
- Ron Weasley and Lucius Malfoy

See "Stamps" section for listing of Harry Potter Postal Cards with pre-printed stamps.

Posters

Posters used in movie theaters are designed for use in the light boxes theaters use to advertise movies. These are printed on both sides with a mirror image on the reverse side so when the posters are lit from behind the picture is more vibrant than a single sided poster would present.

Posters listed below as "double sided" are of this type. Regular posters are printed on one side only and come as "original" (printed when the film first came out) and "reprint." These also can appear with different versions of pictures and artwork. Condition is critical and discounts should be made for tape marks, staple holes, folds, creases, stains, and other imperfections. Rolled posters are preferred over folded.

Following is an overview of what is available. The price range is for posters with small imperfections to mint condition.

Photos are courtesy of MoviePoster.com.

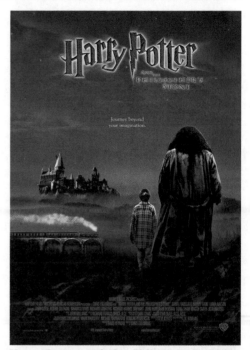

Harry Potter and the Philosopher's Stone: 2001, original regular, double sided, Harry, Hedwig, and Hogwarts at top, 27" x 40". .... **$145-$150**

Harry Potter and the Philosopher's Stone: 2001, original, double sided, First Years boating to castle, 27" x 40". .... **$80-$85**

Harry Potter and the Philosopher's Stone: 2001, original, large, First Years boating to castle, 47-1/2" x 68-1/2". .... **$235-$240**

Harry Potter and the Sorcerer's Stone: 2001, original, double sided, owl carrying Hogwarts letter, 27" x 40". .... **$145-$150**

Harry Potter and the Sorcerer's Stone: 2001, reprint, regular, single sided, "Let the magic begin," Harry surrounded by characters, 26-3/4" x 38-3/4". .... **$18-$20**

Harry Potter and the Sorcerer's Stone: 2001, original, single sided, First Years boating to castle, 27" x 40". .... **$175-$180**

Harry Potter and the Philosopher's Stone: 2001, Harry standing with Hagrid, 26-3/4" x 38-1/2". .... **$17-$19**

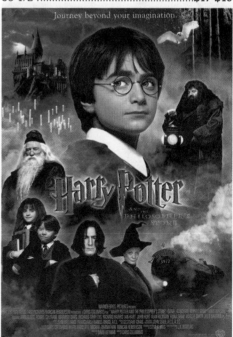

Harry Potter and the Philosopher's Stone: 2001, reprint regular, Harry, Hedwig, and Hogwarts at top, 26-3/4" x 38-1/2". .... **$17-$19**

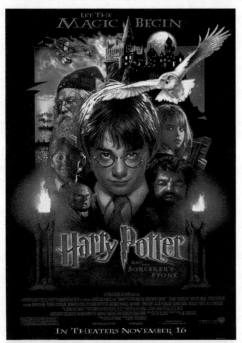

Harry Potter and the Sorcerer's Stone: 2001, original, regular, double sided, Harry, Hedwig, and Hogwarts, 27" x 40".....................**$290-$300**

Harry Potter and the Chamber of Secrets: 2002, original, advance, double sided, "Dobby Has Come to Warn You, Sir," Dobby, 27" x 40"..**$65-$70**

Harry Potter and the Chamber of Secrets: 2002, master print, single sided, Gryffindor vs. Slytherin, Harry above two Quidditch teams, 11" x 17".....................................**$16-$18**

Harry Potter and the Chamber of Secrets: 2002, original, regular style, double sided, "Something Evil Has Returned to Hogwarts," Harry, Ron, Hermione, and Dobby, 27" x 40". ....**$45-$50**

Harry Potter and the Chamber of Secrets: 2002, original, regular style, double sided, Harry holding Sword of Gryffindor, 27" x 40". ....**$45-$50**

Harry Potter and the Chamber of Secrets: 2002, print, Harry and Dobby on his bed, 34" x 24"...**$10-$12**

Harry Potter and the Chamber of Secrets: 2002, print, Hermione, Harry, and Ron over cauldron, 24" x 34". ....**$10-$12**

Harry Potter and the Chamber of Secrets: 2002, original, regular, single sided, Harry holding Sword of Gryffindor, 17" x 25". ....**$13-$15**

Harry Potter and the Chamber of Secrets: 2002, Harry and car flying over Hogwarts, painting print, 26.8" x 38.8".................**$18-$20**

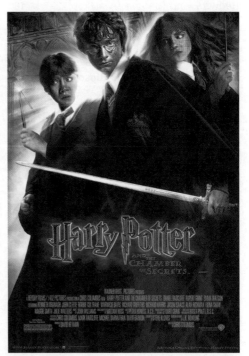

Harry Potter and the Chamber of Secrets: 2002, reprint, regular style, Harry holding Sword of Gryffindor, 26.75" x 38.6". ....**$18-$20**

Harry Potter and the Prisoner of Azkaban: 2004, original, double sided, "Something Wicked This Way Comes," Harry, Hermione, and Ron, 27" x 40"................................**$18-$20**

Harry Potter and the Prisoner of Azkaban: 2006, advance original, single sided, Harry with Lupin and Burrow in background, 24" x 36"..**$60-$65**

Harry Potter and the Prisoner of Azkaban: 2004, original, advance, glossy, single sided, Ron Weasley with Dumbledore in background, 24" x 36"..**$40-$45**

Harry Potter and the Prisoner of Azkaban: 2004, original, advance, glossy, single sided, Sirius Black with Pettigrew in background, 24" x 36"..**$42-$45**

Harry Potter and the Prisoner of Azkaban: 2004, advance, reprint, Harry Potter with Lupin and Burrow in background, 26-3/4" x 38-1/2"..**$18-$20**

Harry Potter and the Prisoner of Azkaban: 2004, advance, reprint, Sirius Black with Pettigrew in background, 26-3/4" x 38-1/2". ....**$18-$20**

Harry Potter and the Prisoner of Azkaban: 2004, advance, reprint, Hermione Granger with Trelawney in background, 26-3/4" x 38-3/4"..**$18-$20**

Harry Potter and the Prisoner of Azkaban: 2004, reprint, Ron, Hermione, and Harry in woods, 26-3/4" x 38-1/2". ....**$18-$20**

Harry Potter and the Prisoner of Azkaban: 2004, advance reprint, close-up Hermione, Ron, Harry, Sirius in background, 26-3/4" x 38-1/2"......**$18-$20**

Harry Potter and the Prisoner of Azkaban: 2004, reprint, Sirius, Peter Pettigrew and Harry in back, 26.6" x 38.6". ....**$18-$20**

Harry Potter and the Prisoner of Azkaban: 2004, reprint, "Secrets will be revealed," Dumbledore, McGonagall, and Ron, 27" x 38.8". ....**$18-$20**

Harry Potter and the Prisoner of Azkaban: 2004, print, Harry holding lantern in potions room, 24" x 34". ....**$10-$12**

Harry Potter and the Prisoner of Azkaban: 2004, print, "Something wicked this way comes," Hermione, Ron, Harry and Dementors in background, 24" x 34". ....**$12-$15**

Harry Potter and the Prisoner of Azkaban: 2004, reprint, "Character will be tested," close-up of Draco, Snape, and Hermione, 26-3/4" x 38-1/2"...................................**$18-$20**

Harry Potter and the Goblet of Fire: 2000, print, Bloomsbury book cover, 24" x 33-1/4". ....**$8-$10**

Harry Potter and the Goblet of Fire: 2005, photographic print, *Life Magazine* cover, Nov. 18, 2005, Rupert, Emma, and Daniel, 11" x 14"..**$35-$40**

Harry Potter and the Goblet of Fire: 2005, print, Harry blasting a spell, 22" x 34". ....**$8-$10**

Harry Potter and the Goblet of Fire: 2005, original, advance, double sided, silhouette of Harry, 27" x 40". ....**$55-$60**

Harry Potter and the Goblet of Fire: 2005, original, advance, single sided, silhouette of Harry, 27" x 40". ....**$45-$48**

Harry Potter and the Goblet of Fire: 2005, reprint, advance, silhouette of Harry, 27" x 38-1/2"...**$18-$20**

Harry Potter and the Goblet of Fire: 2005, reprint, advance, "Dark and difficult times lie ahead," Harry and Triwizard champions, 26.9" x 38.5". ......**$18-$20**

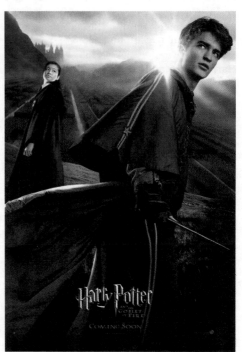

Harry Potter and the Goblet of Fire: 2005, reprint, Cedric and Cho Chang, 26.9" x 38.5". ....**$18-$20**

Harry Potter and the Goblet of Fire: 2005, reprint, Ron and Fleur, 26.9" x 38.5"...**$18-$20**

Harry Potter and the Goblet of Fire: 2005, original, double sided, Harry, Ron, Hermione, 27" x 40"..**$30-$35**

Harry Potter and the Goblet of Fire: 2005, artwork, print, Harry, Ron, Hermione, goblet, and Deathmark, 22-1/4" x 34".............**$8-$10**

Harry Potter and the Goblet of Fire: 2005, reprint, advance, Harry in dragon-fighting outfit, 27" x 38-3/4"............................**$18-$20**

Harry Potter and the Goblet of Fire: 2005, original, regular, single sided, Harry, Ron, Hermione, and Triwizard Champions, 27" x 40"...**$65-$70**

Harry Potter and the Goblet of Fire: 2005, reprint, Harry pointing wand and Mad-Eye Moody in background, 26-3/4" x 38-3/4"...**$18-$20**

Harry Potter and the Goblet of Fire: 2005, reprint, horizontal, Harry, Ron, Hermione, and Triwizard Champions, 38-3/4" x 27"...**$18-$20**

Harry Potter and the Goblet of Fire: 2005, reprint, Harry in tuxedo, Cedric, Moody, and Cho in background, 26-3/4" x 38-3/4"...**$18-$20**

Harry Potter and the Order of the Phoenix: 2007, reprint, "Only One Can Survive," Harry pointing wand and Voldemort in orb, 27" x 38-3/4"...**$18-$20**

Harry Potter and the Order of the Phoenix: 2007, original, advance, double sided, "You Will Lose Everything," Voldemort, 27" x 40"..**$25-$30**

Harry Potter and the Order of the Phoenix: 2007, reprint, advance, "You Will Lose Everything," Voldemort with hands raised, 26-3/4" x 38-1/2"..................................**$18-$20**

Harry Potter and the Order of the Phoenix: 2007, original, regular, double sided, "The Rebellion Begins," Harry and some of Dumbledore's Army, 27" x 40"............**$40-$42**

Harry Potter and the Order of the Phoenix: 2007, original, advance, double sided, Coming Soon, "You Will Lose Everything," Voldemort with hands raised, 27" x 40"..**$25-$30**

Harry Potter and the Order of the Phoenix: 2007, reprint, "Voldemort and the Death Eaters, Dark Arts," Voldemort, 22-1/4" x 34"..**$8-$10**

Harry Potter and the Order of the Phoenix: 2007, reprint, Harry, Ron, Hermione, and Dumbledore's Army pointing wands, 27" x 38-3/4". ....$18-$20

Harry Potter and the Order of the Phoenix: 2007, original, double sided, Imax version, "See it in IMAX," Harry, Ron, Hermione, and Dumbledore's Army pointing wands, 27" x 40"..$25-$30

Harry Potter and the Order of the Phoenix: 2007, reprint, regular, single sided, "The Rebellion Begins," Harry and some of Dumbledore's Army, 26.9" x 38.8".......$18-$20

Harry Potter and the Order of the Phoenix: 2007, original, single sided, "The Rebellion Begins," Harry and some of Dumbledore's Army, 11-1/2" x 17"................................ $12-$15

Harry Potter and the Order of the Phoenix: 2007, print, Harry and his stag, Patronus, 22-1/4" x 34"...$8-$10

Harry Potter and the Half-Blood Prince: 2009, original, advance, double sided, HP6, close-up of Harry with Dumbledore reflection in his glasses, 27" x 40"........................$38-$42

Harry Potter and the Half-Blood Prince: 2009, print, Hermione, 22-1/2" x 34".......$6-$8

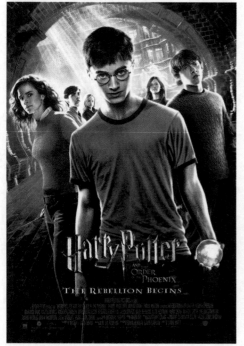

Harry Potter and the Order of the Phoenix: 2007, reprint, Harry holding orb, Hermione, Ron, and Dumbledore's Army members, 27" x 38-3/4". $18-$20

Harry Potter and the Half-Blood Prince: 2009, reprint, Harry holding his wand, 26-3/4" x 38-1/2"....................................$18-$20

Harry Potter and the Half-Blood Prince: 2009, reprint, HP6, close-up of Harry with Dumbledore reflection in his glasses, 26-3/4" x 38-1/2". **$18-$20**

Harry Potter and the Half-Blood Prince: 2009, reprint, Dumbledore in rain, 26-3/4" x 38-1/2"..**$18-$20**

Props and Reproductions

Movie Props

Envelope Prop: Mailing envelope addressed to Harry, actual prop........................**$150-$300**

Golden Snitch: Limited edition of five, display prop made by Warner Bros........**$1,250-$1,450**

Platform Ticket: Prop card from Sorcerer's Stone...**$1,100-$1,200**

Prop Reproductions
Noble Collection
Firebolt (NN7536): 58" replica........**$295-$305**

Godric Gryffindor Sword (NN7198): As seen in Harry Potter and the Chamber of Secrets, 34" sword with the handle set with crystal cabochons comes attached to a wood plaque.
.... **$175-$195**

Harry Potter Glasses (NN7860): 4-3/4" replica in wood case.......................................**$55-$60**

Horcrux Ring, The (NN8177): As seen in Harry Potter and the Half-Blood Prince, plated in 24K gold, ring size 10, comes with display box. ....**$50-$55**

Locket from the Cave, The (NN8133): As seen in Harry Potter and the Half-Blood Prince, comes with display box included. ......**$50-$55**

Lucius Malfoy's Walking Stick (NN7639): 46-1/2" silver plated and set with crystals, 18" long wand is sheathed inside the walking stick. ....**$75-$85**

"Mad-Eye" Moody's Staff (NN7732): 57", hand-painted. ....**$130-$145**

Marauder's Map (NN7888): 15-1/2" x 72" full-size replica printed on parchment paper.
....**$35-$45**

Marauder's Map Case (NN7882): Wooden display case. ....**$30-$35**

Nimbus 2001 (NN7535): 57" replica. **$245-$255**

Proclamation Board (NN7752): 18" in height, crafted in wood, hidden compartments on top holds two pens and eraser (included).
....**$45-$55**

Professor Umbridge's Quill (NN7650): 8" in length. ....**$35-$40**

Puzzles

Images of puzzles are from the collection of Megan Barrow.

Hallmark

Quidditch Match Puzzle and Stickers: Comes with reusable stickers that can be placed on the completed puzzle. ....**$10-$15**

Mattel

"Flying Series" puzzles: 56-piece two-sided mini puzzles..**$1-$2 ea.**

Six different puzzles:
    Chamber of Keys
    Quidditch
    Ron Flying
    Chasing the Snitch
    Harry the Seeker
    Hermione Flying

"Mystery" puzzles: Small pieces for adults and larger pieces for children. Each puzzle includes a plastic decoder strip to find hidden clue images in the completed puzzle. ....**$8-$10 ea.**

Five different puzzles:
    Journey to Hogwarts (260 pieces)
    Fluffy/Forbidden Corridor (300 pieces)
    Potions Class (260 pieces)
    Gryffindor Common Room Entrance
       (300 pieces)
    Gringotts Wild Ride (300 pieces)

Plain puzzles: 350 pieces.................**$5-$8 ea.**
Four different puzzles:
    Hogsmeade
    Hogwarts
    Hagrid's Ride
    Harry and Firenze in the Forbidden Forest

Harry Potter (42761): 550-piece puzzle, released 2001...**$6-$9**

Harry Potter (42784): 300-piece puzzle assortment, released 2000. ....**$5-$8**

Harry Potter (H9960): 24-piece puzzle.. $2-$3

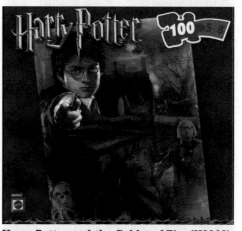

Harry Potter and the Goblet of Fire (H9962): 100-piece puzzle......................................$7-$9

Harry Potter and the Goblet of Fire (H9983): 100-piece puzzle......................................$7-$9

Harry Potter and the Sorcerer's Stone Puzzle (31363): 250-piece puzzle. ....$5-$8

Harry Potter and the Sorcerer's Stone Puzzle (42990): 100-piece puzzle within a puzzle. ....$6-$8

Harry Potter Puzzle (C5554): 100-piece puzzle. ....$7-$9

Hermione Granger and the Sorting Hat Puzzle ....$6-$8

Mini Puzzles

Harry Potter: Mini puzzle, 1/6, 56 pieces, literary art...$2-$3

Hermione Granger: Mini puzzle, 2/6, 56 pieces, literary art...................................$2-$3

Ron Weasley: Mini puzzle, 3/6, 56 pieces, literary art...$2-$3

Draco Malfoy: Mini puzzle, 4/6, 56 pieces, literary art...$2-$3

Vincent Crabbe: Mini puzzle, 5/6, 56 pieces, literary art...$2-$3

Gregory Goyle: Mini puzzle, 6/6, 56 pieces, literary art...$2-$3

United Model 3-D Puzzles

These unique puzzles in United Model's Visual Echo line were released in 2007 with *Harry Potter and the Order of the Phoenix*. They come in two sizes and varying numbers of pieces "using a patented lenticular technology to create a 'magical' 3D viewing experience. Each puzzle uses up to 12 layered images for astonishing 3D depth."

100-piece puzzles: Completed size, 9-3/4" x 7-3/4" ....$5-$8

Includes:
   Order of the Phoenix
      (Dumbledore's Army inside Hogwarts)
   Order of the Phoenix
      (Dumbledore's Army outside Hogwarts)
   Order of the Phoenix
      (the Weasleys)
   Prisoner of Azkaban
      (movie poster)

500-piece puzzles: Completed size, 20" x 16". .... $12-$15

Includes:
   Dumbledore's Army
      (with movie scenes, vertical)
   Goblet of Fire
      (movie poster, vertical)
   Magical Creatures
      (from Goblet of Fire, horizontal)
   Voldemort
      (from Goblet of Fire, horizontal)

University Games

Glow Puzzles: 250-piece puzzles treated with luminous chemicals so that hidden objects are revealed in the dark. Fred Bode paintings. ....$8-$10 ea.

   Hermione Granger and the Sorting Hat
   Mirror of Erised
   Quidditch/Golden Snitch Capture

Harry Potter Magic Puzzles: Set features three two-sided puzzles, one with 60 pieces, the other two with 81 pieces; includes 10 "mind reading" cards and a "magic" spinner to make things move. ....$8-$10

Rubber Stamps
Cedco Publishing Co.

Harry's Life: Four-stamp set with the boy wizard, Hogwarts crest and name, and house name. These foam stamps come with a black ink pad. ....$4-$5

Meeting Harry: Combination set with seven foam stamps with Hagrid, Harry, Ron, and Hermione, and 30 stickers of HP icons, such as a potions bottle, broomstick, and Golden Snitch. Comes with a purple ink pad. ....$8-$10

Plaid/All Night Media

Best Friends: Three-stamp set features Harry, Ron, and Hermione, and an ink pad. ....$4-$5

Charms: Set of four stamps features Golden Snitch, lightning bolt, Sorting Hat, and Harry's eyeglasses. Comes with a gold ink pad. ....$5-$6

Fantastic Creatures: Three-stamp set features Hedwig, Scabbers, and Mrs. Norris. Comes with a brown ink pad. ....$4-$5

Initiation: Deluxe set features Hogwarts Castle and Harry, Ron, and Hermione each under the Sorting Hat. Comes with a black ink pad. ....$8-$10

Tools of the Wizard Trade: Set of five stamps features Harry trying wands at Ollivanders; Bertie Bott's Every Flavor Beans; three stars; broomstick; and cauldron. Comes with a black ink stamp pad...$6-$7

Large Individual Wooden Stamps

Lightning Bolt: ....$6-$7

Quill and Harry glasses, note stamp: ....$6-$7

"This book belongs to" owl/book: ....$6-$7

Winking Hedwig: ....$4-$5

"You Know Who" Lord Voldemort: ....$6-$7

Charms: Set of four stamps features Golden Snitch, Harry on broom, Sorting Hat, and lightning bolt. Comes with an ink pad. ....$5-$6

Stamps

Special care should be taken with mint stamps to preserve their value. Avoid handling stamps with your fingers. Mount the stamps in stamp mounts or in a stock book, available from any stamp store. Keep them away from moisture and extreme temperatures.

Prices are for mint never hinged condition and include postage stamps from around the world as they are easily obtainable in North America.

Albania: *Order of the Phoenix*, 2008, block of four stamps with scenes; also issued as a booklet pane of four. ....**$6.50-$7.50**

Australia: These Souvenir Stamp Sheets are not Harry Potter stamps as the relevant pictures are on the tabs of the stamps and around the border and not on the stamps themselves. Still, they are philatelic and considered collectible. The sheets measure 8-1/4" x 11-3/4".....................................**$16-$20**

– *Prisoner of Azkaban*, Souvenir Stamp Sheet, 2002

– *Goblet of Fire*, Souvenir Stamp Sheet, 2003
– *Half-Blood Prince*, Souvenir Stamp Sheet, 2009

Belgium: Like the Souvenir Stamp Sheets listed at left, Duostamps are not Harry Potter stamps as the pictures of the characters are on the tabs and not the stamps. These are unique to Belgium with an average price. ....**$8-$15**

– Duostamps, Prisoner of Azkaban

– Duostamps, *Order of the Phoenix*   – Duostamps, World of Harry Potter

France: *Order of the Phoenix*, 2007, set consists of:

Three sheetlets of five stamps and five tabs showing Harry, Ron, and Hermione on the stamps. ....**$6-$8**

Postal card with Harry Potter postmark on first day of issue. .... **$1-$2**

Postage paid label.... $.50-$1

Souvenir sheet with Harry. .... **$1-$2**

Booklet of 10 self-adhesive stamps, four of Harry, three of Ron, and three of Hermione. ....**$15-$17**

Great Britain: Commemorating the seven Harry Potter books, 2007, consists of:

Strip of seven stamps showing the covers of the seven books. ....$8-$10
Strip of five self-adhesive stamps with Hogwarts' crest and house crests (sold in sheets of 20, plus 20 labels). ....$6-$8

Souvenir sheet with Hogwarts' crest and house crests. ....$6-$7

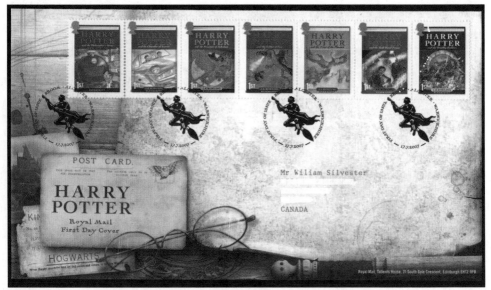

First Day Cover is available for both the strips (**$9-$11**) and the sheet (**$7-$8**).

Indonesia: *Order of the Phoenix*, four souvenir stamp sheets (see note with Australia), 8-1/4" x 11-3/4", 2007.

– The Forbidden Forest

– Dark Arts

– Order of the Phoenix

– Dumbledore's Army

Set of four .... $20-$25

Isle of Man: *Prisoner of Azkaban*, 2004, consists of:

Set of eight stamps.............................. **$12-$14**
(Also available on sheetlets of five, $60-$70
for set of eight.)

Eight postal cards (#32-39) with picture of stamp on front and pre-printed stamp on back......**$5-$6**

Isle of Man: *Goblet of Fire*, 2005, consists of:

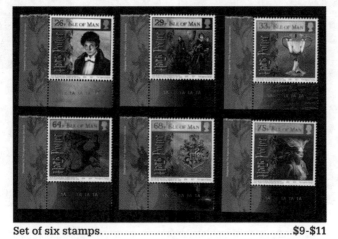

Set of six stamps...$9-$11

Taiwan: *Prisoner of Azkaban*, 2004, consists of two souvenir sheets of six stamps with scenes and characters from the film (initially not sold directly to foreign customers; only available through Canada Post's philatelic bureau). ....$6-$8

Taiwan: *Goblet of Fire*, 2005, consists of two souvenir sheets of six stamps with scenes and characters from the film. ....$5-$6

Postal Stationery

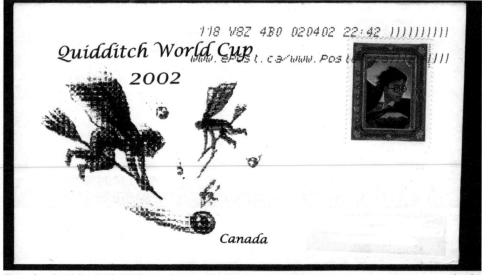

Canada: Quidditch World Cup with personalized stamp, 2002. ....$5-$8

Ireland: *Harry Potter and the Chamber of Secrets* spray cancel on cover, 2002. ....$2-$3

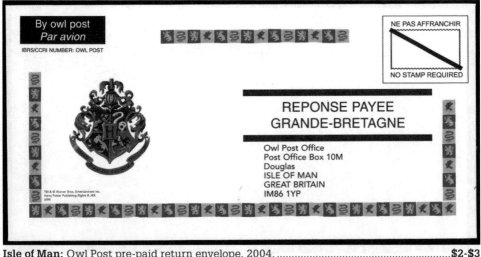

Isle of Man: Owl Post Aerogramme (*Prisoner of Azkaban*), 2004. ....$2-$3

Isle of Man: Owl Post pre-paid return envelope, 2004. ....$2-$3

United States: Owl Station cancels on cards (*Half-Blood Prince*), 2005. (There are a number of these privately produced cards.) ....$1-$2 ea.

Stationery
Andrews McMeel Publishing

Stationery sets feature the art of Fred Bode and contain 16 sheets on heavy stock, with an illustration on one side and writing lines on the other, plus 16 envelopes; six different sets.

Estimated value .... **$10-$15 ea.**
- Hedwig
- Hermione
- Journey to Hogwarts
- Mirror of Erised
- Potions Class
- Quidditch

Scholastic

Harry Potter Deluxe Stationery Kit (ISBN 0-439-28637-9): Lid opens and drawer pulls out, comes with 25 sheets of stationery, 12 envelopes, 32 full-color stickers, double-sided calligraphy pen .... **$10-$12**

Harry Potter Stationery Set (ISBN 0-439-23658-4): Lid opens and drawer pulls out, comes with 10 sheets of stationery, 10 envelopes, sticker sheet, rubber stamp, pocket photo album, and address book. .... **$8-$10**

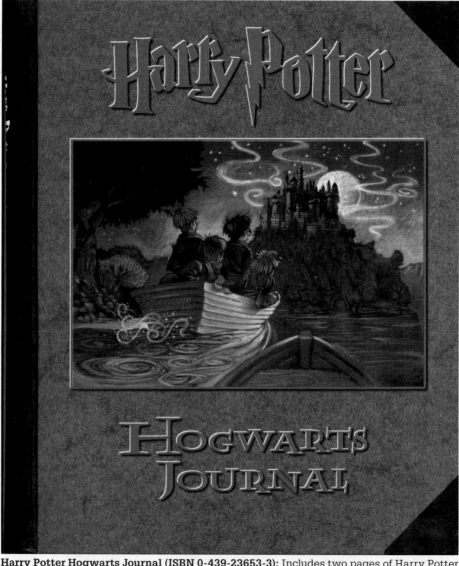

Harry Potter Hogwarts Journal (ISBN 0-439-23653-3): Includes two pages of Harry Potter stickers. ....**$8-$13**

Journals & Diaries
Hallmark

The following are assorted Harry Potter-themed journals and diaries sold in 2000 and 2001. Some came with a matching pen. Most had illustrations by Warner Bros. artist Fred Bode.

Hermione Potions lenticular diary ...... $3-$5

Journal with wand pen .... $15-$20

Magic Quidditch Journal: *With matching pen* .... $5-$7

Magic Wizard's Journal: *With matching pen* .... $5-$7

Quidditch lenticular diary .... $3-$5

Scholastic

Harry Potter and the Chamber of Secrets Deluxe Journal (ISBN 0-439-42521-2): Record your own magical adventures. .... $8-$13

Harry Potter Deluxe Journal and Light (ISBN 0-439-28636-0): 192 lined pages with Golden Snitch in the corners; comes with a built-in pen-shaped light. .... $10-$12

Harry Potter Journals: Three different 144-page books. .... $5-$7

1 – Hedwig cover (ISBN 0-439-23654-1)
2 – House crests cover (ISBN 0-439-20128-4)
3 – Platform 9-3/4 cover (ISBN 0-439-23655-X)

Albums, Organizers, and Planners
Cedco Publishing Co.

Address Books
Blue suede-like address book .... $5-$7
Harry Potter gel pen address book .... $5-$8
Hermione gel pen address book .... $5-$8

Organizers
Room of Keys Student Planner for 2001-2002
.... $6-$7

Photo Albums
Hogwarts album .... $8-$10
Mirror of Erised album .... $8-$10

Warner Bros.

Book Covers (GM564): Released 2000, set of three – red, green, and blue rolled with literary art. .... $2-$3

Hogwarts Logo Fat Book (GM556): Released 2000, coil-bound black book with Hogwarts crest. .... $1-$2

Hogwarts Spiral Notebook (SS837): Released 2000, spiral-bound black book with Hogwarts crest. .... $2-$3

Lightning Bolt Binder (GM565): Released 2000, black binder with "Harry Potter" in gold. .... $8-$10

Photo from the collection of Megan Barrow

Harry Potter Remembrall: Remember special days, addresses, books, movies, websites, TV shows, sports, video games, money, gifts, misc. .... $5-$8

Stickers and Tattoos

Stickers
bsb GmbH

Two sheets of stickers (though it says three sheets on the package): 3" x 5", released in 2001 with non-movie art. Made in Germany but released in North America. Following are some of the more than 20 different stickers available. ....**$3-$4 ea.**

3 – Quidditch Harry, house crests, Snitch.

6 – House crests and banners, Harry, Ron, Hermione on brooms.

11 – Houses crests, Snitch, Harry, Hogwarts (all in purple).

17 – Framed pictures of Harry, Hermione, Ron, Harry riding Firenze.

18 – Fluffy, Norbert, and framed pictures of Hagrid on motorcycle, birth of Norbert.

21 – Framed pictures of Harry playing Quidditch and house crests.

Cedco Publishing Co.

Believe in Magic Set: 38 stickers of Fred Bode's artwork including wands, lightning bolts, eyeglasses, broomsticks, and fantastic creatures. .... **$6-$10**

Big Sticker Books: Contains 24 big stickers (3" x 8-3/4"), 12 different scenes. Released in 2000, "For your Bumper, Notebook, Locker, Whatever!" Non-movie artwork. .... **$8-$10**

27349-02317: Harry Potter

27349-02316: Hogwarts School of Witchcraft and Wizardry

Eureka

Harry Potter Sticker Book (EU-609620): More than 520 theme-based stickers on an easy-to-use pad. Each sticker book contains eight pages (5-3/4" x 9-3/8"). .... **$5-$6**

Hallmark Cards Inc.

Harry Potter and the Chamber of Secrets: Harry, Ron, and Hermione, Ford Anglia, Hogwarts, 2002....................................... **$2-$3**

Harry Potter and the Goblet of Fire: Harry, Ron, and Hermione and crests, 2007...... **$2-$3**

Panini Sticker Books

Though published in Italy, these sticker books were readily available in North America.

Panini has two *Harry Potter and the Philosopher's Stone* collections: The newest has gold packets and features photographic images from the movie, the other is literary art. Albums are sold separately, sometimes with stickers inside; stickers are usually five to a pack.

Empty albums .... $4-$5

Completed albums .... $30-$40

Box of 50 stickers .... $10-$15

Stickers, unopened pack .... $0.50-$1

Stickers, single .... $0.25-$0.50

Harry Potter and the Philosophers Stone (literary): released 2001, album, 144 stickers.

Harry Potter and the Philosophers Stone (movie): Released 2001, album, 180 standard stickers, 18 shiny stickers, 18 gold stickers.

Harry Potter and the Chamber of Secrets: Released 2002, album, 240 stickers, including 12 heat sensitive "magical" stickers (portraits change with the touch of a finger), 24 special embossed metal stickers, and 24 PVC stickers.

Harry Potter and the Prisoner of Azkaban: Released 2004, album, 252 stickers, including 12 glow-in-the-dark and special PVC stickers.

Harry Potter and the Order of the Phoenix: Released 2007, album, 48 pages, 288 stickers, including 12 special foil stickers, glitter stickers, and pull-out poster.

Magical World of Harry Potter, The: Released 2008, album, 32 pages, 216 stickers, including 12 special foil and 12 glow-in-the-dark stickers.

Harry Potter and the Goblet of Fire: Released 2005, album, 246 stickers, including 36 3D stickers and 12 special stickers.

Harry Potter and the Half-Blood Prince: Released 2009, album, 64 pages, 360 stickers including 12 glow-in-the-dark, 36 foil, and 24 satin stickers.

Plaid/All Night Media Inc.

Plaid issued Harry Potter stickers in the All Night Media line. Called "Education of Harry," these are foil stickers with shiny versions of illustrations by Warner Bros. artist Fred Bode. Two sheets of stickers in two sizes (4-1/2" x 7" and 2-1/2" x 7"), released in 2001......**$2-$3 ea.**

84200-38058 – Four pictures, scenes from first book (large size).
84200-37078 – Hagrid, Dumbledore, Snape, and Quirrell in various poses.
84200-37079 – Harry, Hermione, Ron, Draco, books, and Hedwig.
84200-37084 – Harry, Slytherin seeker, and Snitch.
84200-37085 – House crests

Rubies

Halloween Body Décor: Half-Blood Prince package, house and school crests. .... **$3-$4**

Harry Potter Tattoos (0000): Sorcerer's Stone package, house and school crests, lightning bolts, in reverse. .... **$3-$4**

Running Press

Harry Potter Divination Crystal Ball Sticker Kit (ISBN 9780762430109): Released in 2007, includes an easy-to-assemble crystal ball with a three-elephant stand and a book of eight sheets of stickers showing scenes around Hogwarts. .... **$10-$13**

Harry Potter Golden Snitch Kit (ISBN 9780762428212): Released in 2006, includes an easy-to-assemble Golden Snitch with wooden stand and 16-page sticker book. .... **$7-$9**

Harry Potter Sorting Hat Sticker Kit (ISBN: 9780762431465): Released in 2007, includes a knowledgeable 3" tall Sorting Hat and a booklet of eight stickers. .... **$7-$9**

Harry Potter Wizard's Wand Sticker Kit (ISBN: 9780762434268): Released in 2008, includes a three-part assemble-yourself wand and a book of eight stickers with scenes showing Harry using his wand. .... **$7-$9**

Sandylion
Single sheet of stickers (2" x 6-1/4") showing various characters from the books. Released in 2001 by Sandylion Sticker Designs; non-movie artwork. .... **$2-$3 ea.**
PWHP2 – Hedwig, owl post crest, stars
PWHP3 – Hermione, books, potion bottles
PWHP4 – Dumbledore, Harry, Mirror of
Erised, flying keys

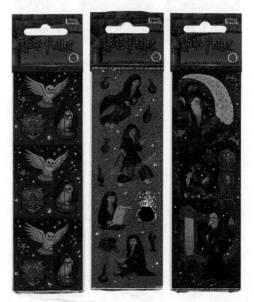

Harry Potter Time-Turner Sticker Kit (ISBN: 9780762429776): Released in 2007, includes an easy-to-assemble timeturner with rotating rings and functional hourglass, as used by Hermione in *Prisoner of Azkaban*, and a book of eight stickers. .... **$7-$9**

Harry Potter Sticker Album (WHP9): 20 specially coated (5-1/2" x 8-1/2") pages to stick down and easily remove stickers. Literary art, released in 2001. .... $3-$4

Harry Potter Sticker Extravaganza Set: 170 stickers on rolls with sticker album and activity scene .... $8-$10

Scholastic

Goblet of Fire promotional sticker set: Issued upon the release of the book *Harry Potter and the Goblet of Fire* in July 2000. These stickers are based upon the artwork of Mary GrandPré, who illustrated all of the U.S. Harry Potter editions. .... $2-$3

Temporary Tattoos
Plaid/All Night Media

Tattoo Stamp Strip: Hermione on one stamp and three potions bottles on the other, 2001, package contains two foam stamps and a black ink temporary tattoo pad. The stamps and inkpad measure approximately 1-1/4" square .... $1-$2

Tattoo Stamp Strip: Argus Filch on one stamp and Harry Potter on the other, 2001, package contains two foam stamps and a black ink temporary tattoo pad. The foam stamps measure approximately 1-3/8" square. .. $1-$2

Tattoo Stamp Strip: Golden Snitch on one stamp and Quidditch player on the other, 2001, package contains two foam stamps and a black ink temporary tattoo pad. Foam stamps measure approximately 1-3/8" square. .. $1-$2

Tattoo Stamp Strip: Solid lightning bolt on one stamp and outlined lighting bolt on the other, 2001, package contains two foam stamps and a black ink temporary tattoo pad. Foam stamps measure approximately 1-3/8" square .... $1-$2

Rubies

Hogwarts House Crests: Features all four house crests, four large and 14 small stick-on tattoos. .... $7-$8

Unknown

Dark Mark, The: Measures approximately 1-1/4" wide and 4-1/4" tall. .... $1-$2

Deathly Hallows Book Promo: Features Number 7 with a lightning bolt and Harry. .... $4-$5

Goblet of Fire: Glow-in-the-dark, 2-1/2" x 4", with nine temporary tattoos, Ron, Hermione, the Hungarian Horntail, Nagini, lightning bolt, Harry, Harry on broom. .... $2-$3

Great Things Mini Tattoo Set: Four black foam stamps and a purple body ink pad in box, Golden Snitch, lightning bolt, the HP flying Snitch logo, and You-Know-Who! eyes. .... $4-$5

Half-Blood Prince: 4" x 6" with six temporary tattoos, school crest, Gryffindor lion, Dark Mark, Harry's 7 logo. .... $5-$7

Half-Blood Prince Promo: Features HP logo with a lightning bolt and Harry and Dumbledore's face in the background. One-time use .... $3-$4

Hogwarts House Crests: Contains one large stick-on tattoo of each house crest – Gryffindor, Slytherin, Hufflepuff, and Ravenclaw – as well as 14 small tattoos of the same. .... $6-$8

Toys

Colorforms

Harry Potter Stick-Ons

Harry Potter and the Sorcerer's Stone (70311): Contains Hogwarts Play Panels (two panels creating four scenes, 3D), Castle Floor Platform, and 34 Colorforms pieces, 2001. ....$3-$4

Mattel

Gryffindor Sword (47430): Measures two feet long with "Gryffindor" on the plastic blade and mythical animals on the handle. At the push of a button it makes six fun sounds simulating sword play, 2003. ....$15-$20

Harry Potter Enchanting Wand: Changes color to create a display of light, 2005. ....$10-$15

Harry Potter Honeydukes Toy Sweets: Little plush sweets with a unique scent that smell like Honeydukes, 2005............$8-$12

Harry Potter Little Lessons: Assortment of collectible miniatures from Divination, Potions, and Herbology classes with a charm bracelet feature, 2005. ....$8-$12

Harry Potter Motorized Spider Swarm Track Set: Released in 2002, this race car set comes with 13 feet of track, four-speed launcher, and motorized power charger booster. The Weasley's Ford Anglia is included and races around the track, knocking off spiders. ....$75-$80

Harry Potter Pet Beast: Spider-like creature from the Dark Forest interacts in a variety of unpredictable ways, 2005...................$25-$30

Harry Potter Quidditch Motorized Competition Set (96899): Released in 2001. ....$75-$80

Harry Potter Relics: Assortment of highly stylized Harry Potter relics found throughout the movies, 2005. ....$8-$12

Harry Potter Wizard Garden: Includes seeds, growing medium, terrarium, mortar and pestle, drying container, and necklace, 2005. ....$10-$15

Nimbus 2000†: 34" handle with noise and vibrating features................$15-$20

Nimbus 2000†: 34" with noise feature only. ....$10-$15

†The vibrating broomstick was apparently withdrawn from sale when parents complained that their children, particularly little girls, seemed to be spending too much time riding it. It was released later without the vibrating feature.

Roarin' Snorin' Baby Norbert (50843): Baby dragon moves its head, tail, and wings and roars with laughter when tickled. It breathes fire (glowing red light) when he sneezes and yawns, falls asleep and snores when tired, 8"x 16", 2001. ....$25-$30

Snitch Chasing Harry: This rotating Seeker figure is a 12" action figure with electronic sounds. Using motion detectors, Harry spins as he pursues the Golden Snitch........$20-$25

Volumes Die-Cast Series Collection

This is a series of 12 books topped with die-cast characters that flip down inside the hollow book covers. They come in a variety of colors with the Hogwarts crest and the title of the book embossed in gold on the front of each, and a crest and H with the volume number on the spine. A single page inside gives details of the figure and displays the trademark and ©

2001 Warner Bros. The books measures 2-3/4" x 3-3/4". The figures measure 2" to 2-1/2".

I have not been able to confirm if Vols. 9-12 were ever released.

These also exist in unauthorized versions with plastic figures and book covers from *Sorcerer's Stone, Chamber of Secrets, Prisoner of Azkaban* and *Goblet of Fire*. There is no inside descriptive page.

Back of box shows four figures.

Vol. 1 – Harry Potter, *The Standard Book of Spells* (Grade 1) by Miranda Goshawk

Vol. 2 – Fluffy, *Fantastic Beasts and Where to Find Them* by Newt Scamander

Vol. 3 – Rubeus Hagrid, *From Egg to Inferno: A Dragon Keeper's Guide*

Vol. 4 – Ron Weasley and Scabbers, *Hogwarts: A History*

Vol. 5 – Hedwig, *A History of Magic*

Vol. 6 – Severus Snape, *Magical Drafts and Potions* by Arsenius Jigger

Vol. 7 – Albus Dumbledore, *Great Wizards of the Twentieth Century*

Vol. 8 – Norbert, *Dragon Species of Great Britain and Ireland*

Vol. 9 – Hermione Granger

Vol. 10 – Mountain Troll

Vol. 11 – Quidditch Harry

Vol. 12 – Professor Quirrell

Vehicles Series

Die-cast metal and plastic characters with turning wheels.

Boat Ride, The (95705): Harry and Hagrid in a small boat... **$13-$15**

Flying Motorcycle, The (95653): Hagrid on a motorcycle... **$13-$15**

Gringotts Vault Cart (95654): Harry, Hagrid, and goblin in a Gringotts cart. .... **$13-$15**

King's Cross Station Trolley (95706): Harry with luggage and Hedwig on a trolley. .... **$13-$15**

World of Hogwarts Playsets

Released in 2002, these detailed playsets are among my favorites, and it is unfortunate the series was not continued with a Chamber of Secrets, Azkaban Prison, Grimmauld Place, or Ministry of Magic. Prices are for new in box condition.

Burrow, The (53934): Comes with Harry, Ron, gnomes, and connecting piece. The Weasley's home opens to reveal an interior as haphazard as the exterior. The right side has stairs leading to a bedroom for Ron and Harry and a fireplace wherein a figure can disappear with the use of Floo Powder. On the left is a peculiar little room over the top of a gnome-infested garden. Turning a bush reveals the gnomes who can then be catapulted out of the yard. ...... **$30-$45**

Forbidden Corridor (50701): Comes with Harry, Hermione, chess piece, and a flying key. This nicely detailed castle-like playset opens to reveal all the challenges of the Forbidden Corridor. Fluffy and the harp are on the top floor with a slide into the Devil's Snare; a room of flying keys is on the right side; on the left is a room with potion bottles. A chess game is on the top, and Quirrell and a revolving Mirror of Erised are on the bottom. ....**$40-$50**

Hagrid's Hut (50699): Comes with Hagrid, Harry, wheelbarrow, crossbow, chairs, and connecting piece. The playset folds open to reveal a three-room hut including Hagrid's bedroom with fold-down bed, living area with roaring fire, hatching dragon egg, and Fang hiding in a closet, all of which are activated by moving a chair. Upstairs is a table, chair, and Hagrid's crossbow. A back door opens into a picture of the living area. ....**$30-$45**

Hogwarts School of Witchcraft and Wizardry (50703): Comes with Harry, Ron, Hermione, Snape, Hedwig, Mountain Troll, Armor, Invisible Harry, and extra tables. The biggest and best of the series, this 11" tall detailed representation of the school opens up to reveal a multitude of rooms, moving parts, and secret passages. There's Snape's Potions class in the dungeon, the library with a roped-off Forbidden Section, the girls' bathroom complete with troll, the Gryffindor Common Room, Flitwick's Charms class, the Grand Hall, and even a pop-up Owlry in the top tower. ....**$150-$200**

Platform 9-3/4 (50700): Comes with Harry, Ron, trolley, baggage cart, and luggage. The playset folds open to reveal, on one side, the King's Cross platforms, 9 and 10 with a secret door between that opens to reveal the 9-3/4 sign. The side of the train folds down to reveal the interior of the platform with

people waiting for the train. On the other side is printed Hogwarts Express. The car behind the locomotive has padded seats and scenery whizzing by the window.....................**$30-$45**

Quidditch Stadium (55275): Comes with Harry, Slytherin seeker, quaffle, bludger, Snitch, ball launcher, and connecting piece. This representation of a Quidditch pitch is designed so that a game can be played by placing the figures on their brooms and turning a dial to move them about, dodging the bludger and trying to score. Two compartments open for storage of the quaffle and Snitch. Unfortunately, the figures with this set are much larger than the figures in the others..**$30-$45**

Whomping Willow: Comes with Harry, Ron, Aragog, Ford Anglia, and connecting piece. This forest-shaped playset opens to reveal the Whomping Willow beating on the Weasley's topless Ford Anglia on the left and the den of Aragog and his family on the right....**$30-$45**

Kaleidoscopes
Schylling Toy Co.

Regular kaleidoscope: 9" long, made of embossed tin, features owl designs and HP Snitch logo. ....**$4-$5**

Wand kaleidoscope: 9" long, shaped like a magic wand. ....**$3-$4**

Kites
International Playthings

International Playthings, Inc., of Parsippany, New Jersey, offered a few Harry Potter designs in its Flight Zone kite line. Each comes with kite line and spinner.

Giant Hex Kite: Harry Potter seeker on this six-sided "Giant Hex" flat model........ **$10-$15**

Quidditch Box Kite: Harry Potter seeker on both sides... **$8-$10**

Triangular Kite (63001): Harry about to get the Snitch on this flat plastic kite with long base. ....**$20-$25**

Model Trains
Bachmann

Hogwarts Express: Released in 2001, this HO scale replica of the Hogwarts Express is painted to resemble the locomotive in the first Harry Potter film. Comes with 4-6-0 locomotive and tender, three passenger coaches, 12 curved, three straight, and one terminal tracks (assembles to 56" x 38" oval), Platform 9-3/4 building, and power pack. .... **$150-$180**

Hogwarts Express: Released in 2002 to correspond with *Chamber of Secrets*, this HO scale replica of the Hogwarts Express is the same as the locomotive in the first Harry Potter film. Comes with 4-6-0 locomotive and tender, three passenger coaches, 12 curved, three straight, and one terminal tracks (assembles to 56" x 38" oval), Platform 9-3/4 building, exclusive Ford Anglia, and power pack. ....**$180-$200**

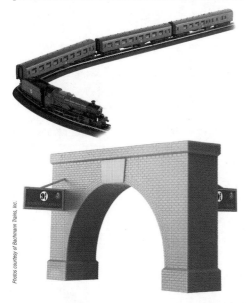

Photos courtesy of Bachmann Trains, Inc.

Lionel

Hogwarts Express G-Gauge (7-11080): Released in 2007, this G-gauge scale replica is battery operated and comes with six C batteries, remote controller, Hogwarts Express locomotive and tender, one passenger coach, 12 curved and four straight tracks, and an owner's manual...........................**$140-$160**

Hogwarts Express Add-On-2-Pack (7-11142): Contains an additional passenger coach and combination car to add to the above. **$120-$140**

Hogwarts Express O-Gauge (7-11020): Die-cast metal locomotive features puffing smoke, headlight, whistle, and passenger cars with interior lights. Comes with locomotive and tender, two passenger coaches, one combination car, one CW-80 transformer, eight curved, three straight, and one terminal tracks, smoke fluid, replacement traction tire, and owner's manual. ....**$320-$350**

View-Master

Originally intended for adults when first introduced in 1939, the famous View-Master reels turned to the youth market in the 1950s. They are now sold by Mattel through the company's Fisher Price division.

View-Master Reels

These are the traditional View-Master reels in packages of three with seven 3D scenes from the movie on each reel. Prices are for opened to mint on card conditions.

Harry Potter and the Sorcerer's Stone – Part 1: Journey to Hogwarts (73632): 2001. ......**$10-$15**

Harry Potter and the Sorcerer's Stone – Part 2: Final Chapters (73633): 2001. .... **$10-$15**

Harry Potter and the Sorcerer's Stone – Part 3: Scenes From Hogwarts Castle (73634): 2001. .... **$10-$15**

Harry Potter and the Sorcerer's Stone – Gift Set (3997): 2001, comes with special purple virtual viewer and three reels different from the above...**$20-$25**

Harry Potter and the Chamber of Secrets (B0113): 2003. .... **$10-$15**

View-Master 3D Windows

Harry Potter and the Sorcerer's Stone: Special 3D viewer was developed for the series of slide cards introduced for this set. They came in packs with five randomly selected slide cards with some in holographic and others in regular windows. Each pack also contains a decoder card to find secret information on the window cards about the books.

View-Master Viewer ....**$7-$10**
Individual cards: 60 different ....**$4-$5**
Collector Case...**$5-$6**

Video Games
EA Games

Electronic Arts, founded 1982, was a pioneer of early home computer games. The company grew by the acquisition of other successful developers, and by the 2000s were one of the world's largest publishers of electronic games. EA's most successful products are sports games and games like Harry Potter that are produced under license.

The prices range from used games with box and instructions to factory sealed games. Games without original boxes and/or instructions sell for less.

Harry Potter and the Philosopher's/Sorcerer's Stone

The first versions of the game were released in November 2001.

PC-CD	**$5-$10**
Game Boy Color	**$2-$5**
Game Boy Advance	**$3-$9**
Playstation	**$5-$7**

Another version was released in 2003.

Nintendo GameCube	**$10-$15**
Playstation 2	**$15-$20**
Xbox	**$15-$20**

The PC version was ported to the Mac (Mac OS 9 and Mac OS X) by Aspyr in 2002. ..... **$10-$15**

Harry Potter and the Chamber of Secrets

Harry Potter and the Prisoner of Azkaban

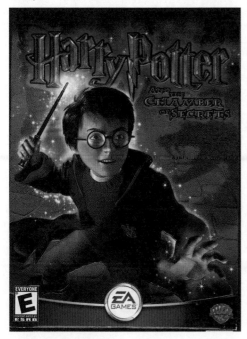

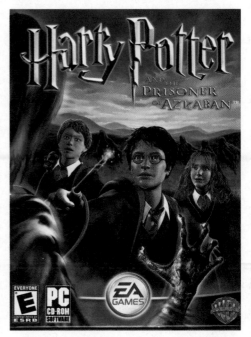

Released in November 2002.

PC-CD	**$15-$10**
PlayStation 2	**$5-$10**
GameCube	**$10-$15**
Xbox	**$5-$10**
PlayStation	**$5-$10**
Game Boy Advance	**$5-$10**
Apple Macintosh	**$5-$10**
Game Boy Color	**$2-$5**

Released in May 2004.

PC-CD	**$5-$10**
Game Boy Advance	**$10-$15**
Xbox	**$10-$15**
Nintendo GameCube	**$10-$15**
PlayStation 2	**$5-$10**
Playstation 2	**$15-$20**

Harry Potter and the Order of the Phoenix

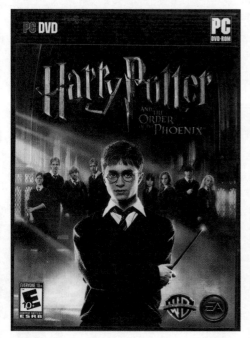

Harry Potter and the Goblet of Fire

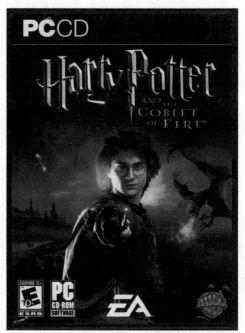

Released in June 2007.

PC-DVD	**$10-$15**
PlayStation 2	**$10-$15**
PlayStation 3	**$10-$15**
Xbox 360	**$15-$20**
PlayStation Portable	**$15-$20**
Nintendo DS	**$10-$15**
Wii	**$15-$20**
Game Boy Advance	**$10-$15**
Mac OS X	**$25-$30**

Released in November 2005.

PC-CD	**$5-$10**
Game Boy Advance	**$5-$10**
Xbox	**$5-$10**
GameCube	**$10-$15**
PlayStation 2	**$10-$15**
Nintendo DS	**$10-$15**
PlayStation Portable	**$5-$10**

Harry Potter and the Half-Blood Prince

Released in June 2009.

PC-DVD	**$15-$20**
Nintendo DS	**$15-$25**
PlayStation 2	**$20-$25**
PlayStation 3	**$25-$40**
PlayStation Portable	**$15-$20**
Wii	**$35-$45**
Xbox 360	**$15-$25**
Mac OS X	**$25-$30**

Harry Potter Collection

Released in September 2004, this is a compilation of EA games, including Sorcerer's Stone, Chamber of Secrets, and Quidditch World Cup.

PC..$15-$20

Harry Potter Interactive DVD Game – Hogwarts Challenge

Released in 2007.

DVD...$3-$7

Harry Potter: Quidditch World Cup

Released in October and November 2003.

PC...$2-$5
PlayStation 2..$2-$5
Nintendo GameCube ....$5-$10
Xbox..$5-$10
Game Boy Advance...............................$5-$10

LEGO Creator Harry Potter

Released in June 2001.

PC...$2-$5

LEGO Creator Harry Potter and the Chamber of Secrets

Released in November 2002.

PC...$6-$9

World of Harry Potter

Released in July 2005, this features the EA Games, Sorcerer's Stone, Chamber of Secrets, Quidditch World Cup, and Prisoner of Azkaban.

PC...$30-$40

Dell Print Studio

The easy-to-use Harry Potter Print Studio is used to make custom letterheads, posters, calendars, greetings cards, party kits, or picture frames from scratch or with predesigned templates. *Goblet of Fire* was available for a limited time as a Dell promo when making an ink specific purchase of three or more.

The Harry Potter and the Goblet of Fire Print Studio

CD for PC..$5-$10

Harry Potter and the Order of the Phoenix Print Studio

CD for PC..$5-$10

Fly

Harry Potter's Marauder's Map and Fly Pentop Computer: "15 interactive games will challenge your movie memory." ....$50-$60

Radica Electronics

Harry Potter 20 Q's Game: New enough to cover all the books and the first five films, this Snitch-shaped game comes with wings, stand, and light. ....$3-$5

Tiger Electronics

Book of Spells, The: Contains an index and graphic information on Harry Potter characters, situations, creatures, and spells. It can be used as a Quidditch rule reference when paired with the Electronic Quidditch Game. Doubles as an organizer and address book................$20-$25

Electronic Quidditch Game: Retractable broom can extend 48" with screen and controls on the handle. ....$25-$30

Fluffy Electronic Game: Converts from watchdog to mini-game, controls and screen are inside the mouths. ....$10-$15

Harry Potter E-Pals – Norbert (36294): The little dragon performs a number of activities and games..$10-$15

Harry Potter Hogwarts Electronic Game: Harry battles the Mountain Troll. ......$10-$15

Harry Potter Magic Spell Challenge, The: Eight levels of play in this wand with magic sounds and voice-activated commands. ....$20-$25

Harry Potter Mini-Action Game – Hagrid (36287): Hogwarts' Groundskeeper travels through the Forbidden Forest rescuing students and Fang. ....$10-$15

Talking Portrait Animated Room Alarm: Fat Lady Portrait outside Gryffindor Common Room; eyes and mouth move and are sensitive to motion up to six feet. ....$25-$30

Electronic Learning Pads

Harry Potter Leap Pad: Book and cartridge, "Above & Beyond Series, Making Movies, Lights Camera Action," ages 4-7. ....**$8-$13**

Harry Potter Quantum Pad: Book and cartridge, Making Movies, "Enter Harry's World of Secrets," ages 8 and up. ....**$8-$13**

Wall Décor

Canvas Art
NECA Inc.

Harry Potter and the Sorcerer's Stone: 16" x 24" stretched canvas, poster art for film. .....**$30-$35**

Harry Potter and Chamber of Secrets: 16" x 24" stretched canvas, poster art for film. ....**$30-$35**

Harry Potter and the Prisoner of Azkaban: 16" x 24" stretched canvas, poster art for film. **$30-$35**

Harry Potter and the Goblet of Fire: 16" x 24" stretched canvas, poster art for film ....**$30-$35**

Collector Plate
Warner Bros.

Harry Potter Holiday Plate: Titled "A Holiday Scene at Hogwarts," from the Witches and Wizards series, released in 2000, limited edition of 1,200, porcelain plate trimmed in 24kt gold, 9-1/4" diameter. ....**$50-$60**

Signs
NECA, Inc.

Hogwarts Express: 18" x 7" wooden sign, reddish-brown with 9-3/4 in circle and Hogwarts Express in gold, display chain included...**$20-$25**

Leaky Cauldron: 13-1/2" black metal sign, witch bending over cauldron silhouette, 2007. ....**$30-$35**

Wall Banners
NECA, Inc.

Gryffindor Banner: Black polyester banner with Gryffindor crest, edged in gold. **$10-$15**

Hogwarts Banner: Black polyester banner with Hogwarts crest, edged in gold. .**$10-$15**

Slytherin Banner: Black polyester banner with Slytherin crest, edged in silver.. **$10-$15**

Rubies

Photo courtesy Rubies Costumes Co. Inc.

Hogwarts Banner (7254): Black polyester banner with Hogwarts crest, 20" x 30" with rope and pole. ....**$10-$15**

Unknown

Gryffindor Banner: Black felt banner with Gryffindor crest, 20" x 30" with rope and pole. ....**$10-$15**

Hufflepuff Banner: Black felt banner with Hufflepuff crest, 20" x 30" with rope and pole. **$10-$15**

Ravenclaw Banner: Black felt banner with Ravenclaw crest, 20" x 30" with rope and pole. ....**$10-$15**

Slytherin Banner: Black felt banner with Slytherin crest, 20" x 30" with rope and pole. ....**$10-$15**

Wallpaper
Priss Prints

Priss Prints (which went bankrupt in 2004), a division of Hedstrom Corp. of Mt. Prospect, Illinois, produced two wallpaper borders dealing with Quidditch and owls. The borders came in standard 5" x 15' size. One was based on Fred Bode's work, the border of which glows in the dark; the other was by an unnamed artist..**$3-$5**

Priss also offered coordinating plastic "Jumbo Stickups" that continue the Quidditch theme. ....**$5-$12**

Wall Plaques
Enesco
CAUTION: Witchcraft and Wizardry: Hermione, wand in hand and book open, polyresin, 5-1/4" x 5".............................**$5-$10**

Entering Gryffindor House/Winner/House Cup: House crest, polyresin, 5-3/4" x 4". ....**$5-$10**

Harry Potter: Harry grabbing for the Golden Snitch, polyresin, 5" x 6". ....**$5-$10**

Hogwarts Student/1st Year: School crest, polyresin. ....**$5-$10**

WARNING: Potions Class in Session: Ron looking at his green mixture, polyresin. ....**$5-$10**

Hallmark
Hedwig the Owl: Scroll, wall decoration; released in 2000. .... **$10-$15**

Hogwarts School Crest: Card wall decoration, 11" x 12", released in 2000. ....**$5-$7**

NECA, Inc.
Gryffindor: Laser engraved house crest, silver on black, 14" x 11". ....**$15-$25**

Hogwarts: Laser engraved school crest, silver on black, 14" x 11". ....**$15-$25**

Slytherin: Laser engraved house crest, silver on black, 14" x 11". ....**$15-$25**

Rubies

Hogs Head Wall Decor (8023): Name plate connected above the head with metal chains and a hanger for mounting. The head is 12" x 17" x 6". ....**$25-$30**

Wall Scrolls
NECA, Inc.
Gryffindor Wall Scroll: 22" x 32" with top and bottom rods..**$18-$20**

Harry Potter and the Order of the Phoenix: One-sheet wall scroll, 22" x 32" with top and bottom rods..**$18-$20**

Houses of Hogwarts Wall Scroll: 22" x 32" with top and bottom rods....................**$18-$20**

Hufflepuff Wall Scroll: 22" x 32" with top and bottom rods..**$18-$20**

Marauder's Map Wall Scroll: 22" x 32" with top and bottom rods...........................**$18-$20**

Ravenclaw Wall Scroll: 22" x 32" with top and bottom rods..**$18-$20**

Slytherin Wall Scroll: 22" x 32" with top and bottom rods..**$18-$20**

Wands
Hallmark

Harry Potter Light-Up Wand: 6-3/4" wand with a red tip that lights up when a button is switched on; includes batteries. .... **$2-$3**

Mattel

Harry Potter Silly Spells Wand (C1840): Released in 2004, makes a number of magical and humorous noises as spells are cast; 13" in length. .... **$10-$15**

Noble Collection

Bellatrix's Wand (NN7976): With display and miniature mask. .... **$35-$45**

Cho Chang's Wand (NN7831): 15" long in collector box. .... **$25-$35**

Dolores Umbridge's Wand (NN7607): 14" long on a display plaque. .... **$35-$45**

Draco Malfoy's Wand (NN7256): 14" long in a collector box. .... **$25-$35**

Harry Potter's Wand (NN7005): 14" long in a collector box. .... **$25-$35**

Hermione Granger's Wand (NN7021): 15" long in a collector box. .... **$25-$35**

Lord Voldemort's Wand (NN7331): 14" long in a collector box. .... **$25-$35**

"Mad-Eye" Moody Wand (NN7270): 11" long in a collector box. .... **$25-$35**

Neville Longbottom's Wand (NN2163): 13" long in a collector box. .... **$25-$35**

Professor Dumbledore's Wand (NN7145): 15" long in a collector box. .... **$25-$35**

Professor Lupin's Wand (NN7199): 14" long in a collector box. .... **$25-$35**

Professor McGonagall's Wand (NN7238): 16" long in a collector box. .... **$25-$35**

Professor McGonagall's Wand (NN7527): 15" long in collector box. .... **$25-$35**

Professor Snape's Wand (NN7150): 13-1/2" long in a collector box. .... **$25-$35**

Ron Weasley's Wand (NN7462): 14" in long in a collector box. .... **$25-$35**

Sirius Black's Wand (NN7081): 15" long in a collector box. .... **$25-$35**

Illuminating Wands

Harry Potter's Wand (NN1910): Illuminating tip, 14" long in a collector box. .... **$30-$40**

Hermione Granger's Wand (NN8028): Illuminating tip, 14" long in collector box. .... **$30-$40**

Voldemort Wand (NN7460): Illuminating tip, 14" long in a collector box. .... **$30-$40**

Wand Sets

Dumbledore's Army Wand Collection (NN7728): Six wands of Harry Potter, Hermione Granger, Ron Weasley, Ginny Weasley, Neville Longbottom, and Luna Lovegood on a parchment-shaped display board. .... **$135-$145**

Triwizard Champions Wand Set (NN7008): 17" high, set includes the wands of Harry Potter, Cedric Diggory, Fleur Delacour, and Viktor Krum and comes with a display stand and cover. .... **$135-$145**

Weasley Wand Collection (NN7495): Two wands of Fred and George Weasley on display stand. .... **$70-$80**

Wand Displays

Dumbledore's Collector Wand Wall Display (NN8106): 11" x 12", holds wand and box (not included) with picture of Dumbledore. .... **$25-$30**

Harry Potter's Collector Wand Wall Display (NN8103): 11" x 12", holds wand and box (not included) with picture of Harry. .... **$25-$30**

Hermione Granger's Collector Wand Wall Display (NN8104): 11" x 12", holds wand and box (not included) with picture of Hermione. .... **$25-$30**

Lightning-Bolt Wand Display (NN7771): 13" long for displaying collector wands. Wand not included. .... **$10-$15**

Lord Voldemort's Collector Wand Wall Display (NN8105): 11" x 12", holds wand and box (not included) with picture of He-Who-Must-Not-Be-Named. .... **$25-$30**

Rubies

Photo courtesy Rubies Costumes Co. Inc.

Photo courtesy Rubies Costumes Co. Inc.

Draco Malfoy Wand (7250) .... **$5-$10**

Harry Potter Wand (7246) .... **$5-$10**

Harry Potter Wand with Light and Sound (7247): Wand lights up, is motion-activated, and makes "3 Magical Movie Sounds."**$9-$13**

Hermione Granger Wand (7249).......... **$5-$10**

Ron Weasley Wand (7248).................... **$5-$10**

Warner Bros.

Harry Potter Wand: The first wand distributed by Warner Bros., it was given out as a promotional item at the first major premiere of *Harry Potter and the Sorcerer's Stone* at select theaters in 2001. The wand is made from wood and comes in a silk-lined wand box. ....**$450-$500**

Photo courtesy of Fulumwer Investibles Inc.

Index

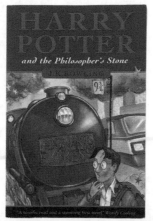

SPELLBINDING REFERENCES

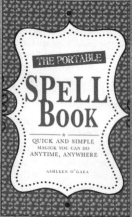

A few charms, a couple chants, a brewing potion or two, and with this book you'll learn how to go about casting spells quickly and easily. Using simple tools and ingredients you find around the house you can conjure effective magick for boosting your energy, protecting family and home, and much more.
Softcover ✶ 224 p ✶ Author Ashleen O'Gaea
Item#Z2656 ✶ $10.95

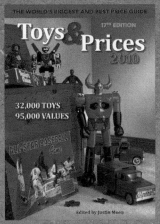

Whether it's Professor Lockhart or Harry, in his Cast-a-Spell mode, action figures are among the most popular toys today. You'll find these popular figures and many more in Toys & Prices, with its 32,000 listings, with 95,000 up-to-date values.
Softcover ✶ 800 p ✶ Author Justin Moen
Item#Z4969 ✶ $21.99

...orld of gnomes, elves, and ...and entertaining book. ...rgy of nature spirits ...hor Edain McCoy ...* this world of

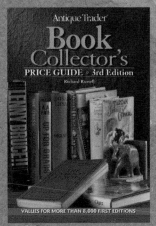

A good book can be a great escape, a cool adventure, source of inspiration and valuable collectible. In this, the only full-color guide to collectible books you'll discover the collectible side of literature found in various genres, including Americana, banned, mystery, westerns and more.
Softcover ✶ 400 p ✶ Author Richard Russell
Item#Z5019 ✶ $24.99

...e publisher at **Shop.Collect.com**